Published by The Evergreen Foundation
Printed by Jostens Commercial Printing, Clarksville, TN

ISBN: 978-1-7923-3277-7

Book design and production: E.T. Hinchcliffe
E.T. Graphics, Central Point, OR

Proofreading and facts: Karen McQueen

Put out the Fire?

Wildfires are destroying our nation's western national forests. These forests belong to all of us. They are our forest legacy and future.

◆

The wildfire pandemic we face has natural and political dimensions.

◆

Both dimensions require our immediate and honest attention.

◆

Trees in several western national forests are now dying faster than they are growing, a result of insect and disease infestations we have failed to control.

◆

Forest scientists estimate we have 90 to 100 million national forest acres in the West that are "ready to burn" – or soon will be.

◆

What should we do about these fires? Let them burn or put them out?

◆

Some Americans believe we should let these wildfires burn themselves out because fire is a "natural" occurrence in forests.

◆

Fires can and do occur naturally, but "natural" does not exclude stewardship when addressing the West's wildfire pandemic.

◆

If we don't put out these mega fires as quickly as possible, the catastrophic losses will continue to accrue. The brutal lesson will come too late as to how to better care for our national forests.

◆

First, put out the Fire! explains why the West's forests are on fire and what we must do to better protect our nation's forest heritage and future.

Thompson Pass above Murray, Idaho

Table of contents

Acknowledgements

I am indebted to many for their help and inspiration with this writing project. The list forms a trapline that stretches back at least 40 years and includes some whose passing from this life I still mourn.

In the here and now, my Broomall, Pennsylvania colleague, Michael Rains, who has written the Foreword for this book and who read every word of every draft; Phil Aune, whose wildfire wisdom and enthusiasm are unrivaled; Rich Stem, a Forest Service retiree for his technical assistance. Rich's encyclopedic knowledge of the National Environmental Policy Act makes him one of the best at navigating its complex forest planning rules; Lyle Laverty, whose resume includes leadership roles in the U.S. Forest Service, the U.S. Department of the Interior and as Director of Colorado's state park system, and the always plainspoken Bill Derr, the conscience of Forest Service retirees who believe that bold forest management is the key to effective fire management.

Jim Petersen

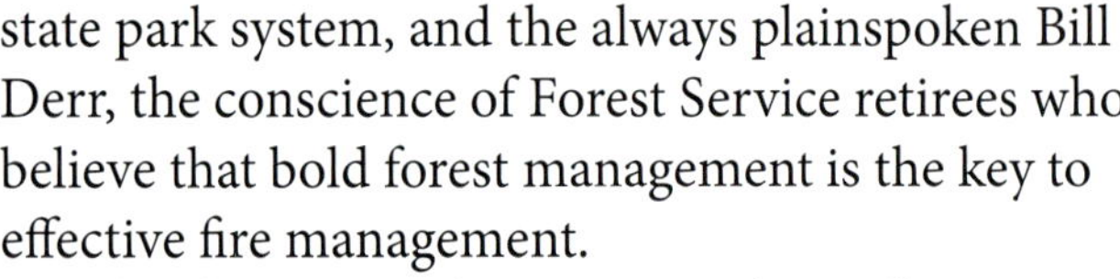

Thanks to Darrel Knops, another colleague and Forest Service retiree, for taking on the thankless job of explaining the connection between our changing climate and our crumbling national forests. We met 30-some years ago in Oregon. He was the Willamette National Forest Supervisor during the awful months when Earth Liberation Front terrorists were threatening his staff. After ELF burned down the Oakridge Ranger District office, the FBI hunted down the suspects. It took nearly 10 years, but they were convicted and jailed.

Thanks are due Peter Kolb, a PhD eco-physiologist at the University of Montana for spending hours and days explaining how forests in the Interior West function, why wildfires are consuming them, what pollen samples taken from the bottoms of lakes tell us about forests that grew in the aftermath of the last Ice Age and the differences between forests that are fire dependent and fire adapted.

Peter recently completed a remarkable video explaining the basic ecology of Rocky Mountain forests.[1]

Thanks to Paul Hessburg, a PhD landscape ecologist with the Forest Service's Pacific Northwest Research Station at Wenatchee, Washington for sharing his wildfire knowledge, which is self-evident in his "Era of Megafires"[2] presentation.

I am indebted to the horde of scientists and technicians who work for the Forest Service's Forest Inventory and Analysis Program in Portland, Ogden, St. Paul and Knoxville. These professionals – men and women representing every forestry discipline – are the census takers for America's forests. The technologies they have harnessed in the last decade are bringing us images from remote forests around the world. Only the most dedicated among us would think it possible to partner with NASA to bring us forest data from the Space Shuttle.

Special thanks to Jim Menlove and Todd Morgan. Jim works for the Forest Service in

Ogden. It was he who first introduced me to FIA data maybe 15 years ago and it is Todd, who keeps me supplied with FIA economic data from his post as Director of the Forest Industry Research Program at the University of Montana's Bureau of Business and Economic Research.

Thanks to my friend Dennis Becker, Director of the University of Idaho's Policy Analysis Group and Interim Dean of Idaho's College of Natural Resources. Dennis is the inspiration for my *Felt Necessities* essays,[3] which began as a presentation to one of his graduate forestry classes. You can find them on our *Evergreen* website.

Major thanks to Duane Vaagen and Mike Petersen for introducing me to forest collaboration. I had first seen it fail in southern Oregon and northern California in the 1980s and had no idea that Duane and Mike were breathing new life into the idea in northeast Washington – Duane as owner of Vaagen Lumber Company at Colville and Mike as Executive Director of the Lands Council in Spokane, two old warriors looking to heal battle scars by bringing the wounded together for the common good.

Roger Johnson, Gordy Sanders and Tim Love were on a similar mission in western Montana. Stewardship Contracting was both new and controversial but they gave it their all anyway – and it worked magnificently. I have dozens of photographs of the Clearwater Stewardship Project that demonstrate what happens when leaders lead – Roger as owner of the Pyramid Lumber Company at Seeley Lake, Gordy as his resource manager and Tim as District Ranger on the Forest Service's Seeley Lake Ranger District.

Stewardship Contracting is commonplace today but they were the only ones brave enough to give it a try. The coalition they started now includes several leading conservation groups including the Blackfoot Challenge, the Kootenai Forest Stakeholders Coalition, the Theodore Roosevelt Conservation Partnership and the Rocky Mountain Elk Foundation.

1 

2 

3 

Former Forest Service Chief, Dale Bosworth, was kind enough to invite Julia and I into his Missoula home to explain why he sees reasons for hope in the emergence of so many diverse collaborative groups – and why collaboratives offer our best and perhaps only realistic hope for pulling western national forests back from the brink of ecological collapse.

Barry Wynsma started writing essays for *Evergreen Magazine* only weeks after he retired from the Forest Service, but we first met several years earlier on a biomass thinning tour on the Bonners Ferry Ranger District in the Idaho Panhandle. John Deere was demonstrating its biomass bundler, a technological marvel that proved too expensive to operate in low value timber.

I have Barry to thank for introducing me to a logger who modified some of his older machines so he could remove very small trees from restoration projects I would have thought impossible. His name is Dave Ehrmantrout. The projects we toured are only a few miles from the bundler project. Every skeptic should see the beautiful result. Dave and his sons are big time artists in the biomass world – and I have the photographs to prove it.

Thanks to my South Dakota friend, Tom Troxel, who early in his career worked on the Kootenai National Forest and for years thereafter managed the Intermountain Forestry Association's office in Rapid City. It was Tom who lured me to the Black Hills National Forest in 1999 to write about Case No. 1, the first federal timber sale in history. Gifford Pinchot helped lay out the sale in what was then the Black Hills Forest Reserve in 1899, six years before the Forest Service was formed.

The story is momentous if for no other reason than the fact that more timber is growing in the Black Hills National Forest today than there was in 1899. Such has been the contribution of forestry when and where it is allowed to flourish.

Tom coaxed us back to the Black Hills last summer. We have begun work on a major Case No. 1 update. Wildfire and collaboration are our main characters. We again see what happens when good people set out to do good things together.

Thanks to Jim Neiman for tossing us the keys to his sawmills at Spearfish and Hill City, South Dakota and Hulett, Wyoming. Were it not for this third-generation family's commitment to its communities, there would not be a viable market for the impressive flow of ponderosa pine thinnings the Black Hills National Forest yields annually while also providing a dazzling array of recreation possibilities.

The Black Hills is one of only three western national forests in which tree growth exceeds mortality. Jim Neiman's employees provide a good deal of the glue that holds it all together. The Nature Conservancy should be so lucky in its effort to find investors for the central Washington sawmill it envisions.

Thanks to Don Motanic, Gary Morishima and the members of the Intertribal Timber Council for teaching me the ways of Indian forestry. Over the last 20 years, we have published three *Evergreen* tribal forestry reports to Congress. They are all good but my favorite is "Forestry in Indian Country: Solving Forestry's Rubik's Cube." You can find it on our website. Click "Magazine Archive' on the toolbar. Tribal forestry's spiritual and cultural underpinnings should be canonized in our national forests. Indians have been successfully farming and managing forests from coast to coast for thousands of years.

I am indebted to Nick Smith and Mike Archer for their informative Monday through Friday news summaries. Mike lives in Los Angeles. We've never met but his *Wildfire News of the Day* [4] is my "go to" for news about wildfires around the world. Really well done.

Nick Smith reminds me of myself 30 years ago. Back then, before the Internet, when cell phones were the size of lunch buckets, we organized a grass roots network similar to his but probably not as large. Nick's *Healthy Forests Healthy Communities* [5] news digest summarizes the comings and goings in forestry and forest communities across these United States, much like the old snail mail clipping services. Give it a try. It's good.

Thanks to my stepson, Eli, and his cousin, Cody, for their fine work on a series of unscripted "man-on-the-street" interviews we recently completed in concert with Nick. The boys picked men and women at random on the streets of Portland and Seattle and asked them what they thought should be done about our wildfire pandemic. Most admitted they knew little about forestry, but to our great surprise, not one of them endorsed the environmentalist call for allowing the West's killing fires to burn themselves out because "it's natural." You can watch these three to four-minute videos on our *Evergreen* YouTube Channel. [6]
Very interesting.

Thanks to my friend, Steve Wilent, who edits *The Forestry Source,* [7] the Society of American Forestry monthly tabloid newspaper. He also teaches forestry at Mount Hood Community College in Portland. Long ago, "in a galaxy far, far away, Steve set chokers on a logging crew. This I did not know until I read his biography.

For reasons I still don't understand, Steve invited me to write an essay for *193 Million Acres: Toward a Healthier and More Resilient U.S. Forest Service*, a fine book he edited that describes the multiple challenges facing our Forest Service. Most who contributed are forest scientists or Forest Service retirees. Why he asked me remains a mystery, but I'm glad he did. You can order his book online. Rob Freres and Lynn Herbert entrusted me with their sawmilling family stories. *Can't Never Could Do Anything* is the life story of Lynn's dad, Milt.

When I asked Milt the secret to his success he said, "My customers became my friends and my friends became my customers. *Santiam Song* is the four-generation story of the Freres family's Freres Lumber Company, an icon in western Oregon founded in 1922 by Rob's grandfather, T.G. Freres. There was no "quit" in T.G. and there is none in his son, grandsons or nephews.

Mike Newton, the only silviculturist I've ever known who has a PhD in botany. He taught and supervised Oregon State University forestry grad-

4 

5 

6 

7 

8 

uate students for 40 years. At 6-foot-5, his long legs served him well in two very different capacities: as an Infantry Platoon Leader in Germany during World War II and much later as a Tree Farmer. Mike's land west of Corvallis was treeless and brush-covered when he bought it in 1960. Now many of the Douglas-fir seedlings he planted are four to five feet in diameter. Such was his expertise in the use of herbicides to control brush that impedes tree growth. Mike is a marvelous and patient teacher. Much of what I know about Douglas-fir I learned from him.

Thanks to Dick Bennett for showing me the first mountain pine beetle I ever saw. He used his jack knife to dig it from a tree trunk on his land above Elk City, Idaho, then laid it gently on my index finger so I could watch it crawl. Then I crushed it.

Dick is a legend among Idaho sawmill owners and was a steady Evergreen Foundation contributor for years. On September 11, 2001, I photographed hundreds of acres of rust-colored beetle kill where his beautiful Tree Farm borders diseased and dying tree stands on the Nez Perce National Forest.

I was in the woods early that morning and did not know until evening that nearly 3,000 of us had been killed that day at the World Trade Center in New York, the Pentagon in Washington, D.C. and a farmer's field in Stoneycreek Township, Somerset County, Pennsylvania in the worst terrorist attack ever on American soil. The fires that are burning our nation's soul have many sources.

C.J. Hadley, a pistol-of-a-woman who allows me to write periodically for *RANGE,*[8] her beautiful and thought-provoking magazine about cattle and sheep ranching in the west – the idyllic life I lived on my grandfather's ranch when I was a boy. Writing periodically for C.J. quiets my soul.

Thanks to Danny O'Reilly, my Bronx cab-driver friend, who was embarrassed to ask me if there were any trees left out west but did anyway. I assured him they still stretched as far as the eye could see. Then he flipped off his meter and took me to his home, where his wife fixed sandwiches for us. Hours later he drove me back to my mid-town Manhattan hotel.

Danny, if this book should ever show up on your radar screen, come see us. We'll make sandwiches and get caught up over glasses of red wine. And because I know you don't know, the Bronx spans 27,180 acres, an area less than 18 percent the size of the 2018 Camp Fire that burned almost 19,000 buildings in and around Paradise, California. Not what we had in mind when we talked forestry and conservation at your kitchen table longer ago than I care to remember.

Among those I want to thank who have gone on but remain inspirations: My 40-year mentor, Bill Hagenstein, who testified before House and Senate forestry committees and subcommittees more than anyone in history. Thanks for the Old Bushmills and soda, the bedroom downstairs, our many midnight chats, breakfast in your "cook-house," our photographic memory and your vast knowledge of the history of American forestry.

Hal Salwasser, Dean of the Oregon State University College of Forestry until shortly before his death in 2014. We met when he was Region 1 Regional Forester in Missoula, possibly 20 years ago. Hal was the first to attempt to describe "New Forestry," a management ethos that veers close to forestry in Indian Country. He had crossed swords with Vice President Al Gore on a couple of issues, which got him banished to the Forest Service's fire science lab at Davis, California. Hal would have made a fine Forest Service Chief, but he cringed every time I brought up the idea in *Evergreen* Magazine.

I once asked Hal what it would take for me to earn a forestry degree at Oregon State. "Why would you want to do that?" he asked. "You've already done more for American forestry than any forester I know." Thanks Hal, but I doubt it.

The late Carl Stoltenberg, who was OSU's forestry school dean during Evergreen's earliest years. Dean Stoltenberg graciously tossed me the keys to Peavy Hall and said, "Talk to anyone you like and learn all you can." It was the beginning of an ad hoc forestry education that I still pursue daily.

On my first visit, I spent a week roaming from office to office. Among those I met: future Evergreen Foundation board member, Con Schallau, a highly-regarded PhD forest economist with the Forest Service's Pacific Northwest Research Station. It was Con who introduced me to the agency's voluminous Resource Planning Act [RPA] assessments. "You need to read these," he said in a

Lookout Pass on the Idaho-Montana Divide

commanding voice. I dutifully did. Back then, the always well-illustrated 400-500-page assessments existed only in print. Now you can Google them.

Thanks to Peter Koch, Robert Buckman and Ben Stout, three of the finest PhD forest scientists I ever knew. They spent countless hours explaining their wide-ranging disciplines to me.

Peter headed the Forest Service's research station at Knoxville, Tennessee for many years. Somewhere in time he patented a lathe for peeling soft southern pine logs into veneer panels for the plywood industry. It made him wealthy.

After he retired, I spent a mind-bending day at Peter's home and lab near Corvallis, Montana, soaking up his exhaustive knowledge of lodgepole pine, a prolific species in the Interior West with a lifespan about the same as humans. Peter's three-volume series exploring its taxonomy, management and use is essential reading for foresters and lumbermen engaged in restoration projects. Lodgepole seeds are sealed inside their cones by a waxy substance that are best opened by the heat of fire. Although lodgepole makes a handsome house log, it tends to overcrowd itself in thickets filled with trees no bigger around than your forearm. Thinning prevents this from happening.

Robert Buckman directed the PNW Research Station in Portland before moving on to Washington, D.C. where he directed research and international programs for the agency, a position that led to his being named vice president and then president of the International Union of Forest Research Organizations, representing 15,000 forest scientists in 110 countries.

We met shortly before he gave up his teaching position at Oregon State. In one of our many conversations, I asked about federal funding for old-growth research. He bristled, collected himself and said something I've never forgotten. He said, "I want to argue that for every dollar the federal government spends on old growth, it needs to spend another dollar studying young forests. There is more biological diversity there than there is in old growth."

Ben Stout was a well-traveled PhD silviculturist who began his long teaching career at Rutgers University. He later saved the University of Montana's forestry school from academic ruin, then went on to direct the National Council for Air and Stream

Improvement research program at Oregon State.

For reasons he never explained, Ben took a special interest in my writing. It was he who introduced me to the diaries of Hugh Miller Raup, Bullard Professor of Forestry at Harvard University and possibly the botany world's most legendary boat rocker. His *1938 Botanical studies in the Black Forest* is a classic.

D.R. Johnson, a tough-as-nails Riddle, Oregon lumbermen who hired me away from the *Grants Pass Daily Courier* to do public relations work for the long-gone North West Timber Association. In June 1971, D.R. called to say he wanted to hire me. He'd loved a series of articles I'd written about forestry in the Douglas-fir region. I'd only been at the *Courier* for a few months so I initially said I wasn't comfortable leaving the paper so soon. At our second lunch meeting he said fixed me with his trademark scowl and said, "How much do you make here?" I reluctantly told him and he said, "I'll double it."

Wes Rickard, a forestry legend

I worked for D.R. long enough to know [1] that I respected him as much as I did my own father and [2] I could not work for him. He was so angry when I quit that I feared he might not sign my last check. Happily, we remained good friends for 39 years. The last time I saw him he was sitting in a wheelchair in his office, too stubborn to go home and enjoy the small empire he'd built from scratch.

Aaron Jones, a lumberman of uncompromising standards and dignity who spent millions perfecting log sawing technologies that were so advanced he was able to patent them. Aaron asked me to help him assemble the post-World War II history of the West's Independent lumbermen – independent in the sense that they did not own timberland, sailed their own ships and answered only to the guy they saw in the mirror. We did it together and it was great fun.

Wes Lematta, a kind and unassuming man who built the largest heavy-lift helicopter company in the world out of a fanciful idea that came to him while he watched P-51s fly over his water-filled foxhole in the South Pacific. They were so close overhead that he could see the pilots that were laying down protective fire ahead of him. "They were going back to warm beds and hot meals and I wasn't," he told me years later. "I wanted to learn to fly after the war."

Columbia Helicopters pioneered helicopter logging in national forests in northern California and southern Oregon in the late 1960s and early 1970s. Wes and I met over bowls of clam chowder in a Gold Beach, Oregon café in June of 1971. I was there as a guest of Siskiyou National Forest Supervisor, Bill Ronayne. Bill wanted me to witness the astonishing lift capacity of the S-64 Skycrane Wes and Jack Erickson had leased from Sikorsky. Nearly 40 years later, Wes asked me to help him assemble Flying Finns, the 50-year history of his company. Despite his failing health, he wrote thank you notes in most of the 900-plus copies he gave to Columbia employees working on five continents.

Early on, I asked Wes how he had overcome the desperate moments when it looked like there might not be enough money to pay the monthly bills. "I just kept working," he said quietly. Then, as if to check the accuracy of his answer, he repeated what he had already told me. "I just kept working."

Wes died on Christmas Eve, 2009, but you can still see his twin-rotor airships working big wildfires here in the West. They cost taxpayers about $10,000 an hour and Wes hated every minute of it.

"Why aren't we thinning these forests before they burn," he asked me many times. We both knew the answer but his question is as valid today than it was 30 years ago, so following Wes's lead, I just keep working.

My friend, John Marker, undoubtedly one of the classiest guys who ever worked for the U.S. Forest Service. We met during the spotted owl wars. He was the driving force behind the founding of the National Association of Forest Service Retirees and an Evergreen Foundation board member for many years. I miss his great wisdom and steady counsel more than words can say.

Jack Ward Thomas, Forest Service Chief after the owl was listed as a threatened species. Jack had directed much of the research leading to the listing. We became friends after he retired and accepted a position as Boone and Crockett Professor of Wildlife Conservation at the University of Montana.

I don't know if Jack knew that John Marker called him "God" after he refused to join NAFSR, but I sought him out anyway because he was brilliant and brutally candid about his successes and failures. Of all the observations he shared with me the one I remember most was his wish for more "by-God humility" in the science and forest policy arenas. I agree.

Robert Bradley Slagle, USMC, World War II, Tinian, Tarawa and Bougainville, who taught me how to drive log trucks because he knew I wanted to learn. R.B. and I traveled a lot of miles over the years, both literally and figuratively.

Larry Brown and Leigh Johnson, fishing buddies for 30-some years – Larry who hired war-weary Vietnam veterans to thin Josephine County Forests in southern Oregon and who gave me his drift boat about a month before cancer killed him. "I don't think I'll be needing it anymore," he said. "You take it back to Montana with you." He was only 61 and I think of him every time I pick up the oars.

And Leigh, an American patriot and congressional dandy who was for years a constant source of forestry intelligence for me. We were born on the same date , February 23, and celebrated our birthdays with Larry for years. He was born the day after Leigh and I and was late most days for the rest of his life.

Leigh pretended to love fly fishing and had an expensive rod to prove it, but what he really loved was the peace the Kootenai River brought him, rare ribeye steaks at the Riverbed Restaurant and vodka tonics on the deck at the Otter Cabin, which overlooked Jennings Rapids. He was so damned fastidious that he had his fishing jeans starched and pressed. But I loved him anyway.

My father-in-law, Wes Rickard, a giant in the world of forestry. He was the old Weyerhaeuser Timber Company's first forest economist and it was he who invented high yield forestry for them in the late 1950s. In answer to all my late night forestry questions, Wes always asked his own question: "What do you want from your forest?" If I could describe what I wanted – better fire protection, more wildlife habitat, older trees or steady income from periodic harvests - he could tell me how to get it – the caveat being soil protection.

"We must protect the soil because without it we have nothing," he'd remind me. The West's wildfire pandemic is incinerating millions of acres of organic soil in which newly planted trees would otherwise grow quickly.

Back on earth, thanks to my 30-year friend, Dave Blackburn, a West Virginia forestry school graduate and a gyppo timber faller in his youth. He is easily the finest fishing guide I've ever known and a marvelous banjo picker who somehow convinced my wife to open her cello case and play for the first time in years. Now they play together at Dave and Tammy's Riverbend Restaurant. I can't read a note or carry a tune but their music is a joy to my ears.

Bruce and P.J. Vincent, Kootenai River friends who stuck by me during the low ebb of my life. Men and women who get their hands dirty every day in forests, fields and mines have never had better friends than these two. Bruce is beyond doubt the most electrifying public speaker I've ever heard. P.J. has been his steady and trusted compass for 40-plus years.

And Julia, my wife and business partner, a fiery red-headed beauty whose laughter and million-dollar smile lift me up when nothing else can. She saved my life many years ago and still insists it was a life worth saving. I hope so.

Jim Petersen

Dalton Gardens, Idaho
July 3, 2019

Foreward

Since my retirement from the United States Forest Service in 2016, I have been talking to Jim Petersen almost constantly, it would seem. Yet, oddly enough, I have never met Jim in person. My connection with Jim has been through the conservation of America's forests. Jim, Founder and President of the Evergreen Foundation, allowed my voice – specifically, the role of "aggressive forest management to ensure effective fire management" – to emerge through his *Evergreen* Magazine.

Jim and I have developed a strong bond and friendship. When he asked me to write the *Foreword* to his book, I was both honored and a little scared, to be frank. Jim writes like no other. His writing style is eloquent, comfortable, informative and contemporary. And, he seems to know everything about America's forests and what's needed for their stewardship. This book is exposé of that vast knowledge.

Michael Rains, U.S. Forest Service, 48 years

Even though I began my Forest Service career as a wildland firefighter, I was never part of the formal "fire organization." But I often intersected with wildland fire during my almost 50 years with the agency by studying the costs of fire suppression and the impacts of wildfire on people's lives and their communities. Especially during the last decade of my Forest Service career, detailed discussions about "improved fire management" were commonplace. As a member of the Forest Service leadership team, we seemed to talked constantly about how better managed forests could become more resilient so wildfires would be smaller, less intense and eventually become a tool for improved forest health -- as opposed to destructive behemoths that destroy everything in their paths. No one disagreed. But real change seemed to always remain elusive.

As one of our country's top journalists, Jim was writing and teaching and pushing for change on this critical issue. I was learning. And, together we were having nothing to do with the notion that destructive wildfires are becoming the "new normal." In our minds, that was simply a convenient excuse for maintaining the status quo. As we often concluded, the current wildfire situation, and the devastation that is taking place year after year, "does not have to be this way." So, when Jim said, "I am going to write a book about fire and what we need to do to address this situation facing our country," no one was surprised. That's Jim Petersen; that's what he does. The phenomenal result: *First, put out the Fire! Rescuing Western*

National Forests from Nature's Wildfire Pandemic.

As the chapters of his book were unfolding, a small cadre of us would comment. Mostly, I would read and from the very beginning became captivated by the incredible historical depth of how fires have and are shaping our lives and communities across America. The book is indeed a history lesson about forest management, protection and wise use and how the lack of professional will to effectively address the relationships between well-managed forests and uncontrollable wildfires has us stuck.

Jim has been a working journalist for -some 50 years. The words in this book will jump out and grab you and not let go. I recall saying as the book began taking its final shape, "...I so wish I could write like that." *First, Put out the Fire!* will take you on an incredible journey that includes a mesmerizing discussion with Danny O'Reilly from the Bronx and instructional wisdom from legendary conservationists like Peter Kolb. With a powerful foundation of the horrific impacts caused by wildfire, the book with draw you in with experiential vignettes; the tug-of-war between conservationists and environmentalists [yes, there is a difference]; a formidable *Question and Answer* segment about forestry; values associated with a complex rural to urban land gradient; and the vibrancy and vision of iconic leadership and the perils associated with lack of focus by those who are afraid to make mistakes; waiting on the sidelines, doing nothing.

I hate what is happening to America's forests. Over the last three decades or so, and most do agree with this, there has been a lack of forest management along the rural to urban land gradient throughout our country. For the Forest Service, this has been due to a shifting of resources away from restorative actions to fire suppression. A paradox has developed. The more resources that are shifted away from management actions, the larger and angrier wildfires have become because forests are not being maintained. The west, due in part to the impacts of a changing climate, is particularly vulnerable. Jim Petersen's book describes this in sobering detail.

Uncontrollable wildfires due to the lack of forest management is the conservation issue of our time. Again, what is happening does not need to happen. We must change this destructive cycle so

The cover of a 2003 edition of *Evergreen* begs a question that remains unanswered 17 years later: What the devil is our federal government's forest management objective? Are we going to manage our national forests or let nature do the work for us? Before you choose, remember that nature doesn't care about human need - and our list of forest wants and needs is long and complex.

American lives, their communities, and the landscapes where we live can be protected. Jim's book, in a very candid, instructional and sometimes humorous way, provides the direction.

Those who read *First, put out the Fire!* will not look at America's trees and forests the same way ever again. I predict your voice will also emerge and standing on the sidelines will no longer be an option. As Jim states, "we are all a part of this American story." Now is our time.

I loved reading this incredible book. I know you will too.

Michael T. Rains

Author:
A Forest Service Vision During the Anthropocene [2017].
Co-Author:
Restoring Fire as a Landscape Conservation Tool: Nontraditional Thoughts for a Traditional Organization [2018].
Managing the Impacts of Wildfires on Communities and the Environment – the National Fire Plan [2001].

"Are there any trees left?"

On a beastly hot afternoon some 20 years ago, I hailed a cab in the Bronx and asked the driver if he could take me to my hotel in Manhattan.

"Sure," he said in one of the thickest Bronx accents I'd ever heard. God only knows how long he'd been driving cabs, but he was Bronx-born, Irish, in his early 60s and he'd never been out of the five boroughs that make up New York City. His name was Danny O'Reilly.

Almost immediately, he asked where I was from and what I did. I said I was from Montana and that I ran a forestry education program I'd started in 1986.

Silence. He was watching me in his rear-view mirror, but I wasn't prepared for his next question.

"Are there any trees left out west?"

Before I could answer he said, "We hear all these stories here about how all the trees out there have been chopped down."

"I know," I said ruefully. "Let me assure you, we have millions if not billions of trees in our forests. You should come out sometime. I'll show you around."

My openness clearly took him by surprise. He reached across the front seat, flipped off his meter at $4.50 and said, "You're my last fare for the day. Let's go over to my place. My wife can fix lunch and we can talk."

And with that he asked dispatch to patch him through to his wife. "Estelle honey, I'm bringing a guy from Montana home for lunch. You'll like him."

I have no idea how often Danny O'Reilly invited his fares home for lunch, but it was great. Homemade pasta and a glass of wine. We must have talked for three hours about his growing up in the Bronx, my growing up in northern Idaho and how amazing it was that our paths had crossed.

"I'm embarrassed about asking you if there were any trees left," he said.

"Don't be," I replied. "I've had people back here ask me if hostile Indians still attack us at night for stealing their land."

"Oh for chrissake," he roared. "Even I know that's not true."

"It's a long story," I explained. "Land ownership was not a concept Indians understood, so tribes often 'stole' one another's places in the wild west. But tribes did not claim ownership in the same way we do with property titles and land deeds, so we simply jammed them onto reservations so they could not slow our so-called 'Manifest Destiny,' the settlement of the West by European whites."

Danny and I talked some about Central Park, beautiful by day but very dangerous by night – and patrolled after dark by heavily armed mounted policemen. I had seen them the previous evening while touring the park in a horse-drawn buggy. Public safety is a big deal in Central Park, no doubt because New Yorkers see the park as a national treasure. It is all that and more. It was a rock quarry before famed landscape architect Fredrick Olmstead worked his magic.

"You would never see that in a park in Montana, Danny" I said of my chance encounter with two mounted policemen. One carried a shotgun, the other an automatic weapon of some kind. Both wore .44 caliber sidearms.

"It's a fact of life here," Danny said of the jaw-dropping firepower I'd seen in Central Park. "Too many people crammed into a small space."

Five boroughs joined together by bridges and

concrete: 1.5 million in The Bronx, Danny's hometown; 1.67 million in Manhattan, where I was staying; 8.6 million in New York City, 2.6 million more in Brooklyn, another 2.3 million in Queens and 479,500 on Staten Island. 17.15 million in all.

More than twice the combined political power of Idaho, Montana, Wyoming, Utah and New Mexico, a chunk of geography I know well.

"But it's different on our street," Danny said as he swung into the car-length driveway beside their home. Estelle greeted us on a front porch covered with blooming potted flowers and vines. Her colorful apron reminded me of the ones my grandmother made every winter.

"We have families and kids and grandkids here," Danny said, his arm sweeping the length of street. "We look out for each other. Kids can't get away with much. Their mothers deputize each other."

Northern Spotted Owl - Mike McMurray

The visual brought back fond memories of my own growing up in Kellogg, Idaho. I described the same scene Danny has just described to me.

"Every mother on Mission Avenue was deputized and the sheriff was Madeline Bottinelli. She made sure we all got up on time for work or school, and if you were sick she brought you a pot of minestrone soup and a loaf of bread hot out of her oven. I was one of two kids on our block who weren't Italian Catholics, so I spoke Italian before I spoke English."

Danny laughed and Estelle refilled our wine glasses. Age separated us but we three had grown up in the same neighborhood: Mission Avenue in Kellogg and Jerome Avenue in the Bronx, 2,512 miles east.

Our afternoon together remains one of the most memorable in my life. It was past seven o'clock when he dropped me off at my hotel. We promised we'd stay in touch but we didn't. Life got in the way. Now I wonder if he and Estelle are still living. Not knowing is its own emptiness.

My chance encounter with Danny O'Reilly completely changed the way I look at the cultural divide that distances rural America from urban America. There isn't that much distance between us. No matter where we live, most of us value many of the same things. Forests being a big one.

Danny had never been out of the five boroughs, but he wanted to know if what he'd heard about the trees out west was true. When I asked him why he said, "I probably won't ever see them but still I want to know they're there."

I've spent years thinking about how Danny's desire to know about trees more than 2,500 miles from his home translates into a more civil forestry dialogue and a better-informed citizenry.

If facts by themselves carried the day, the timber industry would have all the Danny's in our country in their hip pocket. But they don't, which tells me that facts alone aren't going to carry the day where public worries about the welfare of our nation's forests are concerned.

Why is this? I think it's because we are only human. We make mistakes. We don't all value the same things in the same way and we can be very defensive about the by-God certainty of what we believe.

Mark Twain or maybe Josh Billings – no one seems to know for sure - spoke to this human frailty.

> *"It ain't what you don't know that gets you into trouble. It's what you know for sure that just ain't so."*

A modern-day version of this observation might go something like this:

> *"It ain't what you don't know that gets you into trouble. It's the algorithms on your cell phone that deliver the news you want that just ain't so."*

I recently read a fascinating article titled, "Changing others' minds or our own is a tricky business. Here's how to make it happen." Google it if you like. The author is Ozan Varol, a former rocket scientist turned lawyer. He teaches at the Lewis and Clark Law School in Portland, Oregon.

The crux of Varol's 2017 essay is that facts and statistics – the mother's milk of rocket scientists and foresters – rarely change minds or hearts.

Playing Al Gore's Inconvenient Truth on repeat to a room of Detroit auto workers won't change their mind on global warming if they're convinced your agenda will put them out of a job," Varol wrote. "Humans operate on different frequencies. If someone disagree with you, it's not because they're wrong and you're right. It's because they believe something that you don't believe."

The challenge, Varol writes, is to identify the area of disagreement, then adjust your own frequency. Job security is vital to Detroit auto workers, so they won't be moved by pictures of polar bears navigating melting glaciers. Instead, he argues, show the auto workers how renewable energy will provide job security for their grandchildren.

"The trick," Varol opines, is to give your mind an excuse to change your own thinking because, until you give yourself an out, you won't be able to change other minds. Unfortunately, our human tendency is to belittle those with whom we disagree ["I told you so"]. We ostracize ["Basket of deplorables."]. We ridicule ["What an idiot."].

I saw plenty of this behavior during the spotted owl wars in the 1980s and 90s. The timber industry hammered away with its reams of facts and statistics, while environmentalists verbally assaulted loggers and millworkers – those deplorable souls for whom job security was everything.

When the federal government listed the owl as a threatened species in June of 1990, environmentalists declared victory and about 40,000 woods workers lost their jobs. But no minds were changed, the combatants are still living in foxholes and to this day, 29 years after the listing, spotted owl populations are still in free-fall and we don't know why.

How can this be? Simple. The owl was a surrogate – a means for setting old growth forests aside in no-harvest reserves. Environmentalists took this route because the federal Endangered Species Act does not protect "old growth" per se. But it does protect species. Protecting old growth necessitated finding a storyline that could focus the federal government's attention on the need to list the owl.

While I busied myself making the jobs case in small logging towns in southwest Oregon and northern California, environmentalists took their show on the road. Manhattan became a favored destination: great wealth and even greater political influence, the media capital of the nation. What better place to show pictures of "cathedral forests" or mountainous piles of stumps left behind by "greedy" loggers, those "last buffalo hunters."

No one in Manhattan cared about job losses in Cave Junction, Oregon. And why should they? But they did care about protecting old growth in national forests out west. This is why Danny O'Neill asked me if there were any trees left out west. He cared. So do I, which is why I wrote this book in my seventy-fifth year.

First, Put out the Fire! is the summation of what I have learned about wildfire and forest management over the last 33 years. It traces the path that I took to give myself an out, to escape the echo chamber where I lived before I began to think more deeply about why hundreds of thousands of acres of old growth reserved in no-harvest areas in national forests we all love are burning to the ground in catastrophic wildfires for which there is no ecological precedent in our nation's history.

Herein, I chronicle the history of the west's wildfire pandemic, lay out the stark choices we face and offer safe, reliable, time-tested, science-based solutions for pulling western national forests back from the fiery brink of ecological collapse.

Time is short and hope is not a strategy. But by drilling deep into the very direct connection between our changing climate and our wildfire crisis, we can assemble a Green New Deal that taps the creativity and vitality of generations of young men and women who are the future of our nation and our forests.

A word about my title. We face three kinds of fire in our nation's forests: the senseless and very destructive Political Fires that burn in our nation's capital, Bad Fires that are destroying mostly national forests out West where I live, and Good Fires we should be using in combination with some very large-scale gardening techniques to slow our wildfire crisis before it's too late. Our first fire scientists often reminded us that fire was a great servant but a terrible master.

There's a lot of chatter here in the West about how our wildfire pandemic is "the new normal." This is misleading nonsense and it's just plain wrong! I'll have much more to say about this deplorable situation throughout this book, but know this in the interim: In Germany, where forests have been sustainably managed for 500 years, most fires are extinguished within 20 minutes of the time they are spotted!

Conflagrations like the ones that are incinerating our western national forests don't occur as often in heavily forested Scandinavia or northern Europe, but some do in Greece, Spain and Portugal where arson is a means of protesting restrictive land development laws.

Why the big difference here? It's all about what you value – and Europe's citizens place a much higher value on managed forests that yield timber for recreation and eventual harvest. Here we mainly play lip service to what's "natural" and "green," but we haven't a clue what "conservation" requires or how to achieve it.

Our 301,562 square mile national forest estate is falling apart and burning to the ground. That's an area larger than the entire Northeast: New York, Pennsylvania, Maine, New Hampshire, Vermont, Connecticut, Ohio, New Jersey, Maryland, Massachusetts, Virginia, Delaware and Rhode Island!

If Danny O'Neill is still living, he is one pissed off Irishman, and if he is dead he is rolling over in his grave.

Imprimis: getting started

It isn't necessary that you agree with everything you read in this book, or any of it for that matter.

What is necessary is that you be aware of what is happening to our nation's forests, and especially our national forests.

You, me and about 325 million of our best friends share ownership in them – and they are in terrible shape for reasons I'll explain in painful detail.

Don't take my word for anything you read here. Do your homework.

Whatever your environmental passions, hang on to them, but for heaven's sake, learn to think for yourself. Hone your critical thinking skills. Get off your damned cell phone and go to the library. Read, read, read.

We list many websites throughout this book that are maintained by the U.S. Forest Service. Exceptionally well-researched. No agendas. Just the facts.

Attend public meetings where forests and forestry are being discussed. Seek out people with local knowledge and experience. Ask questions of people who hold different points of view. Listen respectfully, even if you disagree.

Join discussion groups. Learn how to plow deep in the common ground. There is no perfect truth and there are no one-size-fits-all answers. What works in one place won't work everywhere. Nature doesn't work this way. Nor do societies.

Volunteer your time in a local collaborative group that is searching for answers to the really contentious questions that revolve around when, where and how to manage our national forests, and when and where to let Nature do the work. Remember that Nature isn't fragile. If it was, we wouldn't be here. There are backup systems galore. We can't see most of them, but they're here.

Nature has all the time in the world. We don't. This is why we need to do everything possible to protect natural systems that are powering the forests we all want and need. If you've got the time, learn this system from the bottom up, starting with the soil that holds the tiny nutrient-rich organisms where new forests take root. One of the first things you'll discover is that the 3,000-degree heat that radiates from big wildfires sometimes melts the organic layer into a waxy substance that rainwater cannot penetrate. It will take nature centuries to repair the damage. Meantime, no forest.

Soil is one of the building blocks of our civilization. In fact, we'd starve to death without it because we wouldn't have a place to grow our food. So I'll have lots to say about soil in this book.

The first place I saw soil melt was on a south-facing slope in southern Oregon that had been ravaged by wildfire. Loggers used a ripper blade on a bulldozer to break it up so water could penetrate the waxy layer. It looked ugly as hell but it stopped the water from pushing a lot of crap downhill into a nearby trout stream.

I recently asked my long-time friend Peter Kolb if he could explain what I'd seen. Peter has a PhD in forest and range ecophysiology. Ecophysiologists study the interrelationship between the normal physical function of an organism and its environment. He teaches in the Department of Forest Management at the University of Montana College of Forestry and Conservation in Missoula.

As you might expect – or maybe not – Peter emailed his answer, printed below in its entirety. It's pretty technical but I'm hoping you will be able to visualize what he describes. Even if you live in a big city and haven't seen what wildfires can do to a forest, you've probably seen what big fires do to big buildings. Hold that image in your mind's eye as you read this.

"Although severe fire effects can lead to serious soil erosion - I have yet to see the kind of soil melt you reference where the soil layer is sterilized. Heat goes the path of least resistance - which is up into the air.

In worst cases I have seen the upper two inches of soil altered by extreme heat, but the term "sterilization" is not correct.

You should also use the word "hydrophobicity" carefully because - although soils can develop some water repellent characteristics - it is mostly due to the water being driven away from soil particles that makes them wetting resistant. This is different from "sterilization" or "hydrophobicity" and is usually resolved by a good rain or snow-pack.

The fine ash left by the burning of thick organic layers is very erosive and can by itself slow down water penetration into the mineral soil by plugging macropores and creating a super water saturated surface layer that by the adhesion and cohesion properties of water can act as a barrier to soil water penetration.

When describing the effects on soil, I prefer to say that big fires can significantly increase the potential for soil erosion and can severely alter surface vegetation. I can show you drainages where I would estimate 75% of the topsoil was eroded in a rainstorm event after a severe fire.

This is particularly true in mountainous areas where soil coverage on bedrock is already very thin. Here fire can transform soil capable of supporting productive growth in trees and other vegetation into an area where exposed bedrock and boulders now account for 50 percent of the surface.

In such cases, it can take 1,000 years or more to rebuild the soil and vegetation conditions present before the fire. Because soils also act as water reservoirs and water filters, the impact on landscape hydrology can be severe because rain and snowmelt simply runs off and isn't stored and filtered in a soil substrate."

Now you know what I saw in southern Oregon and now you also know why I asked Peter to read the entire First, Put Out the Fire! I wanted a rock-solid forest scientist to read what I've written for accuracy and completeness. Peter is nothing if not jarringly accurate and complete!

Circling back, climate change is certainly a contributing factor where our wildfires are concerned, but the West's godawful wildfires and the carcinogenic smoke that annually floods thousands of western cities and towns are not solely the result climate change. Not by a long shot.

Of far greater significance has been our failure to care for our national forests as if we owned them. But wait! We do own them! So we best start paying attention to this shit show. The fate of our national forests is resting in our hands – yours and mine. Our voice matters. If we do nothing, we can expect to get nothing in return

What do you want from your forest?

If you're like most Americans, you want clean air, clean water, abundant fish and wildlife habitat, the beauty and solitude that only a forest can provide and a wealth of year-round outdoor recreation opportunity.

If you live far away from big forests, you probably dream about visiting them someday. Like my Bronx friend, Danny.

We also demand an abundance of high-quality, competitively-priced wood products, and sure as sure can be, the Big Box stores – The Home Depot, Lowes, Menards and 84 Lumber – stock everything you'll need to build a house, fence your yard, or add a family room or a new deck.

We all strive to improve our lives and owning a home most likely constructed from wood is one of those aspirations, so wood is literally and figuratively an essential building block in our lives

It's the same with the food we eat, the clothes we wear, the medicines we take and the energy that lights our homes and keeps us warm in the winter and cool in the summer.

Most of us have no idea where our stuff – the comforts of everyday life – comes from. We just expect that our stuff will always be there at the flip of a switch or the push of a button. And it almost always is.

We live off the land in a much different way than our forebears did. They grew their own food, sewed their own clothes, drilled their own water wells and built their own homes from timber cut from nearby forests or bricks fired from clay they dug from the earth.

Alston Chase, PhD, best-selling author.

We don't do any of this. We just go to the store and get what we need. That's nice but most of us have no idea how to care for or conserve land that provides the necessities of everyday life – especially forests we all love.

We all claim to be environmentalists, but most of us have no idea what it means to be an environmentalist.

More than 20 years ago, I interviewed Alston Chase, a PhD professor who holds degrees from Harvard, Oxford and Princeton, and who chaired the Department of Philosophy at Macalester College in Minnesota until he traded his academic life for that of a best-selling author.

Chase hit the bigtime when Atlantic published his *Playing God in Yellowstone*, a page-turner that describes the misdirected role environmentalists played in the mismanagement of Yellowstone National Park. I wish Chase's book was required reading in our high schools. What passes for an "environmental education" today is disgusting and disingenuous hyperbole. We're doing impressionable young Americans no favors. Remember, 14 year-olds will vote in four years.

Here's a thoughtful quote from our interview, which appeared in the September 1990 edition of *Evergreen*, the forestry journal I started in 1986.

"There is no such thing as leaving nature alone. People are part of nature. We do not have the option of choosing not to be stewards of the land. We must master the art and science of good stewardship. Environmentalists do not understand that the only way to preserve nature is to manage nature."

Chase said something else to me that I will just never forget.

"Environmentalism increasingly reflects urban perspectives.

As people move to cities, they become infatuated with fantasies of land untouched by humans. This demographic shift is revealed through ongoing debates about endangered species, grazing, water rights, private property, mining and logging.

It is partly a healthy trend. But this urbanization of environmental values also signals the loss of a rural way of life and the disappearance of hands on experience with nature. So the irony: as popular concern for preservation increases, public understanding about how to achieve it declines."

Alan Houston, PhD wildlife biologist.

A good place to start to gain some understanding is with a wisdom shared with me more than 20 years ago by my friend Alan Houston, the PhD wildlife biologist who manages the forestry program on the Ames Plantation at Grand Junction in middle Tennessee.

We were out walking on the Cumberland Plateau of a crystal-clear October 1997 morning, looking for his favorite tree – a towering white oak – when he suddenly turned to me and said something so memorable I can still quote it from memory.

"When we leave forests to nature, as so many people seem to want to do, we get whatever nature serves up, which can be very devastating at times, but with forestry we have options and a degree of predictability not found in nature."

What Alan was saying is that Nature is great but It doesn't care about us or the things we want and need from forests:

> Clean air, clean water, abundant fish and wildlife, the beauty and solitude that only a forest can provide and a wealth of year-round outdoor recreation opportunity.

To get our needs met, we must first learn how to care for our forests. Currently, we aren't doing a very good job. In fact, we're doing a terrible job. We're failing our forests, ourselves and future generations.

How bad a job are we doing? Tree mortality now exceeds growth by a ratio of more than three to one in some of our western national forests. These forests are dying faster than they are growing. Their dead wood is fueling a wildfire pandemic for which there are no parallels in the history of our country.

We have an eco-tragedy on our hands. It is morally, ethically and environmentally wrong – and it is not sustainable by any known social, environmental or economic measure, model or paradigm that prescribes a forest conservation ethic.

Many environmentalists are offended by the mere mention of economic losses associated with timber because they consider unmanaged forests to be priceless and irreplaceable environmental assets. As you will discover in these pages, this claim isn't true. Moreover, economics is a social science, not a physical one like biology or chemistry.

There isn't an economics model on earth that can capture the nuances and complexities of human behavior, but we still need a way to describe and measure the social and economic interface that joins humans to their natural surroundings in a continuous cycle of life, death, planting and harvest – something transparent that expresses both the philosophy and practice of forestry.

Maybe a good place to start anew is with a new conservation ethic fashioned from the wisdom of Chief Oshkosh, leader of the Menominee Indian Tribe of Wisconsin from 1827 to 1854.

> *"Start with the rising sun and work toward the setting sun, take only the mature trees, the sick trees and the trees that have fallen. When you reach the end of the reservation, turn and cut from the setting sun to the rising sun and the trees will last forever."*

America's Indian tribes manage their forests with environmental, economic, cultural, medicinal and spiritual goals in mind. They work on a seven-generation time horizon – meaning the management decisions they make in any given year are weighed against the outcome seven generations hence. I'll have more to say about tribal forestry in upcoming chapters, but their land ethic encompasses a management model well worth replicating in our western national forests.

Small dead tree salvage in western Montana

CHAPTER 4

Full disclosure

Misplaced environmental worries and ineffective and often politically-inspired federal forest management policies are the major reasons why our forests are dying and burning in wildfires for which there are no ecological precedents in our nation's history.

We have drifted away from site specific forest management that accounted for all the bits and pieces of a forest – including local social, cultural and economic need. We have adopted a 'command and control' approach that dumbs down diverse forest ecosystems in favor of more generic cookie-cutter approaches that insist on jamming square pegs in round holes.

Site specific management solutions based on what our forests are telling us have given way to process-drive bureaucracies that do a great job of crossing all the "T's" and dotting all the "I's" but do a terrible job of managing forest conditions nature presents.

By default, the U.S. Forest Service has become a Soviet-style bureaucracy that is gripped by a fear that it might do something wrong. Better to do nothing than to risk doing something that will invite congressional wrath. "Don't mess up," [DMU] has become the watchword in the Forest Service's chain of command. Gone are the locally-inspired management decisions that recognized local forest conditions and local social, cultural and economic needs.

The unintended result: We have far too many trees in our federally-owned national forests - the ones we own - for the natural carrying capacity of the land: the aggregate of soil fertility, annual rain and snowfall, elevation, sunlight and the cyclical influences of climatic warming and cooling cycles.

These cycles, which look like sine waves, reveal themselves in soil and pollen samples and tree ring counts. Scientists have collected samples from lake bottoms that date back tens of thousands of years. Muskeg samples reveal that Earth was once warm enough to support redwood trees inside the Arctic Circle.

A few months ago, Peter Kolb [See Imprimis] emailed me some peer-reviewed research that had been done by another PhD scientist he knows. The topic was how forests in Montana have changed through time, and the research involved pollen samples taken from bottoms of several lakes including tiny Foy Lake, which is about a mile from where I lived when I went to work for The Daily Interlake in Kalispell in 1967.

As you might expect, the Foy Lake stuff caught my attention. I was startled to learn that the pollen samples reveal that 5,000 or so years ago the Flathead Valley was mostly a grassy savannah punctuated by clumps of ponderosa pine scattered here and there. Way different than it looks today.

The visual got me to thinking about the many times I've driven to the summit of the Moiese Bison Range for the commanding views it offers of the Flathead and Clark Fork valleys. I still have trouble wrapping my mind around the fact that both valleys were once part of the lakebed that formed Lake Missoula, which covered 2,700 square miles to a depth of about 1,000 feet and held about half the water volume currently held in Lake Michigan.

Are we again entering such a warming period? Will the Flathead Valley and its lush stands of fir, pine and larch be transformed into the grassy savannah it once was - interrupted only by clumps of ponderosa? Possibly, but some climatologists believe our warming period is winding down and a new cooling period has begun. Nothing in nature is ever settled.

I did not write this book to argue for or against climate change. I wrote it to tell you what time it is in the West's national forests. But let's get one thing clear: climate and weather are not the same.

Weather is what's happening outside now. Climate is the longer-term stuff, – the trend lines that sometimes hide mini-warming and cooling trends inside longer term warming and cooling trends. You can see these trends in the growth rings on trees. Rings spaced further apart signal better growing conditions – more sunlight and moisture. Rings tighter together indicate slower growth – not as much sunlight and moisture.

Check out The Laboratory of Tree-Ring Research.[9] Its scientists have mapped the west's climate in reverse for 2,019 years. More on this marvelous laboratory in Chapter 26.

Somewhere around here I have a photocopy of a *Newsweek* article from the 1970s. Environmentalists of that era were on their "next Ice Age" bandwagon. "Global cooling" was all the rage. But when the public didn't bite, they switched to "Global warming." No one blinked. Now we have "Climate Change." Up climate or down climate, the usual suspects can extort money from apologetic captains of industry, no matter what. Easy peasy.

Listen, I get the part about our curbing our consumptive lifestyle but why is it that most of the young people pounding the table about recycling more are also sucking on plastic designer water bottles?

And I know the rich are getting richer and the poor are getting poorer and the middle class is falling behind, but shouldn't that be reason enough to try to grow our private economy? The only money the federal government has is the money it collects from taxpayers who already think they're paying too much.

If we confiscated all the money held by our nation's 585 billionaires we might be able to run our government for a week. Ten days tops. So there isn't much chance that we can tax our way out of debt but couldn't we grow our way out by creating new jobs in both our old and new industries? I think we could.

I also understand that there is a lot of environmental injustice in the world. Everyone should be able to breathe clean air and drink clean water. It's tragic that half of humanity goes to bed hungry and sick every night. Bless Bill and Melinda Gates for taking this on in ways that only the richest and most generous among us could. So here's my take on climate change:

9 

- The *right* Green New Deal holds the potential to solve many of our economic, environmental and social problems but we're not going to get there with solar panels and windmills. They can help but they bring their own environmental impacts. Lots of steel, concrete and glass. Non-renewable resources with big carbon footprints.
- I don't care if you are a climate change believer or a denier. I have neither the time nor the energy to argue about the climate. What cannot be denied is that the West's prolonged drought is fueling an environmental disaster in our national forests.

I also don't care if you are a Republican or Democrat. The fate of our nation's forest heritage should be a non-partisan issue.

What I care about is the wildfire pandemic that annually destroys several million acres of our western forest heritage and future – and I hope to engage you in helping me stop this pandemic in its tracks.

While our pandemic is of enormous public concern here in the West, it seems to be less of a concern in the Midwest and East, though it is slowly moving from west to east and will soon collide head-on with pathogens that are killing millions of treasured hardwoods in the upper Midwest.

My friend Michael Rains – the only guy I know with five degrees from five different universities – frequently reminds me that ridding our nation of Bad Fire necessitates aggressive forest management to ensure that Good Fire can help us better manage the risks that have engulfed western forests.

The "Doomsday Clock," monitored by Beyond the Bomb, an anti-nuclear coalition, reports that it is currently two minutes to midnight on planet earth – meaning two minutes remain before nuclear holocaust destroys all life on earth.

It is also nearing midnight in our national forests. Herein, I explain why this is true and what we must do to avert looming disaster.

Beetle-kill timber near Elk City, Idaho.

Dead tree thicket ready to burn in New Mexico

Full disclosure

In the interest of full disclosure, I must tell you that I am not a forester, a forest scientist or any kind of scientist. I am a plain-brown-wrapper working journalist with 55 years of experience as an investigative reporter and a smattering of experience as a self-employed public relations consultant.

Everything I know about forests and forestry, I have learned by asking stupid questions of very smart people: PhD forest scientists, under-appreciated Forest Service employees and Forest Service retirees who have lived with the land and their successes and failures long enough to have developed a wisdom and capacity for good judgement.

Thirty-three years ago I started The Evergreen Foundation, a non-profit organization dedicated to advancing public understanding and support for science-based forestry and forest policy. For years, we published *Evergreen*, a periodic journal that chronicled the issues and events that were impacting the west's national forests.

More recently, our print editions have given way to the Internet. It's free and its spans earth at the speed of light. My brother-in-law, a big-time web designer in Seattle tells me [1] that content is king in the website world and [2] our *Evergreen* website holds more content than any similar site he's seen.

Click on "Magazine Archive"[10] on the tool bar and you'll find PDF files for most of the print editions we've done over the last 20 years.

When we published our first edition in 1986 there was no Internet and there were no cell phones or speedy laptops, only landlines, fax machines and clunky old desk tops that took about five minutes to boot up. Thus, there are no PDF files for our earliest editions, but by my count we have published 10 *Evergreen* reports that called attention to the west's looming wildfire crisis.

For years, few outside the rural west seemed to care about the horrible environmental damage these fires were inflicting. Now they do.

Why? Because the political forces that have for years swirled around the advisability of leaving the West's federally-owned national forests to "Nature" have collided head-on with the global climate change debate.

10 

The West's largest cities are now engulfed in carcinogenic wildfire smoke for weeks on end every summer, giving rise to a politically uncomfortable question few in Congress are willing to ask: How can the federal government impose new air quality regulations on private industries while refusing to aggressively address a wildfire crisis of its own making? We unravel this question in this book.

The United States Forest Service cares for 193 million acres of publicly-owned forestland. These are our national forests – yours and mine – and they are located mainly in the 11 western states.

Forest Service fire ecologists report that some 80 to 90 million of these acres are in a death spiral. Overstressed by prolonged drought, hundreds of millions of the trees we own are dead or dying. *In some western national forests, especially those across the 1,000-mile stretch defined by the Rocky Mountains of the Inland West, our trees are dying faster than they are growing.*

Trees that are stressed by overcrowding and drought become magnets for insects, diseases and inevitable wildfire. We are losing from six to 10 million acres of trees annually in killing wildfires.

There are many reasons why this is happening, Difficult for most people to understand is the fact that our national forests hold too many trees for the natural carrying capacity of the land – the availability of sunlight, rainfall, soil nutrients and enough growing space

Crammed into groves so dense that walking is difficult, our trees are killing each other in their fight for growing space, sunlight, moisture and soil nutrients. Much of this crisis is of our own doing.

For now, know this: The many sciences of forestry provide the two safest and most effective tools for pulling the west's national forests back from the brink of ecological collapse. But our society is conflicted. Do we cut down our dead and dying trees and put them to good use or do we let Nature burn them down?

My opinion. We Americans owe our national forests a great debt for providing the wood that housed millions of young families, including our veterans, following the Second World War. It's time to pay up. Standing down while they burn down isn't socially or environmentally acceptable.

Let's put out the fire!

We have some soul searching to do

We Americans disagree sharply on the question of how to get the things we all want and need from our national forests. The nation's privately-owned forests do most of the heavy lifting now where lumber and paper are concerned, but how do we get our more aesthetic needs met in our national forests?

Many of us believe we should leave our national forests in the caring hands of Nature. It's a nice idea but if Nature really cared about our wants and needs It [She?] would not be burning our western national forests to the ground.

Americans who live closest to our national forests often have hands-on experience with Nature. They see our forests in a very different light than the fantasy portrayals Hollywood gives us. They know that Nature doesn't give a damn about human need – the things we all want to see in our forests.

They know we – and that's all of us – must share responsibility for our roles in securing the things we want from our national forests.

In a perfect world, Congress – our elected House and Senate members – would be working closely with our federal forest management agencies to make sure that our wants and needs are met, but the world is not perfect, and Congress is as conflicted as we are about the caring part.

If you live in a city or a major urban center on the east or west coasts, your members of Congress are up to their eyeballs in issues that are more important to their constituents than the wildfire pandemic rural westerners are enduring. Many may believe that Nature is our best forester.

By contrast, members of Congress that come from the rural West and have experienced the realities of "Nature" in its starkest form favor a more "hands-on" science-based approach where caring for our forests is concerned, removing dead and dying trees and transforming fire into a tool for cleaning up our forests before they burn them down.

The 2018 Carr and Camp fires are perfect examples of what is happening because members of Congress can't agree on what to do about these fires. The Camp Fire destroyed some 20,000 northern California homes, blackened 380,000 acres and killed 94 people. 94! Driven by high winds, it burned the equivalent of a football field every second. Some died trying to escape in their cars. Others never got out of their houses. Some refused to leave believing the fire would go around them. Bucolic Paradise, California was reduced to ash and ruin.

Clearly, we Americans have some soul searching to do.

We need to ask ourselves why the way our national forests are "protected" has become such a bitter partisan issue and what we can do to mend our political fences. What we have here is as much a moral and ethical dilemma as it is an environmental catastrophe.

The reality is we are not "protecting" anything – not our forests, private property, communities or lives.

If we all want the same things from our forests – and I believe we do – we should be able to find common ground in our shared quest to conserve and share the great gifts our forests provide.

We Americans hold title to 193 million acres of forest and grassland that the U.S. Forest Service cares for on our behalf. These forests are an especially dominant geographic features in the 11 western states.

Eastern white pine seedling in a Potlatch nursery in Minnesota. A significant public-private partnership is backing efforts to restore the species in forests it once dominated.

Time was when Republicans and Democrats from the East, Midwest and West were united in supporting and funding a hands-on management approach that conserved our national forests while providing economic opportunity for those who lived in them. The rural-urban-city chasm that divides us today didn't exist.

We've lost sight of the difference between "conservation" and "preservation." Conservation implies a desire to keep forests functioning. Preservation connotes a desire to keep forests the same. Given ever-changing natural disturbance patterns [fire, wind, ice, flooding, insects and diseases] it is impossible to preserve forests the same way we preserve jams and jellies, but we try anyway because some of us still cling a belief that forests "untrammeled by man" are somehow better than forests where the presence of people is easily seen.

The truth is that we can't preserve or restore forests to some legislated snapshot in time for the same reasons we can't freeze communities or people in the pictures we like best. I'd like to see my mother and father look like they looked when I was 10 years old, but they've both been dead for more than 30 years. Life goes on. We either go with it or it leaves us behind. That's the "nature" of things that make up the lives we lead. Fostering expectations that run counter to these truths isn't heathy for us – or our forests.

The journalist in me wants to know what's happened to media scrutiny. Where has it gone? Why isn't anyone asking the hard questions about the roots of our great cultural divide and the damage it is doing to our forests? This arena that we call "life" provides fertile ground for enterprising journalists in the hunt for the very direct connection between climate change and our changing forests. What we are facing is the most critical conservation issue of our time. Why the silence?

Few of today's working journalists realize that the increasing threat that killing wildfires pose is reversible. Are they that poorly educated or have they simply chosen to side with the "let nature care for our forests" crowd? It seems so but I have a hard time believing they're all idiots or that they don't care about people living in rural American. But some of them have bought into the environmentalist claim that rural Americans are too stupid and greedy to know what's good for them. Remember what Alston Chase said about hands on experience with nature? It resides in rural America, not on Wall Street inside the Beltway.

What we have here is a tragedy of the commons, a phrase social scientists use to describe serious disruptions in shared resource systems, like our national forests. Tragedy occurs when individuals and groups, acting independently according to their own self-interests, behave contrary to the common good of all users.

The identifiable self-interests here include:

- Small, family-owned logging and sawmilling outfits that want to be involved in restoring natural resiliency in our national forests.
- Conservationists who are working with the family-owned outfits because they favor forest restoration because they've seen the results.

Part of the Whittier Fire in Los Padres National Forest burns out of control.

- Huge private landowners who don't give a damn if our national forests burn to the ground because they don't want any competing wood fiber on the market, especially publicly-owned fiber.
- Environmental groups that hate the timber industry on principle and don't trust any science except their own.
- Big time Wall Street CEO's who have developed the disgusting habit of sucking up to the climate change crowd.
- Elected officials who play to the myriad self-interests and worries of voters. The late House speaker, Tip O'Neill, said it best. "All politics is local."

These self-interests hope to convince us that they and they alone have our best environmental interests at heart and that their positions are the correct ones. Seemingly well-meaning groups have been transformed into multi-million dollar global organizations that prey on people who want to help "save the planet" but don't know how. Independent thought and creative problem-solving genius are routinely suppressed in favor of group think and "settled science." Trust me, in nature nothing is ever "settled."

Most of us never question the veracity of unsubstantiated claims about the "last of" this or the "destruction" of that or the "end" of whatever. We're too busy or we think someone we trust is watching the store on our behalf. Worse, we trust the news our algorithms deliver daily to our cell phones.

The problem with algorithms is that they only deliver news that fit our usage pattern. You're a timber beast so you get all the news that reinforces your point of view. You're a tree-hugger so you get all news that reinforces your point of view. We live in echo chambers and we're never going to learn anything new!

We allowed ourselves to be deceived by some of the best bullshit artists in history, special-interest groups that prey on our gullibility and our fears. No need for me to name names because we all have our built-in biases – me included – but I will say that the cost of our negligence is enormous.

Annual wildfire losses in our nation run into the millions of acres. More than 100 million acres have burned over the last 20 years. That's an area larger than three times the combined size of Rhode Island, Connecticut, Delaware, Maryland, Hawaii, New Jersey, Massachusetts, New Hampshire and Vermont. The damage equates to hundreds of billions of dollars.

The many sciences of forestry provide the tools we need to reverse the disastrous forest growth and mortality trend lines in our national forests, but first we need to heal the partisan divide that has us debating whether Nature should do the heavy lifting, or whether we should.

Many oppose cutting down these trees because they oppose logging on principle. Others say the environmental damage these killing wildfires are doing far exceeds the more temporary impacts of logging.

More recently, others have expressed concern for the health impacts of the millions of tons of carcinogenic wildfire smoke that Westerners breath for months on end every summer. They think storing carbon in environmentally benign wood products makes more sense than storing it in our lungs.

One of our greatest failings has been a failure to understand the difference between Good Fire and Bad Fire. Bad Fires are destroying our western national forests. Good Fires are purposefully set by professional foresters to dispose of woody debris under controlled conditions before Bad Fires strike.

When professionally-trained foresters talk about "fuels management" this is what they're talking about. They call their purposefully-set fires "prescribed fire," Good Fire being "management prescription."

Many private forestland owners use Good Fire in combination with the selective removal of dead, dying trees or undesirable tree species. Removing these trees before they burn promotes growth in healthy trees that are left in the forest.

Where our national forests are concerned, when professionals talk about "forest management" they are talking about the selective removal of dead, dying or undesirable tree species.

Removing trees from western national forests that hold too many trees is a fundamental first step to restarting the growth process in residual trees, and restoring their natural resistance to disease, insects and wildfire.

Forest management first, then fuels management. Why forest management first? Because it is too dangerous to start a prescribed fire in a forest that holds so much dead wood. Removing most of the dead and dying trees first keeps prescribed fire from climbing into residual trees. Keeping the fire on the ground allows it to consume woody debris on the forest floor.

What do my journalist's sensibilities tell me about the debate between timber beasts and tree huggers? I don't understand why we don't clean up the mess we've made before our forests burn.

Cleaning up the mess we've made will save millions of beautiful trees from a fiery death and we avoid storing carcinogenic carbon-laced wildfire smoke in our lungs.

My journalist's sensibilities also tell me the forestry world is overlooking the convergence of its best storylines: the intersections between climate change and our changing forests and the powerful natural roles played by carbon sequestration and photosynthesis.

I'll have more to say about these storylines later but first consider the power of these often-overlooked truths:

- As trees grow they absorb carbon as carbon dioxide and release oxygen into earth's atmosphere. This process is called photosynthesis. It is powered by the free, non-polluting energy of the sun.
- Young, fast-growing trees store, or sequester, large amounts of carbon in what are called "carbon sinks."
- As healthy trees age, the rate at which they tore carbon slows and eventually stops. In some ecosystems, different tree species live for centuries while others live little more than a decade.
- Live trees may hold the carbon they sequestered while growing. Dead trees release their stored carbon into the atmosphere as their wood decays but a small fraction is added back to the soil in which they grew.
- When trees burn in wildfires, both live and dead trees release their carbon into the atmosphere very quickly. Big wildfires release thousands of tons of carbon-laced smoke.
- Trees transformed into wood products continue to sequester carbon. If your house is constructed from wood, it acts as its own carbon sink.
- Cradle-to-grave analysis – also known as "life cycle analysis" tracks the environmental impacts of various structural building materials through their manufacture and use to their eventual disposal.
- No product – not steel, aluminum or concrete – can match wood's minimal impact measured in terms of energy consumption or its impact on air and water quality.
- Two next generation wood products – cross-laminated timbers [CLT] and mass panel plywood [MPP] are earning high praise from the news media and architects.
- Both CLT and MPP are manufactured from small-diameter trees, the very trees that many forest ecologists believe we must remove from our dying national forests as quickly as possible, before killing wildfires strike.
- CLT and MPP seem like better places to store wildfire-related carbon than our lungs. The tagline on old Caterpillar advertisement speaks to this: "*There are no easy answers, only intelligent choices.*"

No matter your point of view where logging is concerned, know this: Nature isn't waiting around for us to settle our differences. It is using insect and disease infestations and inevitable wildfire to clean up the mess we've made.

Because these forests belong to all of us – Easterners, Midwesterners and Westerners -- we share responsibility for their care and well-being. Westerners sense greater urgency because their lifestyle, with its new emphasis on exercise, healthy eating, and living well in the great outdoors, is being incinerated in the largest and most destructive wildfires in our nation's history.

The National Aeronautics and Space Administration landed its latest robot on Mars in November 2018. If NASA can land a robot on a planet 300 million miles from earth, government scientists can sure as hell figure out how to put the Good Wildfire Genie to work stuffing the Bad Wildfire Genie back in her bottle.

Eliot Ivy helps replant a clearcut on Coquille tribal forestland in southwest Oregon. *Coquille Indian Tribe*

Who can we trust?

Where might we go for better-balanced information we can trust?

In my 50-plus years as an investigative reporter, I've learned to trust the U.S. Forest Service and its many data bases, all of them available free of charge on the worldwide web. Most of their research is rock-solid but often misrepresented by special interest groups with different agendas.

I've also developed trust relationships with a quite diverse group of forest scientists, many of them Forest Service employees.

I wish the Forest Service was less timid and more forthcoming with what it knows. I was a big admirer of their historic and steadfast refusal to "take sides" in public dust-ups that swirl about the way that the venerable agency does its work.

Many friends who worked in the timber industry disagree with me on this point and I understand why. They were financially ruined by the collapse of the federal timber sale program that followed the government's June 1990 decision to list the northern spotted owl as a threatened species. Some even lost their families in the emotional upheaval that followed.

They blame the Forest Service for the listing decision. I don't. The political winds had reversed course in the 20 years leading to the listing. Outside the rural west too little public support remained for the post-war federal timber sale program designed and developed by the Roosevelt and Truman administrations. As economic miracles go, it had outlived its usefulness.

It would be another 20 years before our federal government realized that its bygone timber program had not outlived its environmental usefulness.

My memories of the Forest Service begin in the 1950s. Robert Stout, a ramrod straight ranger working on the Wallace District of the old Coeur d'Alene National Forest came to Sunnyside Grade School every spring. He wore a spotless and perfectly pressed uniform that every kid wanted to touch. But none dared.

Years later I learned that Mr. Stout – and he was Mr. Stout to us – was a war hero, a veteran of some of the South Pacific's bloodiest battles. He was a Marine to the depths of his soul. Like many GIs, he had joined the Forest Service after the war.

In the early 1950s, one of our big weekly news magazine – I no longer remember which one – conducted a national opinion survey to see which federal agency the public admired most. There were two: The United States Marine Corps and the United States Forest Service.

Back then, the line separating the Corps' image from the Forest Service's was almost indistinguishable. The uniform Mr. Stout wore was patterned after his Marine green and khaki service uniform, and his military bearing told us that the line separating Ranger Stout from Sergeant Stout was very thin.

Much has changed in the Forest Service, most good, some bad. On the good side, the agency's workforce is far more diverse than it was when Robert Stout visited our classroom every spring.

On the bad side, the Forest Service's workforce is in free fall. Since Fiscal 1992, close to 14,000 professionals with the skill sets needed to reduce wildfire risk in our national forests have been let go as more and more of the Forest Service's annual budget is consumed by the same wildfires that are consuming western forests. This makes no sense!

Forest Inventory and Analysis' (FIA) GEDI [Global Ecosystem Dynamics Investigation] relies on data collected in partnership with the National Aeronautics and Space Administration's Space Station orbiting 254 miles above Earth. Here is the link to the GEDI website GEDI website[11] which contains colorful schematics, additional information to explore, and important mission details.

The skill sets lost include foresters, down 74 percent; engineering technicians, down 72 percent; professional engineers, down 51 percent; forestry technicians, down 49 percent; interdisciplinary team leaders, down 45 percent; and wildlife biologists, down 38 percent. In the aggregate, a 54 percent loss in the skill sets needed to reduce the risk of wildfire. Meantime, staffing on fire lines has been increased 132 percent because – guess what – we have more wildfires to fight!

The predictable result this strategic misallocation of personnel is that more than half the Forest Service's $5.8 billion annual appropriation is now spent fighting forest fires, leaving too little for preventive measures – like thinning trees from forests that have grown too dense to sustain themselves.

If you've ever managed a household budget you will readily identify the underlying problem facing the Forest Service: Not enough money at the end of the month. Congress needs to get serious about the funding forest restoration work in Condition Class 2 and 3 forests. By my back-of-the-envelope estimate, the Forest Service is short about $3 billion a year. Less in the long term, but near term many skill sets need to be replaced.

All of this is explained in painful detail in a July 2019 report compiled by the National Association of Forest Service Retirees [NAFSR]. I know this organization well and think highly of the thousands of years of collective experience its 700-plus members bring to the table. Sustaining the Forest Service: Increasing Work Force Capacity could have just as easily been titled Burning an Empire, after Stewart Holbrook's 1943 book by the same name.

If this report isn't the Forest Service's autopsy, it's a close approximation – close enough that I'd recommend you take a few moments to read it sometime soon.

11

The North Santiam River's Little North Fork drainage near Lyons, Oregon drains thousands of acres of well-managed private timberland. Cody Shotola-Schiewe

It includes a letter to Agriculture Secretary, Sonny Perdue. The Forest Service has been part of the U.S. Department of Agriculture since 1905 so the buck stops on Perdue's desk, though I suspect he wishes it didn't. Most of our Ag Secretaries have been ag politicos who saw the Forest Service as the ugly stepchild they wished would run away from home.

See NAFSR's Workforce Capacity Study [12] Congress has been squeezing the life out of the Forest Service's capacity to care for national forests since the federal government listed the northern spotted owl as a threatened species in 1990. On-the-ground treatments needed to reduce the risk of deadly wildfire have been crushed by layers of conflicting and redundant restrictions that the Forest Service's motto – Caring for the land and serving the people – an impossible dream.

At the very moment in time when more professional help is needed on the forestry side, the resources – human and monetary – are being shifted to a losing battle against pandemic wildfire. I think Congress and the Forest Service have this whole thing backwards. We can't hope to contain the risk of wildfire – much less reduce it – until we first deal with the reasons why the risk is so damned high.

Congress steps up with billions of dollars whenever the Federal Emergency Management Agency [FEMA] needs money for floods, hurricanes or earthquakes. And what does the Forest Service get when the firefighting bills roll in? It gets to shift money from its forestry budget to its fire budget, fueling the agency's fire culture while snuffing out its forest conservation culture. This is a terrible strategic blunder.

Congress would like you to think it fixed its "fire borrowing" problem last summer. It didn't fix anything. The Forest Service is still at least $2 billion short in its $5.14 billion budget for Fiscal 2019. Closer to $3 billion in my opinion.

I'll have more to say about this sorry mess in later chapters. For now, remember this: any private business that is forced to shed 30 to 50 percent of its workforce while spending half its annual budget propping up bad decisions made years ago will soon be filing Chapter 13 bankruptcy papers. But the Forest Service soldiers on, repeatedly changing its priorities, and taxpayers pick up the tab.

And so the question: "Who can we trust to honestly answer tough questions about the state of our forests? Who brings the most reliable information to the table: facts, figures, field research that can be replicated and forest management techniques that have survived the test of time?"

My "go to" source list

It's the Forest Service. No one else is even close. Here's my list of "go to" Forest Service websites that answer most of the difficult questions facing Americans who love forests and find something morally and ethically reprehensible with the whole idea of simply standing down while our forests burn down.

Where wildfire is concerned, the best Forest Service website is managed by The National Interagency Fire Center [13] in Boise, Idaho. During wildfire season, it is often updated several time each day.

For more general information about the Forest Service, the agency's main website [14] is huge, and leads to many other related sites.

The Forest Service websites I refer to almost daily are those maintained by the agency's Forest Inventory and Analysis Program. [15] In my opinion, FIA data is the gold standard. No other organization – public or private – can match its exceptional breadth or depth.

The Forest Service's decadal *Future of Forests and Rangelands* [16] should be your constant desk reference. It is encyclopedic in length, but I know of no agency document that provides more comprehensive information.

Especially valuable are the RPA reports, named for the 1974 Resources Planning Act, which

12 

13 

14 

15 

16 

mandated a decadal forest planning process and required the Forest Service to prepare detailed progress reports. You can download these reports on the Internet. They're long but filled with useful thumbnail information.

The Forest Service also maintains impressive, content-rich websites for its four regional research stations: Portland, Oregon; Ogden, Utah; St. Paul, Minnesota; and Knoxville, Tennessee. and their in-house Forest Inventory and Analysis [FIA] programs. Both FIA and the research stations have been around since the 1930s so their wells are very deep.

Pacific Northwest Region, Portland [17]

Northern Research Station, St. Paul [18]

Rocky Mountain Research Station, Ogden [19]

Southern Research Station, Knoxville [20]

These websites present impartial and meticulously researched information we can use to make informed, science-based choices about protection, conservation and management of our national forests.

The Forest Service gathers its information from several sources. It's field survey plots date from the 1930s and now number in the hundreds of thousands. They are scattered across five regions: West Coast, Interior West, North Central, Northeast and South. Explore each region. [21]

Field survey crews follow a protocol described in a three-ring binder that covers every survey requirement. I have a copy of the manual. It's about 300 pages long!

Advancing technologies, including cloud computing, allow forest scientists to layer and display complex data sets in a dazzling and colorful array of interactive "story maps" that describe what you are seeing. This link[22] leads you to one such map from FIA's St. Paul, Minnesota station and includes user instructions. Simply move your mouse and be amazed by the fine-scale detail. All 3,146 counties, boroughs and parishes are accessible. You can ask the system for data on most forest and urban

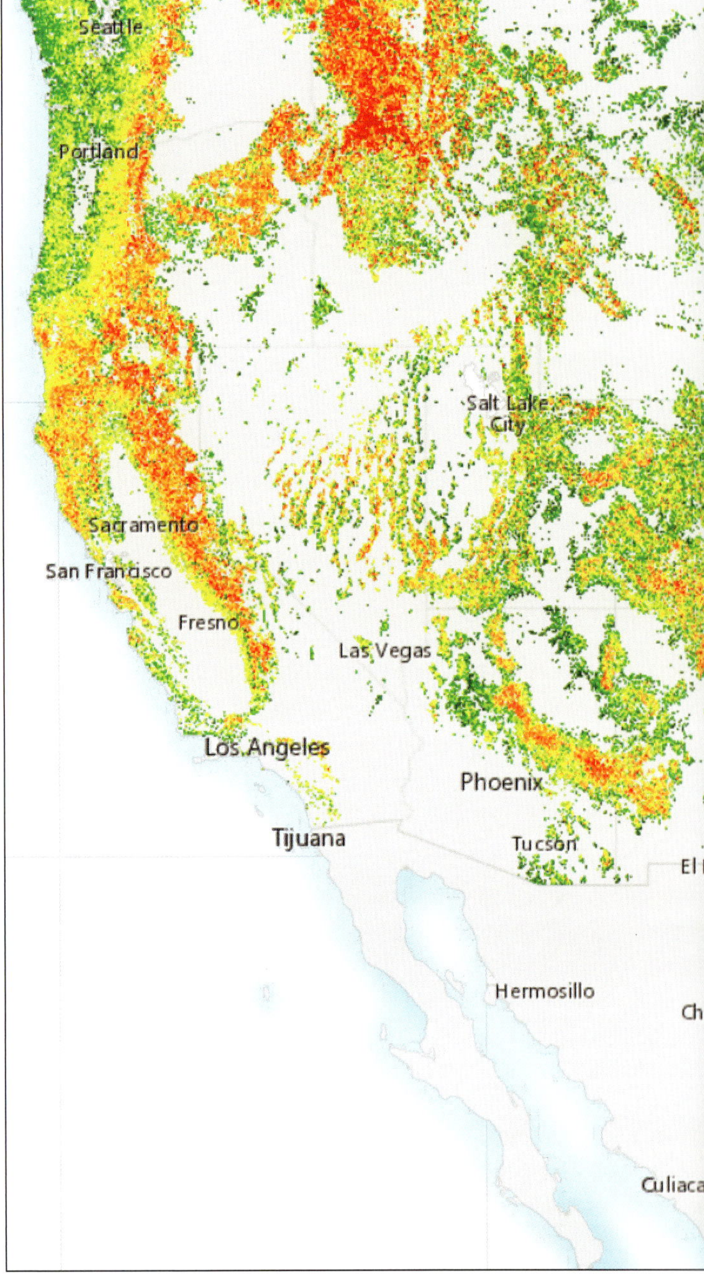

forest topics: tree species, forest health, problems with insects and diseases. Now name it and it's probably there. You should be able to find your own neighborhood.

Cloud computing has enabled forest scientists to merge and display data from multiple sources. Not just field surveys but also aerial photography, drones and LIDAR. Light Detection and Ranging

17 

18 

19 

20 

21 

22 

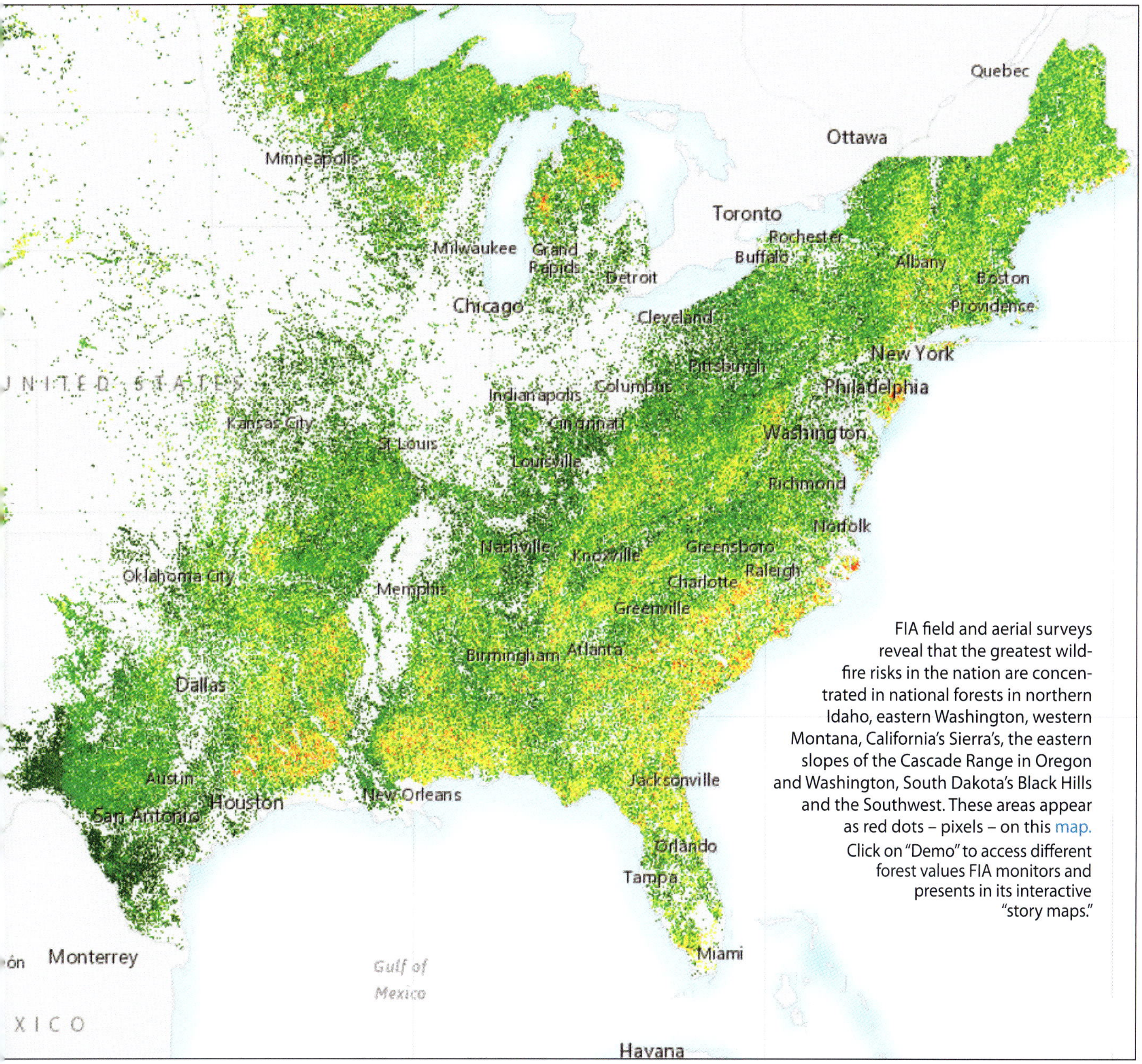

FIA field and aerial surveys reveal that the greatest wildfire risks in the nation are concentrated in national forests in northern Idaho, eastern Washington, western Montana, California's Sierra's, the eastern slopes of the Cascade Range in Oregon and Washington, South Dakota's Black Hills and the Southwest. These areas appear as red dots – pixels – on this map. Click on "Demo" to access different forest values FIA monitors and presents in its interactive "story maps."

[LIDAR] equipment uses pulsed laser light to create three-dimensional images of its target.

Believe it or not, the Forest Service has also teamed with National Aeronautical and Space Administration [NASA]. A camera on the Space Station now transmits data back to Earth that displays forest conditions globally. We dig more deeply into data collection in Chapter 25. Meantime, here are links to some story maps from the Portland FIA station that you can explore. Every station has these.

Forests of California, 2017 [23]
Forests of Oregon, 2016 [24]
Forests of Washington, 2016 [25]
Forests of coastal Alaska, 2014 [26]

23

24

25

26

map

This is what these maps look like in print. I know this is a lot to absorb, but I'm damned sick and tired of hearing environmentalists whine about how the Forest Service doesn't know anything about our forests, so we should just leave them to "nature" because anything we do will do more harm than good. That's bullshit.

Trust me, we know a great deal about forests – certainly enough to push back on the wildfire pandemic that is incinerating the West's national forests. What we lack is the political will to use the knowledge we have.

We have partnered with FIA many times over the years. You can learn more about FIA on our website.[27]

Our magazine archive also includes a much-praised essay on another Forest Service entity that contributes significantly to our common good: the Forest Products Laboratory at Madison, Wisconsin. The report is titled *Giant Minds, Giant Ideas.*[28]

If you really want to beat yourself up, read the Forest Service's 2010 update of its Resource Planning Act assessment. *Future of America's Forests and Rangelands.*[29] 13 chapters, maybe 300-pages, fact-filled and thought-provoking.

Anyone who tells you we don't know enough to make intelligent and well-balanced forest management choices, doesn't know what the hell they're talking about.

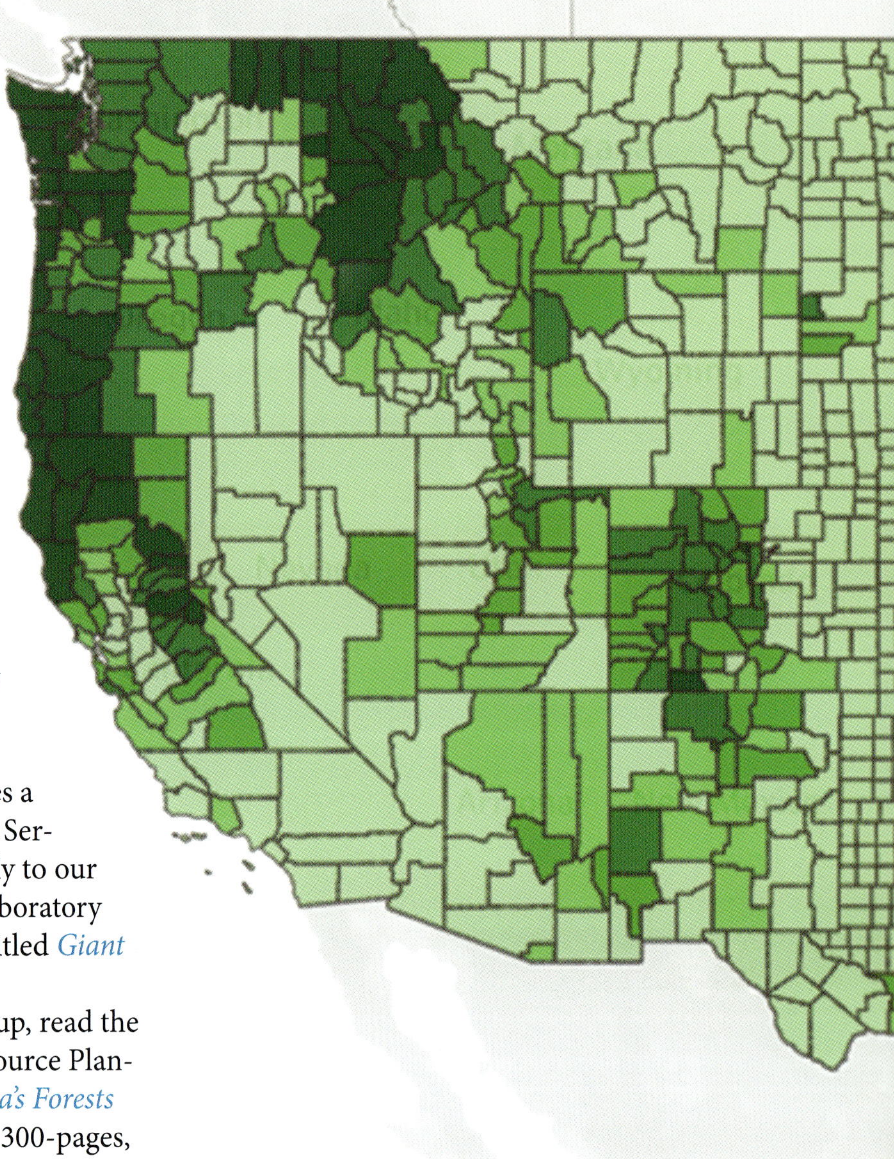

Mex

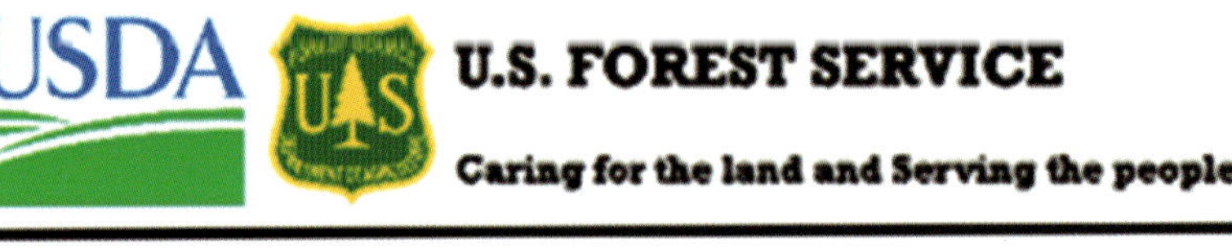

© 2019 Mapbox © OpenStreetMap

Land area in Forest (Percent)

0%

27

28

29

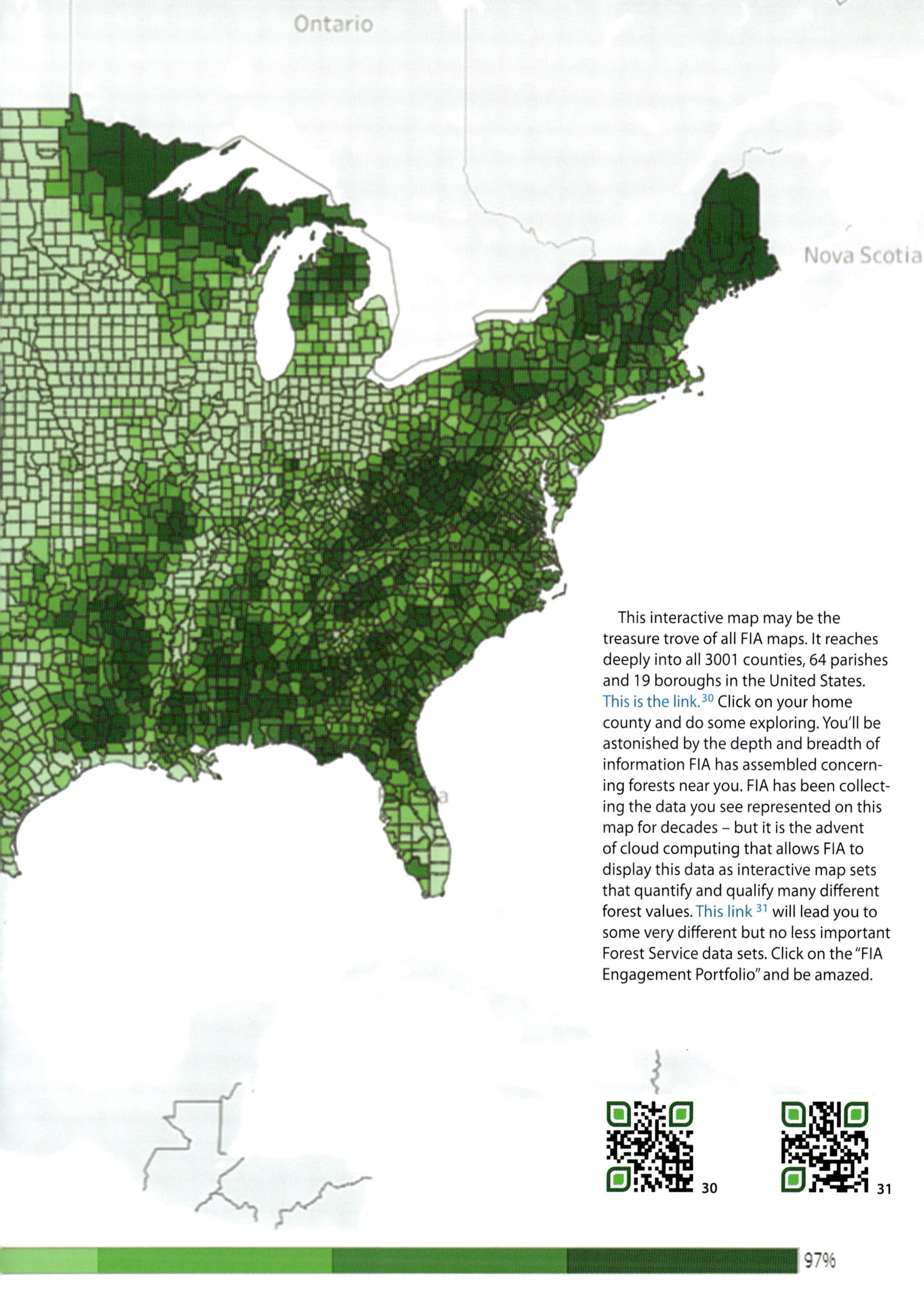

This interactive map may be the treasure trove of all FIA maps. It reaches deeply into all 3001 counties, 64 parishes and 19 boroughs in the United States. This is the link.[30] Click on your home county and do some exploring. You'll be astonished by the depth and breadth of information FIA has assembled concerning forests near you. FIA has been collecting the data you see represented on this map for decades – but it is the advent of cloud computing that allows FIA to display this data as interactive map sets that quantify and qualify many different forest values. This link [31] will lead you to some very different but no less important Forest Service data sets. Click on the "FIA Engagement Portfolio" and be amazed.

30

31

A long way to go and a short time to get there

Fire ecologists estimate we have about 30 years in which to reduce the risk of catastrophic loss in forests we all love. Wildfire will claim the rest. Time is short.

On a scale of 1-10, we are approaching 10. Over large areas dead trees crisscross one another like pickup sticks. Walking is difficult, even for deer and elk.

Our fixation with global climate change is clouding our ability to see and understand the cause and effect relationships that are fueling our western wildfire pandemic. Much of what is wrong in our forests can be rectified in a matter of years for a fraction of the cost of proposed Green New Deal, which makes scant mention of our western wildfire crisis and its estimated impacts on climate change.

Making headway depends totally on a much-improved understanding of the relationships between wildfire, the carcinogenic smoke wildfires spew into earth's atmosphere, photosynthesis and carbon sequestration and our myriad forest wants and needs.

Our nation's historically stormy relationship with wildfire and our more recent worries about the impacts of active forest management – logging included - have blurred our ability to understand the symbiotic relationship between fire, forests and forestry's capacity to enrich our lives.

Our forests have been the focal point of rigorous public debate since our national forest system was created in 1905. In the early going, the debate centered on the best methods for protecting and managing our national forests – and with good reason. Thousands of lives and millions of acres of timberland were lost between 1871 and 1918: Peshtigo, lower Michigan, upper Michigan, Hinkley, Wisconsin, Moose Lake, Yacolt, Cloquet and the Great Idaho/Montana 1910 Fire incinerated everything in sight: towns, homes, lives. Wildfire was Public Enemy No. 1. Our goal was to "run smoke out of the woods."

Amid a wildfire crisis that annually consumes half the U.S. Forest Service's $5.8 billion budget- the debate has shifted to whether we should be managing our national forests at all, or whether we should let Nature – insects, diseases and wildfire do the managing for us.

How's Nature doing? Great, if you don't mind the damned mess these wildfires have created while cleaning up the bigger social and environmental mess that we've created for ourselves in our refusal to accept responsibility for finding common ground in the forest caring department.

And how are we doing? Again, the U.S. Forest Service estimates that between 80 and 90 million national forest acres are in what fire ecologists call "Condition Class 2 or 3." Class 3 forests are ready to burn. Class 2 forests soon will be. Over the last 25 years, about 100 million acres have been ravaged by insects, diseases and wildfire. For purely political reasons – and not because of a lack of "how to" knowledge, we have done little to stop this unfolding crisis.

To see the tragic result, go back to the story maps displayed in the last chapter. All those red and orange pixels you see in the Interior West represent dead or dying forests. You can see the same thing in national forests in Arizona, New Mexico, California, Wyoming, Colorado and eastern Oregon and Washington. We have an unholy mess on our hands.

What can we do to reverse the disastrous

course we are on? Start by ignoring the hucksters who say you must choose between Nature and Forestry. These are false choices. Reject them. We need Nature and Forestry. The two aren't mutually exclusive, but they are different. Nature is reactive. Forestry is proactive.

The role I hope you will accept as an owner of our national forests is to publicly advocate for sustainable, science and experience-based problem-solving. There is no other predictable or reliable way for us to get our wants and needs met.

We have a long way to go and a short time to get there.

Monte Dolack, a Missoula, Montana graphic artist, drew this striking 1910 Fire commemorative poster.

Our pesky wants and needs

In February 2017, I was invited to speak to a graduate level forest policy class in the University of Idaho's College of Natural Resources. Forest policy has long been a fascination for me, owing to my interest in two of history's forgotten geniuses: Supreme Court Justice, Oliver Wendell Holmes Jr. and George Perkins Marsh, a former diplomat turned author and orator.

I titled my UI speech *Felt Necessities: Engines of Forest Policy* – a tip of the hat to Justice Holmes, who first used the phrase in a book of essays he assembled in 1881 titled *The Common Law*.

Describing the underpinnings of the nation's legal system, he wrote:

> "The life of the law has not been logic. It has been experience: the felt necessities of the time, the prevalent moral and political the ories, institutions of public policy, avowed or unconscious, even the prejudices which judges share with their fellow men, have had a good deal more to do with the syllogism in determining the rules by which men should be governed. The law embodies the story of the nation's development through many centuries, and it cannot be dealt with as if it contained only the axioms and corollaries of a book of mathematics."

Holmes' observation got me to thinking about the social and political forces that have driven the evolution of federal forest policy through time. I was able to trace this evolution forward from the Civil War, beginning with a remarkable little boat-rocking book titled *Man and Nature*, written by Marsh in 1864, the year before President Lincoln was assassinated.

"Man is everywhere a disturbing agent," Marsh wrote. "Wherever he plants his foot, the harmonies of nature are turned to discord."

Marsh, a native Vermonter and a former foreign diplomat who spoke seven or eight languages [despite being nearly blind from childhood] had been upset by the conversion of forestland to farmland in the Northeast . His book caught the attention of the scions of wealthy industrialists – the so-called "robber barons" living in luxury in New York City. Their money and political influence spawned our nation's conservation movement.

But it was Marsh, a scion of Vermont wealth, who lit the torch. Many consider him to be America's first conservationist. Perhaps he was, but Man and Nature was not his first foray into the public discourse.

In 1847, Marsh delivered a speech before the Agricultural Society of Rutland County, Vermont that will have a familiar ring to you. Here's what he said:

> "Man cannot at his pleasure command the rain and the sunshine, the wind and frost and sun, yet it is certain that climate itself has in many instances been gradually changed and ameliorated or deteriorated by human action.
>
> The draining of swamps and the clearing of forests perceptibly effect the evaporation from the earth, and of course the mean quantity of moisture suspended in the air.
>
> The same causes modify the electrical condition of the atmosphere and the power of the surface to reflect, absorb and radiate the rays of the sun, and consequently influence the distribution of light and heat, and the force and direction of the winds."

So there you have it – the first climate change

warning issued 172 years ago. In today's vernacular, Marsh was a "citizen scientist," a self-taught amateur whose visual observations formed the basis for his beliefs. Although he made no specific reference to "climate change" in his 1847 speech, the mere fact that it survives to present day says something about his great influence on the formation of our nation's earliest conservation efforts.

If you're interested in tracking the still evolving history of our nation's conservation movement, you'll find much of it chronicled under "Felt Necessities"[32] on our Evergreen Foundation website.

Charlie Petersen on the Coeur d'Alene River in northern Idaho, a prized cutthroat fishery and scene of more than a century of logging and replanting.

32

Hope is not a strategy

Write this down somewhere close by so you can refer to it whenever you get bogged down in some of the finer points in this book:

> *"Hope is not a strategy, and science is a process, not a religion."*

This wisdom comes to us from a very pragmatic scientist, my friend Peter Kolb, who earlier explained how the searing heat of wildfire impacts soil layers. Peter and I have worked hard to keep local knowledge and science front and center while elected officials and various public interest groups debate strategies for pulling the west's national forests back from the brink of ecological collapse.

What Peter is saying here is that hoping things are going to get better is not going to get us off the dime. I'd add that leaving our mess to Nature isn't going to get our forest wants and needs met.

Peter is also telling us thatt, unlike Biblical teachings that haven't changed much in 2,000 years, science is an ever-evolving process. I'd add something memorable an old lawyer friend told me 30 years ago: "What is science today will be witchcraft tomorrow."

Debating the many underlying causes of this collapse and the killing wildfires that accompany it is a foolish waste of time. We need to stop shooting the messengers because, if my fire ecologist friends are correct – we have no more than 30 years in which to rescue the 80 to 90 million acres the Forest Service says will likely burn if we don't do something proactive about it.

If 90 million acres, we're talking here about 140,625 square miles of dead or dying national forest land. That's an area only slightly smaller than Montana, our fourth largest state. It is an areas larger that 45 of our 50 states!

The math here is simple. Divide 90 million acres by 30 years:
90 million = 3 million acres of forest restoration work per year for 30 years.

We won't even get close to three million acres unless [1] Congress increases the annual Forest Service budget by at least $2 billion, [2] we learn how to settle our differences in town hall meetings, not courtrooms [3] the Forest Service more aggressively uses the tools Congress has provided for forest restoration and [4] we greatly increase our human resources – the men and women who will do the heavy lifting in forestry and forest products manufacturing. At the moment, we don't have sufficient people or manufacturing horsepower to treat three million acres annually over the next 30 years.

And the crisis we face is actually much worse than my math because dividing 90 million acres by 30 years does not move us ahead of forest density in Condition Class 2 and forests. To get ahead, we need to treat seven to eight million acres annually over the next decade. If we don't we'll never catch up to the crisis.

About 15 years ago, I asked a forest ecologist friend how long he thought it would take to treat insect and disease infested forests in the Intermountain West from Mexico to Canada. After a long pause he said, "Maybe 50 or 60 years." I knew he wasn't a fan of the timber industry, I asked what fate awaited to the Interior West's sawmills 50 or 60 years hence.

"We won't need them anymore," he replied confidently.

“Really,” I replied. “What happens to the forests we treated in Year 1? Won’t we need to thin them in perpetuity to keep insects and diseases in check?

After an even longer pause he smiled and said, “I guess we’ll still need them.”

This is why expanding our current capacities in forestry and forest manufacturing are so important – unless, like many Americans, you are content to leave western national forests in Nature’s care.

Before you decide, remember Alan Houston’s warning:

> *“When we leave forests to nature, as so many people seem to want to do, we get whatever nature serves up, which can be very devastating at times, but with forestry we have options and a degree of predictability not found in nature.”*

Peter Kolb, a PhD forest and range eco-physiologist at the University of Montana, amid beetle-killed lodgepole pine on Garnet Mountain northeast of Missoula.

CHAPTER 10

"Stop doing that!"

Environmentalism and conservation aren't the same. Not even close.

Conservationists recognize the dual necessities of hands-on forest management: thinning first, then prescribed fire. They understand the difference between Good Fire and Bad Fire.

Hard core environmentalists believe Nature [Bad Fire] should do the managing.

There is no critical thinking, no need to propose solutions or alternatives, no need to develop an in-depth knowledge of local cultures, communities or ecosystem processes that have driven forests forward for eons. You simply wrap yourself in shrouds of naturalness and shout "Stop doing that!" to the high heavens.

Conservation is far more difficult. It demands the best of our listening, thinking and "roll up your sleeves" problem-solving skills. It necessitates collaboration with others who hold different values and points of view.

Whoever said "the devil is always in the details" was right. Expanding our conservation knowledge base and selecting management choices that reflect specific forest needs requires a more detailed understanding of how nature works. Picking the best choices – and there is often more than one - demands mutual respect and good listening skills. We can't get bogged down in ideologies or unsubstantiated personal beliefs. Plain brown wrapper environmentalism makes no such demands on its purveyors.

Many Americans have a fascination with restoring our national forests to pre-settlement conditions, meaning what our forests looked like before European settlement began in the 1600s. Unfortunately, Nature's clock does not run in reverse, so this isn't possible.

Peter Kolb has reminded me many times that managing forests for a snapshot in time – say pre-European settlement - is not science.

"It seems like such a lovely idea," I said the first time he mentioned snapshots in time to me. Why isn't it science?"

"Because it argues for the long-disproven notion of natural equilibrium," he replied. "It's the so-called "steady state" theory which says that, left untouched by man, forests perpetuate themselves in perfect balance."

I remind Peter that many people still believe that Nature's invisible web of life exists in perfect harmony, which is why they insist that we leave the managing to Nature. In turn, he reminds me that there is no scientific evidence that our forests have ever existed in perfect balance.

"Chaos is constant in nature," he says. "Pre-European forests were the result of ever-changing climatic trends and the presence of Indians, who used fire as a land management tool."

If we accept Peter's claim that chaos is constant in nature –- and it certainly seems to be at the moment – we can't turn back the clock in our forests, but we can go forward using forestry's many tools to deliberately create the forest conditions that can deliver our felt necessities: clean air, clean water, abundant fish and wildlife habitat, the beauty and solitude that only a forest can provide and a wealth of year-round outdoor recreation opportunity.

But where to begin? Peter advises that we assess every forest for its range of variability and its risks, then determine what management processes fit best, or as he says, "Find out how, where and when to create functionality and natural resilience."

"In other words," I reply, "Stop trying to drive square pegs in round holes and steer clear of the one-size-fits-all cookie-cutter approaches that Congress seems to favor because it's easy."

"Yes," he says triumphantly, noting that Intermountain mixed conifer dry site forests that blanket much of the Interior West are an excellent example of the need to pay attention to what nature does.

"Contrary to what many say, most species found in our Intermountain forests are *fire-adapt-*

EF! Blockade in Elliot State Forest in the Oregon Coast Range, 2009.

ed, not fire-dependent," Peter explains, emphasizing the fire adapted part. "In my opinion, there are no fire-dependent species in the forests of the Northwest, but there are many fire-adapted species. As the terms imply, dependency denotes a requirement for existence, whereas adaption is a modification for competitive reproductive advantage."

Fair enough but keeping track of the biggest pieces on Nature's Ouija board is daunting, especially for citizen scientists: Fire adaptive or dependent species; seral species, which favor sunlight; climax species, which favor shade; to say nothing of plant associations prevalent in different forest ecosystems, and the differences that characterize disturbance-dependent and fire-dependent species.

No wonder Congress continues to favor legislation that attempts to force Nature into unworkable one-size-fits-all regulatory models. Square pegs in round holes.

A good analogy here is Obamacare – the Affordable Care Act. We all get tossed into the same hat, even though we have different health care needs, because it is politically less risky than tackling the underlying problems that are undermining the architecture of our health care system. Obamacare forestry.

Nature's architecture defies such simplification. There are no nuances, there is no averaging down and there are no winners and losers. Thus, square pegs cannot be pounded into round holes and the kinds of cookie-cutter solutions that Congress prefers are doomed to failure.

Every person who works with land knows this. Experience – failure as much as success – has taught them how to craft management plans that fit nicely within the prevailing landscape based on forest types, forest conditions, dominant tree species, climate, elevation, aspect, soil type and myriad other natural and human factors that have shaped and reshaped forest landscapes through time.

In short, people who work land work with Nature's moving parts, some visible, some not, but always there.

Few foresters have ever served in Congress, so we should not be surprised that the laws and regulations governing national forest management are based on the direction and strength of prevailing political winds, not the moving parts.

Following World War II, those winds blew strongly in the direction of active management of our national forests. We had a nation to house. Millions of GIs returning from Europe and the South Pacific were anxious to get married and start families. They needed jobs, mortgages, houses and wood – lots of it.

A good case can be made for the fact that the Truman Administration saw our national forests as economic engines capable of powering the nation's post-war transition from wartime to peacetime footing. They were right for the time.

Now the political winds are blowing strongly in a no-management direction, a result of the nation's wider belief that managing forests conflicts with our new wants and needs: clean air, clean water, abundant fish and wildlife habitat, the beauty and solitude that only a forest can provide, and a wealth of year-round recreation opportunity.

The wider truth is that these current wants and needs cannot be met unless we manage our national forests in ways that contain the risk factors associated with wildfire – the insect and disease infestations that are killing millions of trees that then fuel horrific wildfires.

Sadly, it has become politically expedient to feign concern for our national forests by casting votes that favor a no-management approach. Nature is simply cleaning up the mess that Congress refuses to clean up because it lacks the political will to challenge forestry's naysayers.

A parting wisdom from our friend Peter Kolb. Association is not causation. Thus, carrying a pack of matches in your pocket for 30 years isn't likely to cause lung cancer, but lighting up a pack of cigarettes every day for 30 years probably will. Likewise, letting Nature manage our national forests might not kill us, but the carcinogenic wildfire smoke we breathe for months on end just might.

Remember Alston Chase's admonition:

> *There is no such thing as leaving nature alone. People are part of nature. We do not have the option of choosing not to be stewards of the land. We must master the art and science of good stewardship. Environmentalists do not understand that the only way to preserve nature is to manage nature.*

Answers to your most frequently asked questions

Before we continue it might be useful for me to answer the six questions I am most frequently asked in the question and answer periods that accompany my many speaking engagements. And if you care to read some of my speeches [33] you will find them on our website. Now the Big Six:

- **How much forest land is there in the United States?**

U.S. Forest Resource Facts and Historical Trends, [34] a very informative 64-page booklet prepared by the U.S. Forest Service's Forest Inventory and Analysis [FIA] Program, answers this and other questions in considerable detail. The brochure is 64 pages long, so hardly a brochure but a very interesting read. If you don't have time at the moment, here's a quick summary:

- In 1630, there were about 1.023 billion acres of forestland in the United States. Since then, some 256 million acres – about 25 percent of total forestland - have been converted to other uses including 989 million acres of agricultural land.
  By 1910, more than 300 years after the English built their first settlement at James town, Virginia, about 754 million acres of forestland remained, but we are again gaining ground in the forestland department.
- Today, we have about 766 million acres of forestland, plus another 138 million acres in urban forests, some 904 million acres in total or about 34 percent of our nation's 2.26 billion-acre land base and about 88 percent of our 1630 forestland base is still forested.
  That's not bad considering the millions of acres of forestland we've permanently cleared for other purposes: farming, ranching, highways and cities and towns that span thousands of square miles and millions of acres.

33 

34 

- **Who owns America's forests?**

The Forest Service's Forest Inventory and Analysis Program divides U.S. forest ownership into four classifications:

1. National Forest - that's all 326,766,748 of us. Together, we own 75 percent of all public forestland in the West.
2. Other publics - you if you live in a state or county that owns timberland. Counties own most of the public forestland in the East. States own most of the "other public" land in the West.
3. Private corporate – you if you own shares in the company. There are 166,000 of you in the U.S. and you own an average 775 acres. One percent of you own more than 5,000 acres, and you own 73 percent of all the corporately-owned forestland in the U.S.
4. Private, non-corporate – there are about 11 million of you, including enrolled members of Indian tribes; four million of you own 61 percent of all the private forestland in the U.S. You own an average 66 acres which you hold as individuals, members of families, trusts, estates or partnerships.

Sophie Petersen and her first big rainbow with guide, Dave Blackburn, on the Kootenai River in northwest Montana.
In distant Louisiana, southern pine seedlings grow quickly in clearcuts on privately-owned land.

5. In total, 56 percent of all forestland in the U.S. is privately owned and 44 percent is publicly owned. But the ownership pattern differs dramatically. West of the Mississippi River, 70 percent of all forestland is publicly owned, but east of the Mississippi, 81 percent is privately owned.

Forest Resources of the United States, 2017 [35] is a PDF report summarizing most aspects of public and privately owned timberland in the U.S. by region: North, South, West and total U.S. At 146 pages, it is both long and dreary, but it's what we had before cloud computing and sophisticated graphics programs saved our sanity. It's how I learned.

Here's a map [36] that provides an absolute wealth of data right down to the county level for those 3,000-plus counties in the U.S. Use your mouse to scroll up and down the map, then click on the links below the map. This is fun stuff.

The terms "forestland" and "timberland" are references on this link. Forestland is just that – forestland. But timberland is defined as land that is capable of growing at least 20 cubic feet of wood per acre annually. There are millions of acres public and privately-owned timberland in the U.S. that are capable of growing more than 60 cubic feet per acre annually.

Not all public forestland is available for harvest. No harvesting is permitted in congressionally designated Wilderness Areas or in areas reserved as habitat for fish, plant or wildlife species protected by the federal Endangered Species Act.

- **Is timber harvesting regulated in the United States?**

No matter the ownership classification – public or private – owners are required to obey all federal and state environmental laws and regulations. Among the laws that control, limit or forbid forest management activity:

- NEPA, National Environmental Policy Act, ratified by Congress in 1970 and signed into law by President Richard M. Nixon
- Clean Air Act of 1972, supported by President Nixon, but vetoed by him because of its "budget-wrecking" provisions; veto overridden by Congress
- Endangered Species Act, ratified by Congress in 1973, and signed into law by President Nixon
- Forest and Rangeland Renewable Resources Planning Act [RPA], ratified by Congress in 1974 and signed into law by President Gerald Ford
- National Forest Management Act [NFMA], an amendment to RPA, ratified by Congress in 1976 and signed into law by President Ford

Many western states also have their own forest practices laws. Oregon, Washington and California have reams of regulations designed to protect air and water quality and to ensure prompt replanting of harvested lands. In Oregon, landowners who refuse to comply with replanting standards risk having their land confiscated and sold at public auction.

The bottom line. What you hear from rabid environmentalists about "logging without laws" and loggers "chopping down the trees wherever they want" is just plain crap. Logging and reforestation are well-regulated on public and private timberland in the United States. No acre escapes the watchful eyes of federal, state and sometimes county agencies.

- **Do landowner management objectives differ?**

Yes they do and you can learn a great deal about these objectives from the Forest Service's *National Woodland Owner Survey.* [37] FIA does this survey, too.

FYI, one-third of the U.S. is forestland – about 800 million acres. Here's the ownership breakdown:

- 36 percent families and individuals
- 31 percent federal government
- 19 percent corporations
- 9 percent states
- 2 percent Indian tribes
- 2 percent other private
- 1 percent local governments

35 
36 
37 

Public approval of landowner management objectives varies widely as does public reaction to their harvesting methods.

Visually pleasing techniques that favor periodic tree thinnings score high with the public, regardless of their ecological value.

Visually unsightly techniques, like clearcutting, often invite public criticism, despite its ecological value when done correctly.

Families that own Tree Farms get lots of applause for their emphasis on thinnings designed to create or maintain continuous forest cover and canopies – habitats for multiple bird, plant, animal and amphibian species.

The big landowners that clearcut their timber rarely hear public applause because their main objective is to maximize profits by leveraging the principles of accepted sustainable forest practices. Profits are distributed to shareholders, sometimes millions of them whose retirement investments include Real Estate Investment Trusts and Timber Investment Management Organizations that advise institutional investors in the management of their timberlands.

Federal resource management agencies adhere to a congressionally prescribed management model that makes it virtually impossible for the Forest Service to do the work necessary to reduce the fast-growth risks posed by insects, diseases and incendiary wildfires in our national forests.

The late Forest Service Chief, Jack Ward Thomas, called this model "the Gordian knot," a "crazy quilt" of conflicting environmental laws and regulations administered by different federal agencies with conflicting mission statements. It "works" like this:

When Congress ratifies a new environmental law it assigns the rule-making to the federal agencies that will enforce the law – the U.S. Forest Service, the U.S. Fish and Wildlife Service, the National Marine Fisheries or the National Oceanic and Atmospheric Administration. Conflicts arise from the fact that these agencies march to very different drummers. Getting them in step is nearly impossible.

Agency conflicts involving differing rules interpretations are inevitable, but at the end of the day they all rise from Congress' obsession with one-size-fits-all cookie-cutter approaches to forest management and regulation.

Worse, these conflicts provide fertile ground for special interest lawyers who make a good living suing on "process," generally defined as a failure to dot all the "I's" and cross all the "T's' found in thousands of pages of conflicting rules and regulations that govern landowner conduct. When the federal government loses one of these nuisance lawsuits, taxpayers pick up the tab.

Federal resource management agencies try to resolve their conflicts through a court-mandated process called "consultation," but the process often provides still more fertile ground for lawyers because competing federal resource management agencies jealously guard their own turf.

There were times during the spotted owl war when other agencies ganged up on the Forest Service in a way that made it appear the agency had done something wrong when it hadn't. No one benefitted from the public lynching that followed. Nor have owls benefited from the minimalist forest management strategy that was shoved down the agency's throat. It was based on deeply-flawed population models that was subsequently discredited by a Rutgers University statistician.

In my 33 years as an investigative reporter, I have yet to encounter an intentional violation of rules and regulations by the Forest Service, but media coverage of perceived law-breaking is often lacking in accuracy or completeness, especially in cases involving U.S. Forest Service management activities that took years to plan and cost millions of taxpayer dollars.

Reducing the frequency of unintentional violations necessitates a much needed reconciliation of conflicting agency forest policies, rules and regulations. It is this mess that invites litigation – a zero-sum game that teaches not one forestry lesson and has sadly transformed the Forest Service into an organization seemingly incapable of defending its own honorable legacy, further exacerbating our wildfire crisis and adding to the cultural divide that distances urban Americans from their rural brethren.

Not surprisingly, many Americans living in urban-metropolitan areas applaud the Forest Service's emphasis on minimal human influences and perceived protection for aesthetic values including outdoor recreation and fish and wildlife habitat. The wildfire crisis facing us in western national

Maple grows prolifically in northern Michigan forests as does well-spaced red pine in the Minnesota's Chippewa National Forest.

The North Fork of the Flathead River in northwest Montana is a favorite with fly anglers. Logging and wildfire have shaped and reshaped this beautiful drainage.

forests has only recently shown up on their radar screens and many aren't sure what it means or what they can do about it, which is why many are counting on Nature to fix the problem.

Americans living in rural areas have been living with our wildfire crisis for years and most are utterly dismayed by federal inaction and the environmental damage insects, diseases and wildfires are doing in and around their communities – many of them completely surrounded by national forests that are falling apart.

They're also angry about the monetary losses their county governments and schools are suffering in the aftermath of the collapse of the federal timber sale program that once fueled their local economies.

High-paying jobs in logging and sawmilling have been difficult to replace and predicted increases in tourism-related employment jobs have never materialized. Nearby national forest campgrounds have limited capacity and private businesses have been reluctant to invest given the summer-long economic downdrafts created by wildfire smoke that can reduce visibility to a few hundred feet.

The federal government is the largest landowner in these counties and, unlike private landowners, Uncle Sam does not pay property taxes. The financial impact is crippling in counties where the government sometimes owns 70 to 90 percent of the entire county land base. Counties do get some money from small timber sales, more from recreational fees and some from federally-appropriated "PILT" funds [payments in lieu of taxes] but these are a pittance compared to what is lost because our federal government does not pay property taxes.

Worse are the uncounted losses that occur when federal forests within counties don't contribute their share to value-added wood processing infrastructures that convert low-value wood into high-value wood products. These contributions are measured in family wage job losses in logging, trucking, sawmills, plywood plants, forestry and equipment sales and repair. The very fabric of the community is compromised – its grocery stores, gas stations, restaurants, car dealerships, banks, hardware and clothing stores, schools, hospitals and churches.

Many Americans don't care about the plight of the west's dying timber towns. Like my cabdriver friend, Danny O'Neill, they simply want to know the trees they may never see are still there, protected from loggers. It's a hard pill for the locals to swallow. Summer after summer, they are surrounded by wildfires that kill trees that were once the economic lifeblood of their communities.

In my travels, I've seen my share of unsightly clearcuts and clearcuts in the wrong places. I squirm a little when I see them because I know most of you don't like them. But I also know that some tree species – Douglas-fir for example – need full sunlight to sprout and grow. Clearcuts also provide habitat for thousands of plants, neotropical birds and small mammals that are food sources for birds of prey. These habitats don't exist in the deep shade of old growth forests.

I've known and interviewed many loggers. They work in the woods because, like foresters, they prefer the company of trees to people. They are conservationists who take great pride in their work. One I know and admire has a quote from famed conservationist and author, Aldo Leopold, on his email page:

> *"A conservationist is one who is humbly aware that with each stroke of his axe he is writing his signature on the face of the land."*

Most private forestland owners – especially the small ones – live by the creed Leopold advanced in his 1949 Sand County Almanac. If you haven't read it, you should. Leopold lays out some important principles regarding land ethics and he explores the often-spiritual relationship between people and land. You can buy a copy on Amazon for about 12 bucks.

Landowners who are Leopold followers are the leaders in applying "close to nature" management practices that replicate natural processes, treating insects and diseases before they become infestations, removing dead and dying trees that host insects and fuel wildfires, maintaining wildlife habitat, sheltering stream corridors to prevent erosion and keep water temperatures cool. This is the day-by- day caring and conservation stuff we should be doing in our national forests but aren't doing. Why?

Personally, I favor the more holistic approach embraced eons ago by our nation's Indian tribes. Forest-owning tribes do a splendid job of accounting for cultural, spiritual and economic values that should be important to all of us.

Many states and small private landowners have begun to adopt the Indian forest management model. Many county extension foresters who advise small forest landowners also sing from the same song book.

Over the last 20 years, our non-profit Evergreen Foundation has published three editions of *Evergreen* Magazine in partnership with the Intertribal Timber Council, the organization that represents the federal interests of U.S. tribes that own and manage timberland.

Our most recent edition, *Forestry in Indian Country: Solving Federal Forestry's Rubik's Cube,* published in 2014, contains a short essay describing tribal forestry's foundation. I co-wrote it with my colleague, Gary Morishima. I think you'll like it because it speaks to the same environmental values most Americans hold:

> *"We are Indian People. As the First Stewards, we have cared for the Land since time began. Our natural resource management practices are footed in traditions, knowledge and wisdom handed down to us by our ancestors over countless generations.*
>
> *Our Creator has entrusted us with the care of our land and its resources. In exchange, He has blessed us with precious gifts of life: Foods, clothing, medicines, fuel, shelter and goods for trade and commerce – the means to nurture our bodies, minds and spirits.*
>
> *We share a deeply-felt responsibility to protect the land for those who will follow in our footsteps. The future of our peoples depends on stewardship of the natural resources that are both our heritage and legacy.*
>
> *We care for Earth so that She will continue to care for us. We are part of the Land and the Land is part of us. It is the Indian Way."*

If you'd like to know more about "the Indian Way" of managing forests, you will find three editions profiling tribal forestry in *Evergreen's* archives:

- *Progress and Promise, June 1998* [38]
- *Models of Sustainability for our Nation's Forests?* Winter 2005-2006 [39]
- *Forestry in Indian Country: Solving Federal Forestry's Rubik's Cube,* Spring 2014 [40]

Evergreen's "Anchor Forests" [41] section contains a series of essays and videos profiling Tribal Forestry practices in a collaborative proposal developed by the Intertribal Timber Council. The videos feature tribal members and are especially powerful.

- **Shouldn't there still be places in our national forests where Nature rules?**

Aldo Leopold certainly thought so, and so do I. Designated wilderness areas act as a control mechanism from which we can gauge our success in areas where forest management is both permitted and suitable. And some areas are better suited to wilderness designation because they are remote and beautiful or because they provide unique habitats for wildlife.

We Americans own about 110 million acres of designated Wilderness. This is an area larger than all but two states: Alaska and Texas. These areas are protected under the aegis of the 1964 Wilderness Act.

Leopold, a 1909 Yale Forestry School graduate, was instrumental in the creation of our country's first designated Wilderness area on the Gila National Forest in New Mexico in 1924. Including the later-designated Aldo Leopold Wilderness and the Blue Range Wilderness, it spans 558,000 acres.

It would be another 40 years before Congress ratified the 1964 Wilderness Act. Its' principal author was Wilderness Society Executive Director, Howard Zahniser. Here's his definition, the end product of 60 drafts and eight years of work:

> *"A wilderness, in contrast with those areas where man and his own works dominate the landscape, is hereby recognized as an area where the earth and its community of life are untrammeled by man, where man himself is a visitor who does not remain."*

Stripped of Zahniser's fine writing, motorized travel and logging are forbidden in designated Wilderness. There are no roads. Only hikers and horseback riders are welcome

38 

39 

40 

41 

– a limitation that has generated lots of controversy since 1964. Many believe we should make our Wilderness areas as accessible as our national parks.

We Americans also own another 55.8 million acres of inventoried roadless land. Under the Clinton Administration roadless rule, reconstruction and new roads are forbidden in these areas save for dire safety needs. Some 4.2 million roadless acres have been formally recommended for Wilderness designation.

Within the 193-million-acre National Forest and Grasslands System cared for by the U.S Forest Service there are about 45 million acres reserved because of their cultural, spiritual, biological or historic significance; also no-harvest reserves established to protect the habitat for fish, wildlife, amphibious, reptile or plant species deemed threatened or endangered under the aegis of the Endangered Species Act, plus research natural areas, recreation areas or national monuments, and areas that federal or state forest regulators deem too risky for active forest management.

Early conservationists divided themselves into two camps where wilderness ewas concerned. John Muir, who co-founded the Sierra Club, advocated for Wilderness. Gifford Pinchot, the principal architect and first Chief of the U.S. Forest Service wasn't keen on the idea. Nor was his greatest supporter, President Theodore Roosevelt, namesake of the 29,920-acre Theodore Roosevelt Wilderness designated by Congress in 1978 in North Dakota.

Our National Forest System owes its existence to Roosevelt and Pinchot, who saw to its creation in 1905. Both believed the nation's early national forests should be managed for the resources they held that could contribute to our country's westward expansion. Here are two quotes – one from Breaking New Ground, Pinchot's autobiography,

The Great Smokies near Cosby, Tennessee. In October, there is no prettier place on earth. Deciduous hardwoods dominate forests east of the Mississippi.

Aftermath of a thinning on the Siskiyou National Forest in southern Oregon. This beautiful area was incinerated in the 500,000-acre Biscuit Fire in 2002. Less than one percent of the burnt timber was salvaged. The rest was left to rot and reburn in a 2018 fire.

Foresters at Pinchot's home in Washington, D.C. Pinchot founded SAF with the able assistance of six of our nation's earliest professional foresters.

First Pinchot:

> *"Without natural resources, life itself is impossible. From birth to death, natural resources, transformed for human use, feed, clothe, shelter and transport us. Upon them we are dependent for every material necessity, comfort, convenience and protection in our lives. Without natural resources, prosperity is impossible."*

Now Roosevelt:

> *"And now, first and foremost, you can never afford to forget for one moment what is the object of our forest policy. That object is not to preserve forests because they are beautiful, though that is good in itself; nor because they are refuges for the wild creatures of the wilderness, though that, too, is good in itself; but the primary object of our forest policy, as of the land policy of the United States, is the making of prosperous homes.*
>
> *It is part of the traditional policy of home making in our country. Every other consideration must come as secondary. The whole effort of the Government in dealing with the forests must be directed to this end, keeping in view the fact that it is not only necessary to start the homes as prosperous, but to keep them so. That is why the forests have got to be kept. You can start a prosperous home by destroying the forests, but you cannot keep it prosperous that way."*

The fact that most Americans no longer share the conservation ethics inspired by Roosevelt and Pinchot reflects our nation's ever-evolving felt necessities. But how about this wisdom from Chief Oshkosh. You may remember it from Chapter 1.

> *"Start with the rising sun and work toward the setting sun, take only the mature trees, the sick trees and the trees that have fallen. When you reach the end of the reservation, turn and cut from the setting sun to the rising sun and the trees will last forever."*

Try your hand at conservation and management with this marvelous interactive National Wilderness Preservation System Map [42] prepared by Lisa Ronald, Wilderness Institute, College of Forestry and Conservation at the University of Montana.

- **What exactly is active forest management?**

Active forest management – as the term applies in our national forests – is science-based, sustainable into the foreseeable future and designed to achieve one or more of these environmental objectives:

- Reduce the risk of catastrophic wildfire in forests that have been weakened by a natural overcrowding of trees and the increasing presence of insect or disease infestations that inhibit growth and natural resiliency.
- Protect wildlife habitat or create missing wildlife habitat types.
- Increase biological diversity by increasing plant species.
- Remove excessive diseased or dead trees from forests that hold too many trees for the natural carrying capacity of the land.
- Protect rural communities that are surrounded by forests and grasslands wherein the wildfire risk is high because of the presence of insect and disease infestations.

In our national forests, the Forest Service is responsible for designating lands that are "suitable and available" for active management. Logging and reforestation can legally occur on these lands without environmental harm.

No management activity, including harvesting, is permitted in designated Wilderness areas or areas that have been reserved as habitat for designated threatened or endangered species.

Roadless areas are also off limits pending final determination as to their highest and best use. Some of these lands will likely be designated as Wilderness. Other lands may be added to the suitable and available land base. Many roadless areas actually have old roads built by early settlers, loggers and miners.

Management objectives vary widely among the nation's million-plus private forest landowners. To explore these, go back to the link to the National Woodland Owners Survey. And remember, forest landowners aren't lawbreakers.

42 

Public enemy number 1

For decades, our nation's conservation ethic demanded that all wildfires be quickly extinguished. The quicker the better.

In the 1940s, Forest Service smoke jumpers bragged about "10 o'clock fires." It was their way of reminding themselves that they were expected to put out their wildfires by 10 a.m. the morning after the fires were spotted. Twelve of the Forest Service's finest died on a steep slope in western Montana in 1949 in pursuit of this ideal. More on them later.

Born of the Puritan admonition to waste not, want not, our nation's determination not to squander its natural resources morphed into a fear of wildfire following a series of deadly blazes. Wildfire became Public Enemy No. 1 and viewed through history's long lens, it's easy to see why.

In Wisconsin, the Great Peshtigo Fire swept over 1.2 million acres on October 8, 1871. The conflagration is thought to have been started by a meteor shower that ignited logging slash. 1,500 were killed. It was the greatest loss of life in a wildfire in U.S. history. My great grandparents escaped with the clothes on their backs.

That same night, the Great Chicago Fire burned one-third of the city to the ground, leaving 100,000 homeless. The fire started in a barn southwest of the city's center. It killed more than 300.

Unbelievably, White Rock and Port Huron, Michigan were leveled by fire the same night Chicago burned. At least 50 were killed and 1.2 million acres of timber were lost. No cause was ever established, but an unusual October drought had settled over Michigan's Upper Peninsula.

The September 1902 Yacolt Burn set the stage for the federal wildfire forest policy that persisted until 1988. The fire ravaged a half-million acres of virgin timberland in northwest Oregon and southwest Washington. More than 60 died.

In the aftermath, George S. Long, General Manager of the Weyerhaeuser Timber Company, led the formation of the nation's first privately funded wildfire fighting cooperatives. He had good reason. Weyerhaeuser lost several billion board feet of old growth timber it had purchased two years earlier as part of what was then the largest land sale in the United States since the 1803 Louisiana Purchase.

The Great 1910 Fire – by far the largest in U.S. history – would eventually put the U.S. Forest Service in the firefighting business alongside the privately-funded fire cooperatives. Hurricane-force winds drove the August 1910 fire into a firestorm that consumed three million acres and eight billion board feet of virgin timber in northern Idaho and western Montana, most of it in only 48 hours.

Seventy-eight untrained and poorly equipped firefighters, most recruited from the streets of Spokane, Washington, died. Half of Wallace, Idaho was destroyed, and several small Montana communities were leveled. My grandmother loaded her belongings on a railroad flatcar, covered them with bedsheets she had soaked in Pritchard Creek and road through a firestorm to safety.

Gifford Pinchot was furious. Although President William Howard Taft had fired him for insubordination in January of 1910, eight months before the 1910 Fire, the fiery former Forest Service chief was revered by working journalists who found him to be far more quotable than his

Image courtesy of the Library of Congress

Gifford Pinchot, first Chief of the U.S. Forest Service.

replacement, Henry Graves.

Pinchot was thus invited to write an essay for the December 1910 edition of *Everybody's Magazine*, a 500,000 circulation muckraker favored by A-list writers of the day: Jack London, A.A. Milne, George Bernard Shaw, O. Henry and Eleanor Hoyt Brainerd.

Pinchot pulled no punches in his bare-knuckle assessment of Congress' refusal to adequately fund the Forest Service, a problem that persists to present day.

> *"This cruel waste of national property and human life is a heavy shadow upon the door steps of certain members of the Congress...*
>
> *If the forest supervisors had been provided with the proper equipment, if money had been appropriated to make trails, buy tools, horses, supplies, and engage a sufficient force of foresters, this fire would not have occurred...*
>
> *It is all loss, dead, irretrieable loss, due to the pique, bias and bull-headedness of a knot of men who have sulked and planted their hulks in the way of appropriations for the protection and improvement of these national reserves."*

It was vintage Pinchot – a well orchestrated and very public temper tantrum that played on the sentiments of wealthy conservationists he knew personally. And it worked perfectly. Wildfire would remain Public Enemy No. 1 for the next seventy years.

Everything in Pinchot's life was meticulously scripted including *The Use Book*, a 142-page "how to" manual completed in 1905 that was given to every ranger the Forest Service hired. Its unambiguous message would resonate through the agency for decades. An excerpt:

> *"Forest reserves are for the purpose of preserving a perpetual supply of timber for home industries, preventing destruction of forest cover which regulates the flow of streams, and protecting local residents from unfair competition in the use of forest and range.*
>
> *They are patrolled and protected, at Government expense, for the benefit of the community and the home builder.*
>
> *We know that the welfare of every community is dependent upon a cheap and plentiful supply of timber; that a forest cover is the most efficient means of maintaining a regular stream flow for irrigation and other useful purposes; and that the permanence of the livestock industry depends upon conservative use of the range.*
>
> *The injury to all persons and industries which results from the destruction of forests by fire and careless use is a matter of history in older countries and has long been the cause of anxiety and loss in the United States.*

The protection of forest resources still existing is a matter of urgent local and national importance. This is shown by the exhaustion and removal of lumbering centers, often leaving behind desolation and depression in business.

You will see to it that the water, wood, and forage of the reserves are conserved and wisely used for the benefit of the homebuilder first of all, upon whom depends the best permanent use of lands and resources alike.

The continued prosperity of the agricultural, lumbering, mining, and live-stock interests is directly dependent upon a permanent and accessible supply of water, wood, and forage, as well as upon the present and future use of these resources under businesslike regulation, enforced with promptness, effectiveness, and common sense.

In the management of each reserve local questions will be decided upon local grounds; the dominant industry will be considered first, but with as little restriction to minor industries as may be possible; sudden changes in industrial conditions will be avoided by gradual adjustment after due notice, and where conflicting interests must be reconciled the question will always be decided from the standpoint of the greatest good of the greatest number in the long run."

Pinchot expected a great deal of his newly hired rangers and his well-known penchant for detail and organization could be jarring. A sampling of the sections in The Use Book:

- Page 6: History and objects of forest reserves
- Page 7: Relation of forest officers to the public
- Page 12: Private and State rights
- Page 13: Jurisdiction
- Page 14: Duration of and charge for permits
- Page 16: Grazing
- Page 20: Sale of timber
- Page 49: Roads and trails
- Page 53: Canals, ditches and reservoirs
- Page 56: Private railroads and telephone lines
- Page 58: Protection against fire
- Page 72: Marking reserve boundaries

On and on it went. Nothing was overlooked, not even field and office equipment and records, reports and correspondence. Pinchot thought of everything, even a reference guide rangers carried in their shirt pockets.

Many rural westerners wish *The Use Book* were still in use. The land management principles espoused by Pinchot and Roosevelt began their fall from grace nearly a half-century ago as the public's interest in timber harvesting declined and public desire to "protect" forests increased. But as the public's obsession with all things environmental increased so too did the frequency, size and destructive force of the West's wildfires.

How to stay current? Gain some perspective? Turn down the noise generated by the snake oil salesmen and blame gamers who make their livings selling fear. Utilize the best information sources where wildfire is concerned.

The National Interagency Fire Center [43] [NIFC] in Boise, Idaho. was founded in 1965 by the Forest Service, the Bureau of Land Management and the National Weather Service. Now the National Park Service, Bureau of Indian Affairs and the U.S. Fish and Wildlife Service are also involved.

Although NIFC mainly coordinates federal and state responses to wildfires, the agency also played critical roles in the anxious hours and days that followed the April 19, 1995 Oklahoma City bombing and the September 11, 2001 World Trade Center terrorist attacks. This is a first-rate outfit with a long history of keeping the wagons circled as tightly as possible.

The data NIFC compiles [44] is our proverbial canary in a coal mine. It warns us that if we don't get our act together in very short order, our national forest losses to wildfire could easily double or triple over the next decade. Is anyone listening? Does anyone care? I sure as hell hope so!

43 

44 

Forest Service Ranger, Ed Pulaski, hid his 45-man crew in this mine tunnel during the 1910 fire. Six died but the rest survived the firestorm that passed over them. Some 1,500 died in Wisconsin's 1871 Peshtigo Fire. This artists rendering depicts thousands more who sought safety in the Peshtigo River.

CHAPTER 13

Congress weighs in

Embers from the Great 1910 Fire were still glowing inside stumps and fallen trees when Congress ratified the Weeks Act in March of 1911, creating six new national forests, authorizing the purchase of private lands along navigable rivers in the eastern United States and encouraging closer cooperation between the Forest Service and state and private firefighting cooperatives.

Although politically symbolic, the Weeks Act did little to improve the wildfire situation. The 1918 Cloquet Fire, started by sparks from a passing train, leveled 38 Minnesota communities, killed 453, injured 52,000 and burned 250,000 acres. But it would still be another 16 years before Congress got serious about the nation's wildfire epidemic.

In 1924, some 14 years after Gifford Pinchot lambasted Congress for its ill-advised failure to fund firefighting equipment for the country's national forests, the House of Representatives finally got serious about wildfire. The Clarke-McNary Act, so-named for its sponsors, New York Congressman, John Clarke and Oregon Senator, Charles McNary, was enacted June 7, 1924.

Charles McNary was 28 years old when Yacolt burned. He'd grown up on his grandfather's farm near Salem, Oregon, studied law, economics, science and history at Stanford University [1896 to 1898], served as Dean of the Willamette Law School [1908-1913], then secured an appointment to the Oregon Supreme Court in 1913. At 39, he was the youngest jurist on the court. He was appointed to the U.S. Senate in 1917, following the death of Henry Lane, then won election to the Senate in November 1918.

Although he was well-regarded across the political spectrum, McNary, a Republican, was a progressive at heart. He supported of President Franklin Roosevelt's plans for publicly financed and owned hydroelectric development of the Columbia River as well as Roosevelt-inspired New Deal regulations aimed at refloating America's Depression-wracked economy.

But it was McNary's friendship with fellow Republican, Henry Cabot Lodge, who was Chairman of the Senate Foreign Relations Committee, that got him appointed Chairman of the Senate's Irrigation and Reclamation of Arid Lands Committee and the Senate Agriculture and Forestry Committee.

Given McNary's political roots in farming and forestry, his Senate assignments made sense, but it was his considerable debating skill that brought McNary to Lodge's attention and secured his favorable place in the U.S. Senate's inner circle.

By 1924, McNary had hit his stride. He combined his constituent interests in expanding the National Forest System, reforestation of cutover timberland and fire protection, co-sponsoring the landmark Clarke-McNary Act. Years later, the pious Bill Greeley, the third Chief of the Forest Service, admitted that he had closeted himself in the Senate cloakroom so that he could pass favorable questions to supportive Senators during floor debate.

Clarke-McNary laid the groundwork for ramping up the Forest Service's capacity to battle wildfires in national forests. Federal equipment and crews would soon join privately-funded cooperatives formed after the disastrous 1902

U.S. Senator, Charles McNary and New York Representative, William Clarke, were the driving political forces behind the 1924 Clarke-McNary Act, putting the Forest Service in the wildfire fighting business alongside three already established and privately-funded fire fighting cooperatives in Idaho, Oregon and Washington.

Yacolt Fire killed 65 people in western Oregon and Washington.

Yacolt began as a series of small fires. Coastal winds blew them together, forming a colossus that leveled a half-million acres of virgin timber. Burning debris drifted across the mile-wide Columbia River near Cascade Locks, Oregon.

Early federal efforts to confront the west's wildfires were hampered by poor road access in national forests, but by the 1940s, the Forest Service could measure the success of its work. What no one understood was that the federal government's effort to stuff the Wildfire Genie back in her bottle without altering the manner in which national forests were managed would only make her angry – very angry.

There are tons of colorful charts and graphs that display the historic result of our nation's seemingly futile effort to stuff the Wildfire Genie back in her bottle and keep her there. As the frequency and destructive force of our killing wildfires has increased, so has the finger-pointing. Environmentalists and loggers blame one another and most everyone blames the Forest Service for doing too much or too little about wildfire. Who to believe? What to believe?

Again, I think the U.S. Forest Service is your best source of unbiased information.

There are many reputable sources [45] that offer charts and graphs that display the historic convergence of harvesting and wildfire – meaning the points at which it seemed like firefighters were gaining the upper hand and the points where it becomes clear that wildfire is winning. You can see a definite correlation between the congressionally mandated reduction in national forest timber harvesting and increases in the frequency and size of wildfires.

On the following pages are the acres burned numbers for 1980-2018. Many more bad years than good since 2000. Tame by comparison in the 1980s and 90s.

45 

Number of Acres Burned in Wildfires – 1980 to 2018

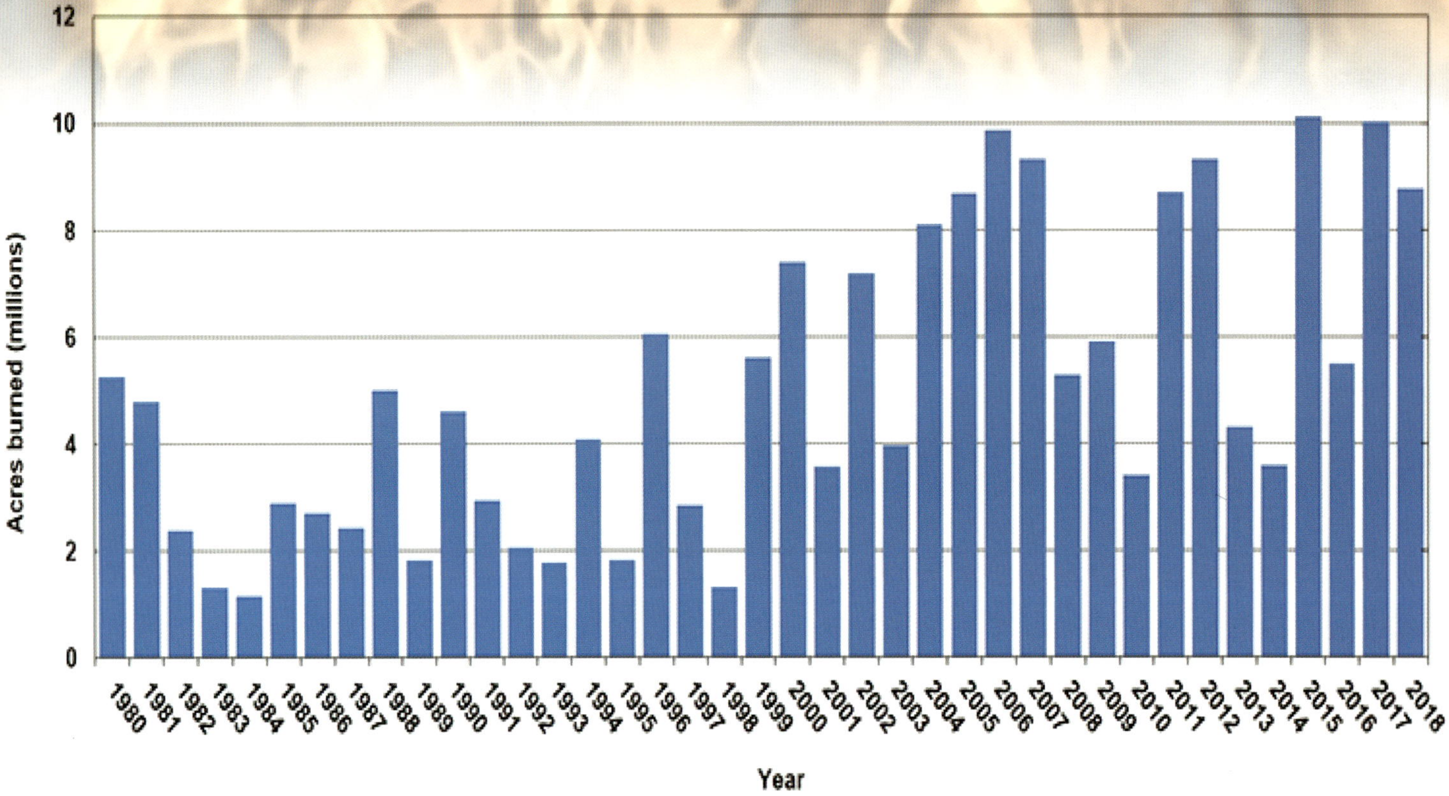

Acres burned (millions)
12
10
8
6
4
2
0
1980
1981
1982
1983
1984
1985
1986
1987
1988
1989
1990
1991
1992
1993
1994
1995
1996
1997
1998
1999
2000
2001
2002
2003
2004
2005
2006
2007
2008
2009
2010
2011
2012
2013
2014
2015
2016
2017
2018
Year

Annual mortality exceeds annual growth in National Forests east of the Washington Cascades.

Hundreds of millions of trees are dying from insect infestations and root diseases that attack forests that hold too many trees for the carrying capacity of the land. Wildfire is inevitable.

Thinning can restore natural resiliency, enabling remaining trees to grow again. Soil and water quality are protected, as are outdoor recreation opportunity and timber, mainstays in Washington's economy.

Imagine a solid block of wood the dimensions of the Seahawk's CenturyLink Stadium stretching more than one mile into smoke-filled skies. This is our annual loss – now more than 327 million cubic feet per year.

Congress is providing tools the U.S. Forest Service can use to restore lost resiliency. Good Neighbor Authority permits the Washington Department of Natural Resources to help the understaffed Forest Service significantly increase its forest restoration capacity.

Conservation groups and their collaborative partners are rolling up their sleeves. With 9.3 million National Forest acres in our state, we have a lot of restoration work to do - and no more than 30 years in which to get it done.

evergreen magazine

Evergreen State No More?
Million cubic feet
300
200
100
0
-100
268,950
327,203
-58,253
19,156
Gross Annual Growth
Annual Mortality
Annual Net Growth
Timber Removal

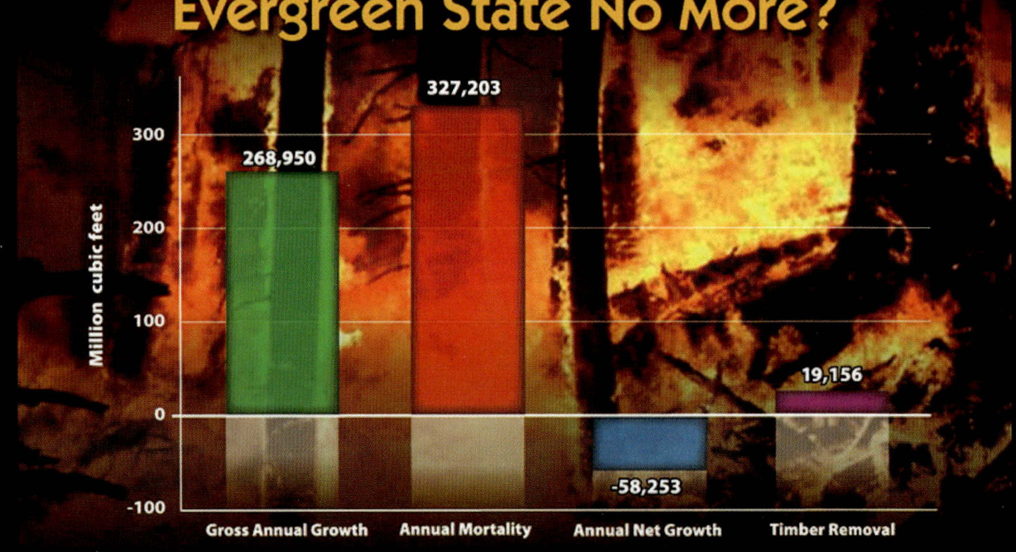

Annual mortality will soon exceed annual growth in Idaho National Forests.

Millions of trees are dying from insect infestations and root diseases that frequent forests that are under great stress.

Thinning stands that hold too many trees for the carrying capacity of the land will restore natural resiliency, enabling residual trees to grow again.

Wildfire is inevitable in dying forests. Fish and wildlife habitat is incinerated, water quality and soil productivity are spoiled, year-round recreation opportunity and timber, mainstays in Idaho's economy are lost for decades.

Imagine a solid block of wood the dimensions of a football field stretching 1.82 miles into smoke-filled skies. This is our annual loss – now more than 555 million cubic feet per year.

Congress is providing tools the Forest Service can use in diseased and dying forests. Good Neighbor Authority permits the Idaho Department of Lands to help the Forest Service significantly increase its forest restoration capacity. The first GNA projects are on the Clearwater-Nez Perce, Payette and Idaho Panhandle National Forests.

evergreen magazine

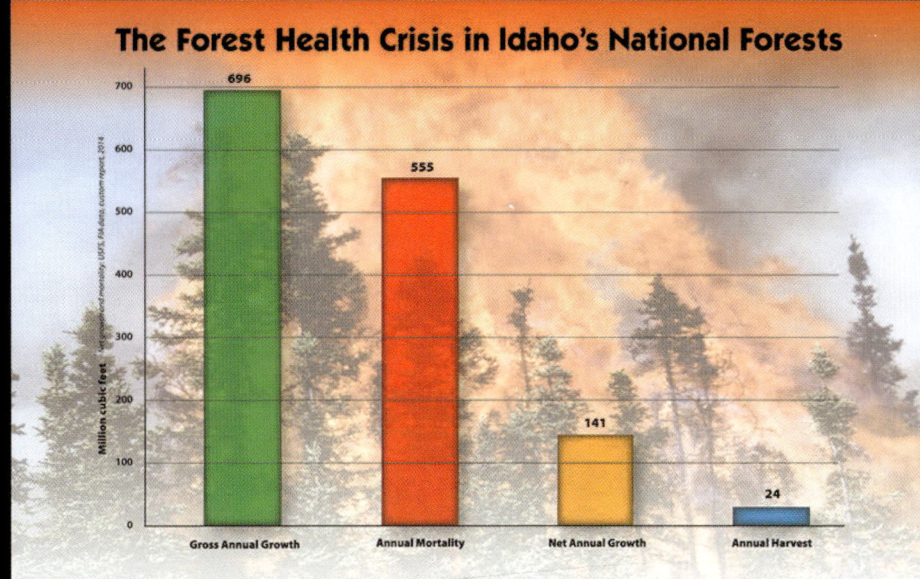

Annual mortality will soon exceed annual growth in Montana's National Forests.

Millions of trees are dying from insect infestations and root diseases that attack forests that hold too many trees for the carrying capacity of the land. Wildfire is inevitable.

Thinning can restore natural resiliency, enabling remaining trees to grow again. Soil and water quality are protected, as are outdoor recreation opportunity and timber, mainstays in Montana's economy.

Imagine a solid block of wood the dimensions of Washington Grizzly Stadium stretching 1.67 miles into smoke-filled skies. This is our annual loss – now more than 510 million cubic feet per year.

Congress is providing tools the U.S. Forest Service can use to restore lost natural resiliency. Good Neighbor Authority permits the Montana Department of Natural Resources to help the understaffed Forest Service significantly increase its forest restoration capacity.

Ironically – and tragically - Montana's serial litigators have pushed the state's family-owned sawmills to the brink of economic collapse. As these mills go out of business, so goes Montana's opportunity to pull its National Forests back from the brink of ecological collapse.

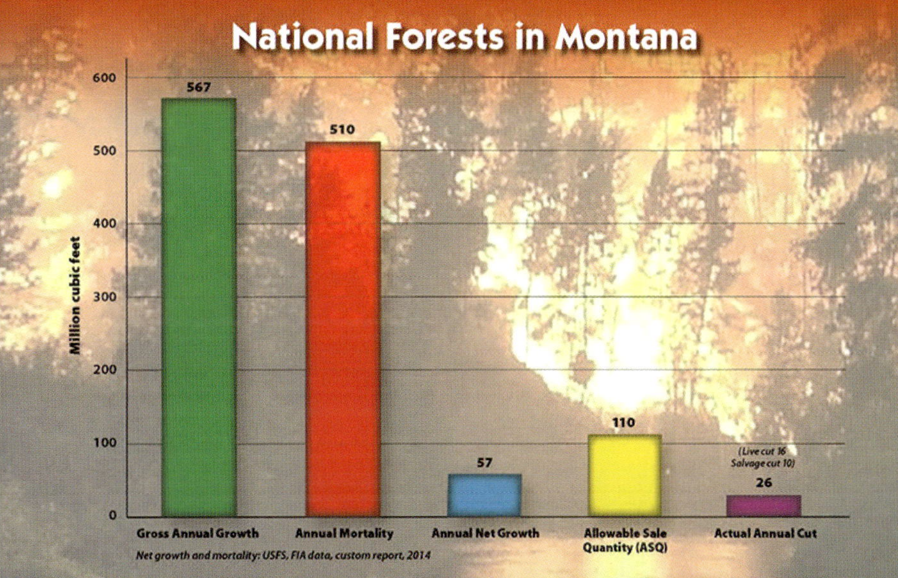

California's National Forests are in crisis. Annual mortality has surpassed 68 percent of annual growth. Next year will be worse than last year, which was worse than the year before.

Millions – perhaps billions - of trees are dying from insect infestations and root diseases that attack forests that hold too many trees for the carrying capacity of the land. Wildfire is inevitable.

Thinning can restore natural resiliency, enabling remaining trees to grow again. Soil and municipal water quality are protected, as are fish and wildlife habitat. So too are air quality and the many year-round recreation opportunities California's National Forests provide.

Imagine a solid block of wood the dimensions of the Rose Bowl stretching 2.18 miles into smoke-filled skies. This is our annual loss – now more than 663 million cubic feet per year.

It's hard to believe that California's political and conservation leaders are willing to stand by - ignoring forestry's many proven management options - while their state's National Forests die and burn in horrific wildfires. Where is the "can-do" spirit of innovation for which Californians are known globally?
National Forests.

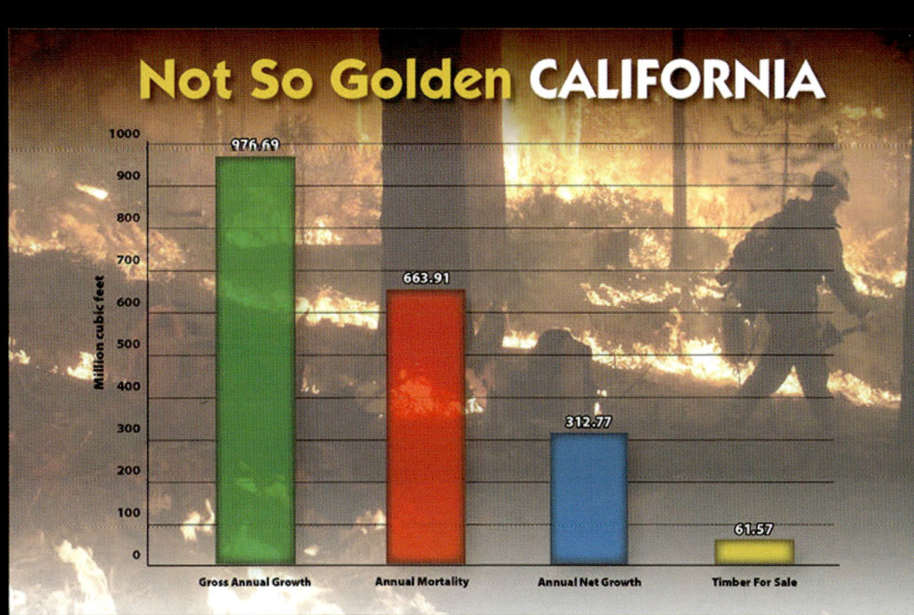

Black Hills green

There are national forests in 40 of our 50 states. 154 in all. Each tells its own story. Some were born beautiful. Others became so with a lot of help from people like you who cared enough to lend a helping hand. Some were once beautiful but are now in crisis.

If I had to pick one that I think best embodies what Gifford Pinchot and Teddy Roosevelt envisioned 114 years ago, it would be the Black Hills National Forest. I know of no other publicly-owned forest where the forestry, conservation and community stories converge so seamlessly on the head of a pin.

There is a sense of unity and purpose here that is rare in western national forests, but it took a raging mountain pine beetle epidemic to force Black Hills residents to realize that they could lose the forest they loved if they didn't find ways to settle their differences – and deal directly with the beetles. There are great civics lessons to be learned here, lessons in the rights and duties of citizenship.

The Lakota Sioux moved into the Black Hills of South Dakota and Wyoming around 1750, some 25 years before the Declaration of Independence was signed. They called the 7,700 square mile expanse "Paha Sapa," meaning "The hills that are black," a reference to their foreboding darkness when viewed from the Great Plains that surround them.

The closer you get to them, the greener they look. It is as though a deep green island somehow broke away from forests in northeast Wyoming or perhaps even southwest Montana, much as the Aleutian Island chain broke away from Kamchatka Krai, 1,200 miles across the Bering Sea, during the Early Eocene warming period, 30 to 50 million years ago.

East, across the Great Plains, the forests closest to the Black Hills are the mixed conifer and hardwood forests of Minnesota and Missouri. But these South Dakota stands are almost pure ponderosa pine. You have to go west to find lookalikes near Lame Deer and Ashland, Montana.

Save for the one-seventh of the 1.25 million-acre Black Hills National Forest located in Crook and Weston counties in Wyoming, the entire forest is confined to five South Dakota counties: Pennington, Custer, Lawrence, Fall River and Meade. Scattered clumps of ponderosa also grow in Todd, Mellette and Tripp counties in central South Dakota, but the rest of the state is mostly prairie – farmland.

A convergence of factors – including sunlight, moisture,. soil type and frequent cone crops – are major reasons why ponderosa pine thrives in the Black Hills. But the most important factor – by far – in modern history has been the very positive impact of hands-on forest management.

For convenience sake – convenience being an easily followed paper trail – let us stipulate that modern history begins with Case No. 1, the first federal timber sale in history, awarded to the Homestake Mining Company in December of 1899. I know of no other national forest that can point to one timber sale and say, "This is where and how it all started." Every national forest had a first timber sale somewhere in time, but there is only one Case No. 1.

There is also only one *first photographic record* of what the Black Hills looked like before white settlement began. It was assembled in 1874 by William Illingworth, a commercial photographer from St. Paul, Minnesota, who was hired by the federal government to make a photographic record of the movements of General George Armstrong's Black Hills expedition. The expedition is memorialized on 59 four-and-one-half by eight inch glass plate negatives that reveal what the expedition's entourage saw in the Black Hills.

There are earlier photographs of the old West – John Carbutt's 1866 photos of the Union Pacific's run across the Great Plains, Timothy O'Sullivan's 1868 pictures of Shoshone Falls on the Snake River in southern Idaho, William Henry Jackson's 1871 photographs of Lower Yellowstone Falls, and a photo of John Wesley Powell's 1871 camp near present-day Green River, Wyoming,

But Illingworth's Black Hills series functions as the beginning point for amateur and professional photographers who have attempted to replicate his work over the last 50 years. I have twice attempted to retake Illingworth's photo taken from clifftops overlooking the Castle Creek Valley, but his photo can't be duplicated because tall ponderosas block the view.

Of all the attempts, the two finest are Yellow Ore, Yellow Hair, Yellow Pine, assembled in 1974 by Donald Progulske and Richard Sowell for the South Dakota State University Agricultural Experiment Station, and Exploring with Custer: The 1874 Black Hills Expedition, a beautiful coffee table book published in 2002 by Ernest Grafe and Paul Horsted.

What these two exceptionally well-documented books reveal is that the Black Hills seen by Custer's heavily armed expedition in 1874 look nothing like the Black Hills we see today. The hills are much greener now than they were then because there are probably twice as many trees. This after 120 years of steady timber harvesting and perhaps 10 mountain pine beetle epidemics.

You can be forgiven for wondering how this could be. The answer begins with Gifford Pinchot's very measured and quite detailed approach to Case No. 1. He understood the political significance of the federal government's first regulated timber sale. Indeed, he had traveled west in 1896 with an investigative team selected by Wolcott Gibbs, a Harvard University chemist and president of the National Academy of Sciences.

The team's worrisome report was key to President Cleveland's February 22, 1897 decision to designate 13 forest reserves in the West, including the 967,680-acre Black Hills Forest Reserve. Homestake had opposed the reserves because their mining operations at Lead consumed millions of board feet of free timber cut from forests within an eight mile radius of Deadwood.

Homestake was far from alone in its opposition to the Black Hills Forest Reserve. The aghast editor of the Custer Weekly Chronicle declared that the forest reserves "...may be safely regarded as one of the most vital blows at civilization, so far as the Black Hills is concerned, that has ever been perpetrated by the ruler of any nation in the history of modern or ancient times."

The Chronicle was right about one thing. Timber – not gold - was the economic lifeblood of the Black Hills. Without timber, there would be no mines, no towns, no nothing. In its subsequent report to Congress, the National Academy of Sciences acknowledged as much.

"It is evident that without Government protection, these forests of the Black Hills, so far as their productive capacity is concerned, will disappear at the end of a few years and...their destruction will entail serious injury and loss to the agricultural and mining population of western North and South Dakota."

Pinchot echoed this opinion in a later report in which he sought to demonstrate that federal regulation and Homestake's cooperation had been key to the success of Case No. 1. "There is no other forest in the United States," he wrote, "in which practical forestry is more urgently needed, or in which results of such importance may be more easily achieved upon. Its preservation depends the timber to supply a great and rapidly growing mining industry."

When Pinchot met with Homestake's manager, Tom Grier, and company attorney, Gideon Moody, in November of 1897, on the tail end of a two week inspection tour, he was acting as the special envoy of Interior Secretary Cornelius Bliss, a fact that spoke to his exceptional political connections in scientific circles: Franklin Hough, first Chief of the Division of Forestry, Charles Sargent, Director of Harvard University's Arnold Arboretum and of Garden and Forest magazine, George Bird Grinnell, a zoologist and conservationist who had taken part in Custer's 1874 Black Hills expedition and Prussian-trained Bernhard Fernow, the first professional forester in the United States and the third Chief of the Division of Forestry.

Hough, Sargent and Fernow had written voluminously about the need for the federal government to designate forest reserves and regulate logging on public domain land. And Pinchot's mentor, Sir Deitrich Brandis had developed a workable system for conservation and use in India's teak forests.

But with all due respect to Pinchot's political cache, it seems likely that Tom Grier had read the tea leaves well in advance of their three-hour

There are millions more trees in the Castle Creek Valley in South Dakota's Black Hills today than there were when Custer expedition photographer, William Illingworth, photographed it in July 1874. Publicly popular wildfire suppression is the main reason. Follow this link [46] to comparative photographs take from the cliffs above the valley.

46

meeting. The three hours isn't much time in which to close the books on the era of free government timber, a 13-year period in which town-builders and miners cut at least 1.5 billion board feet of free public domain timber under the aegis of the 1878 Free Timber Act. Phony mining claims were used to steal more timber after Congress passed the 1891 Forest Reserve Act.

Given the enormity of the day, Grier undoubtedly counseled with George Hearst, Homestake's principal owner and a familiar face on Wall Street after the company listed its stock in 1879. They needed timber for the Lead mine and the only way to legally get it was to apply for the permit to harvest Case No. 1.

But Pinchot needed Homestake's backing as much as they needed his. Getting Grier and Moody to sign on to the tenets of forest conservation advanced by Brandis, Fernow, Hough and others would not be easy. Pinchot's assurance that government regulation would be based on use and good science proved to be the tipping point.

Grier submitted Homestake's application to Interior Secretary Bliss in April 1898. It described the size, location and number of trees to be cut in eight sections along the company's railroad tracks about four miles southwest of Nemo. The company paid $1 per thousand board feet – a board feet being a board one-foot by one-foot and one inch thick – 13 million board feet of saw logs and 5,100 cords of smaller logs. $14,967.32 – chump change in George Hearst's world.

Pinchot's Case No. 1 rules were necessarily straightforward:

- Trees less than eight inches in diameter were to be left to grow.
- Seed trees totaling 482 board feet per acre – two trees per acre - were also to be left to naturally reseed logged areas.
- Treetops and other logging slash were to be piled for burning.
- Trees larger than eight inches in diameter had to be used as timber or lumber and could not be cut into less valuable cord wood.

Logging commenced a few days before Christmas 1899. Over the next eight years, rugged men armed only with crosscut saws and axes cut timber from about 2,000 acres scattered across a 5,100 acre expanse.

Pinchot's forestry training and his conservationist instincts would prove correct. By 1924, ponderosa pine standing volume on the Case No. 1 site averaged 2,129 board feet per acre, a five-fold increase in growth. Although the results were impressive, the Forest Service increased the seed tree requirement from 482 board feet per acre to 2,611 board feet.

The hopeful picture that was unfolding in the Black Hills was a far cry from the doom and gloom that Agriculture field agent Per Axel Rydberg had predicted in 1892. The hills had been "made bare by the ravages of lumbermen, mining companies, fire and cyclones."

Only "stumps, fallen logs and the underbrush remained," Rydberg wrote. He predicted that "it will be no wonder if in a short time the dark pine forest is gone and the name 'Black Hills' has become meaningless."

Recovery would take time and effort, but Pinchot had seen the future in Bear Gulch near Spearfish. He discovered "a beautiful and vigorous forest of great potential value." Mining engineer, Henry Chance, saw the same thing in the southern reaches of the Black Hills, a hundred miles south of Lead.

"It is impossible to travel the Black Hills, especially through their southern portion, without being charmed by the beauty of the country," Chance wrote in 1891. The beauty he described is a close approximation to what the hills look like today.

In 1968, the Forest Service commemorated the harvest of the two-billionth board foot since Case No. 1. Its factual representation was a 203-year-old seed tree that had grown eight inches in diameter since 1899 and held 400 board feet of timber, a four-fold increase over the average-sized Case No. 1 tree. The site had since been harvested four more times.

"With harvest of the two-billionth board foot, the Black Hills will have produced as much or more wood than there was estimated to have been standing when logging started in 1899," a Rapid City Journal reporter wrote following the 1968 ceremony. "Case No. 1 is more than history. The old sale area has been a proving ground for forest management. Here the basic precepts of careful logging were first laid out."

Case No. 1 and William Illingworth's 1874 photographs provide starting points that are rare in western national forests. Black Hills residents can turn to these visual and quantifiable benchmarks as often as they see fit to reassure themselves that the best way to protect their forests is to keep following Pinchot's lead.

But Pinchot was not infallible. While his Case No. 1 harvesting plan met with the approval of his conservationist friends, he – and they – greatly underestimated the killing power of the mountain pine beetle. The first documented beetle sightings came in 1895 near the Wyoming border, but nothing was known about them, so nothing was done.

Reports of widespread beetle damage first reached Pinchot after Bernhard Fernow resigned from the Division of Forestry in 1898 and Pinchot was named its fourth Chief. In 1901, he hired young Andrew Hopkins, a self-taught West Virginia entomologist, to investigate the situation.

Hopkins, Pinchot and his field assistant, E.M. Griffith, traveled to the Black Hills in September 1901. In four days, they rode from Spearfish via Iron Creek and Bear Gulch, South Dakota, to Rifle Pit and Cement Ridge in Wyoming, then back to Little Spearfish Creek and Lead.

Hopkins collected 4,363 beetle specimens, described how they attacked trees, including the gallery-like tunnels they left beneath the bark and even speculated using trap trees to control beetle damage – a method used today. He named the beetle Dendroctonus ponderosa – later corrected to D ponderosae to conform to nomenclature rules regarding gender in Latin names. Roughly translated, "the pine-destroying beetle" of the Black Hills. Scientists have been studying them since Hopkins' report was published in 1902.

Of decades of findings, these are the alarm clocks that announce the arrival of big trouble in the Black Hills:

- Mountain pine beetles return at 20-30 year intervals and gradually disappear 10-15 years later.
- The most vulnerable forests hold an over abundance of trees.
- Trees are less vulnerable when they are widely spaced.
- Air turbulence in more open stands apparently disrupts pheromone flow – pheromones being the primary attractants female and male beetles emit to invite other beetles to join in the feast.
- Left unchecked, mountain pine beetle epidemics can kill millions of acres of ponderosa pine.

They are merciless and well-equipped killers. A virtual metropolis of organisms travel with them: mites, nematodes, fungi, yeasts, bacteria and other deadly organisms including blue stain spores that block water pathways in the tree's sapwood layer. Aerial photographs taken over the last 15 years chronicle the beetle's relentless march through once green forests.

Forest Service entomologists report that the quarter-inch long beetles organize their attacks through smell, touch, sound, site and taste. Once beneath the bark, adult beetles bore vertically, laying their eggs and spreading fungus spores as they go. When their eggs hatch, they transform themselves into tiny white grubs that leave the tree laterally, cutting off the flow of nutrients the tree needs to survive. These spores are the source of the blue stain we see in some pine boards

Reddish brown needles announce the inevitable result of the previous year's fatal invasion. Also inevitable are the stand-replacing wildfires that clean up the mess the beetles leave behind.

John Ball, a PhD entomologist at South Dakota State University, has been studying Black Hills beetles for years. Although he speaks with jarring clarity, his message is much the same as other scientists who study the cause and effect relationships between forest density and beetle outbreaks.

"What we have in the Black Hills is a tree epidemic, not a beetle epidemic," he says. "It is a very unnatural condition caused by the presence of too many trees, a result of not allowing wildfires to burn. This was a stockman's paradise a century ago, about 50 percent trees and about 50 percent grassland. Much, much different than it looks now."

The predictably candid Ball believes there are only two ways to slow the advancing beetles. One is to forget the people component and let big wildfires take care of the beetles. The other is to continually thin the Black Hills National Forest so as to reduce the threats posed by beetles and fire. Black

Hills residents have overwhelmingly chosen the latter strategy. "Nature," though lovely, is simply too unpredictable.

Unfortunately, the biggest ponderosas in the Black Hills – the ones everyone admires most – act as motherships for advancing beetles. In dense stands, they move easily from tree to tree. Once relocated, they bore into the bark, leaving telltale whitish-rust masses of pitch that announce their presence. Their march continues until the epidemic subsides naturally or ponderosas are thinned to a defensible density.

Evidence of the latest beetle attack was first spotted the Beaver Park Roadless Area in 1997. It is subsiding now, thanks to the herculean efforts of three public-private collaboratives, but by 2010 high resolution aerial photography revealed that at least 25 percent of the Black Hills - some 128,000 acres – was under siege. Indeed, the attack appeared to be the worst since an 1870s assault from which the bustling mining camp that became Deadwood drew its name.

To accurately track events that unfolded in the Black Hills between our 1999 visit and our 2009 return, we assembled a timeline beginning in 1997 – the year the Forest Service released its revised forest plan for the Black Hills National Forest and, notably, the year beetles were first spotted near Beaver Park. It would grow exponentially over the next 20 years.

The revised forest plan reduced the annual harvest level on the forest from 118 million board feet to 83.8 million feet. It was appealed by the Black Hills Forest Resources Association and environmentalists – environmentalists because they felt the 32.2 million board foot reduction was insufficient and the association because it knew the reduction would impair wood processing infrastructure it viewed as key to containing pine beetle outbreaks.

The revised forest plan languished for two years before Forest Service Chief, Mike Dombeck decided there were some wildlife issues that had been overlooked, so he sent it back for further analysis. His decision prompted additional litigation by environmentalists who felt they were playing a winning hand. The downstream result was that no timber was sold on the forest in 2000.

In August of that year, the Jasper Fire burned 98,854 acres around the Jewell Cave National Monument west of Custer. Though small compared to wildfires burning in the Southwest, it was huge by Black Hills standards – and it was only the first of several wildfires that scorched another 92,910 acres between 2001 and 2005, setting off alarm bells all over South Dakota.

South Dakota Senator, Tom Daschle, who was then Senate Majority Leader, stepped into the fray in August 2001, hosting a forest summit at Rapid City that drew more than 600 people including the entire South Dakota delegation, Forest Service Chief, Dale Bosworth and Governor Bill Janklow. Daschle encouraged the formation of a citizen council under the aegis of the 1972 Federal Advisory Committee Act [FACA] to help the Forest Service sort through its more contentious issues.

A settlement agreement was reached with environmentalists that allowed some timber sold under the 1997 plan to be harvested but, mired in its own inertia, the Forest Service did not act on Daschle's FACA recommendation until early 2003. Meantime, the mountain pine beetle outbreak was reaching epidemic levels.

In hopes of slowing the advancing beetles, Daschle added language to a supplemental 2002 Defense Appropriations Bill that allowed some specific projects to move forward on the Black Hills National Forest. But it was too late for Pope and Talbott's mill at Newcastle. It closed July 7, 2000, throwing 75 out of work. Abe Friesen, the company's wood processing vice president, noted that the Forest Service had not offered any timber for sale since October 1, 1999.

In the spring of 2003, Forest Supervisor, John Twiss, acted on Daschle's FACA suggestion, forwarding his request that an advisory board be formed to Forest Service Chief, Dale Bosworth, who quickly approved the idea and the 16-member Black Hills National Forest Advisory Board was formed.

The federally constituted board was the second of three citizen groups formed in the Black Hills. The first was the Black Hills Regional Multiple Use Coalition formed in 1991 in response to multiple Black Hills Sierra Club proposals to designate new wilderness areas within the Black Hills National

Forest – an idea that continues to meet with considerable local resistance in both South Dakota and Wyoming. Its members included a diverse array of interests: ranching, forestry, minerals, geology, local governments and multiple forms of motorized recreation.

The third group formed in the Black Hills did not initially have a formal name, but it included some 50 "conservation leaders" who convened as a committee of the whole in 2010 in hopes of hammering out a coordinated approach for pushing back on advancing beetles.

In the course of our research, we interviewed leaders from the three groupss: Forest Service retirees, Hugh Thompson and David Thom and Jim Sherrer, a Tree Farmer and retired CEO of an orthopedic clinic in Rapid City.

Thompson is an ardent supporter and long-time member of the multiple use coalition. He also represented the Crook County Wyoming county commissioners on the Black Hills Forest Advisory Commission for six years.

Thom, a Certified Forester, coordinated the work of the Black Hills Mountain Pine Beetle Working Group, a spin off the conservation leaders group formed in 2010.

Jim Sherrer chaired the Black Hills Forest Advisory Board's forest health subcommittee for several years. His Tree Farm, about three air miles from the Crazy Horse Memorial, was directly in the path of advancing beetles.

"We inherited a real mess," he said of his decision to join the advisory board in 2003. "People on the political left and right were unhappy. Some groups favored allowing pine beetles and wildfires to run their course. Others wanted to harvest beetle-infested timber. Beetles were evident on about 400,000 Black Hills National Forest acres, we were in the midst of a long drought and up to our eyeballs in litigation. It was a battle royal for sure."

Fuels reduction – removing as many beetle-killed trees as possible – quickly became the board's highest priority, but there were other nagging problems that required immediate attention, so the board divided itself into subcommittees: off-road vehicle travel management, invasive species and beetle response/forest health. Because Sherrer was a tree farmer he was picked to head the beetle response/forest health subcommittee.

"I became the voice for private landowners," Sherrer said. "We have close to 300,000 acres of private land locked inside the Black Hills National Forest and some 475,000 acres if you count all the private ownerships in The Hills. Many landowners blamed the Forest Service for their beetle problems. I wasn't interested in assigning blame. My interest was in solving the problem."

Two years before the advisory board was formed, Sherrer hired a logger to begin thinning forests on his property, the goal being to remove beetle infested trees so as to create sufficient defensible space in case of wildfire.

"We removed about 8,000 trees," he said. "Thank God for Neiman Enterprises. They bought our logs. Without them, we would not have had a market for most of the diseased trees removed from private lands or the Black Hills National Forest. Their presence was a real blessing."

With grant monies secured from the South Dakota state legislature, Sherrer turned his forest into a training ground for tree marking crews. Marked trees were removed and Neiman bought the ones that had lumber value.

"It was plain old common sense," Sherrer said. "No government study was needed to understand the scope of the problem or what needed to be done to resolve it."

"Common sense" got a big boost in December 2003. President George W. Bush signed the bipartisan Healthy Forests Restoration Act. Daschle actively supported the measure in the U.S. Senate, which voted 99-0-1 in favor of passage. The lone abstention was that of Massachusetts Senator, John Kerry, who declared that it "took a chainsaw to our national forests." Kerry's histrionics aside, the Act continues to serve as a model for forest restoration projects in diseased and dying western national forests.

Despite HFRA's tight focus on hazardous fuels, woody biomass, watershed protection and insects and diseases, it would be another seven years before 50-some Black Hills conservation leaders issued an "all hands on deck" call for help and ideas – and another five years to hammer out an agreed upon approach to slowing reoccurring beetle epidemics and – more broadly – a set of strategic recommendations for managing the Black Hills National Forest.

A logger delimbs a fallen tree in the Black Hills National Forest a few miles from iconic Mt. Rushmore.

The still nameless group drew representatives from city, county, state and federal governments, private timberland owners and the forest products industry. Some favored an aggressive harvesting strategy in beetle-killed timber, others favored a more measured approach. A few saw the epidemic as a natural cycle in ponderosa pine. Meantime, aerial photographs revealed seas of red-orange trees scattered across 430,000 acres of the Black Hills.

"We were driven by our responses to natural events," David Thom said of the diverse group's eventual compromise. "Faced with the threat of more to come our hope was to develop a strategy for getting more work done on the ground by working together."

Pinedale, Wyoming's Biodiversity Conservation Alliance sued in 2011 in hopes of blocking implementation of the Black Hills National Forest's Phase II Amendment. The amendment, which incorporated more aggressive strategies for reducing the risks posed by both pine beetles and wildfire, had been completed in 2005.

That same year – 2011 – Black Hills lumbermen endorsed a quite successful strategy developed in Alberta after pine beetles from British Columbia moved into the province's forests. Its main tenet: Don't chase beetles. You'll never catch up to them. Try to get ahead of them by treating forested areas they are most likely to attack next. Prioritize your work based on spread and population growth. Cut and burn. Cut and burn. Cut and burn.

Hugh Thompson attests to the patience and dedication necessary to find consensus among such diverse stakeholder opinions. During his six years on the Black Hills Forest Advisory Board he attended 66 public meetings, none of them close to his ranch in the rolling hills eight miles off Wyoming State Highway 24 enroute to Belle Fouche. "Counting preparation time, I'd guess about 600 hours," Thompson said of his six years as an advisory commission member. A lot of road miles too."

Although Thompson never worked in the Black Hills during his long Forest Service career, he quickly returned to his boyhood roots in Wyoming after he retired.

"It's home," he said of his ranch. From his front porch, it is 33 miles to the visible horizon in the Black Hills National Forest. If you squint, you can see Black Elk, the granite spire on which Gutzon Borglum made his decision to carve the faces of four U.S. presidents on Mount Rushmore.

"The Hills were a mess," Thompson said of his decision to join the Black Hills Regional Multiple Use Coalition. "Pine beetles were everywhere and it looked to me like the Forest Service had turned inward and pretty much lost its way where active management was concerned."

There is a steady determination in his voice when he recalls that the group responded in writing "and great detail" to every Forest Service request for public comment concerning its management plans for the Black Hills National Forest. "It took a lot of diligence and hard work on our part," he said of the group's steadfast opposition to both the Sierra Club's Wilderness designation and the alarming pine beetle advance.

"We wanted to make sure the Black Hills did not lose its strong and viable wood processing structure" he explained. Without loggers and sawmills the thinning work that must be done continually in The Hills would not have been possible, much less affordable."

David Thom's leadership group issued their first formal communique in 2012 – a report titled Black Hills Regional Mountain Pine Beetle Strategy. It catalogued the largely unsuccessful 15-year effort to slow the beetle epidemic and called for a more localized and comprehensive approach to address "unique situations present in the Black Hills." To drill more deeply into the situation, Thom's leadership group formed the Mountain Pine Beetle Working Group and went back to the drawing board.

The three Black Hills citizen groups caught their first big break in 2012. The court tossed the environmentalists' 2011 lawsuit challenging the Forest Service's Phase II planning amendment – a ruling subsequently upheld in 2014 by the Tenth Circuit Court of Appeals. The Biodiversity Conservation Alliance closed its doors shortly after the appeals court ruled. Reportedly, it had been counting on the money it figured it would be awarded by the appeals court.

It seems likely that both courts noticed that the entire South Dakota congressional delegation was now fully engaged with the Forest Service: letters, meetings with Chief Bosworth in Washington, D.C., field hearings and meetings with Bosworth in South Dakota, testimony before congressional natural resource committees, and support for Forest Service funding in the 2014 Farm Bill.

Nor could the justices have missed Governor Dennis Daugaard's Black Hills Initiative. "More than one-third of the Black Hills National Forest – over 400,000 acres – has been infested by mountain pine beetles and the outbreak shows no sign of relenting," the South Dakota governor said in August 2011.

"Hundreds of businesses and thousands of employees in the logging, forest products and tourism industries depend on a healthy, well-managed forest for their livelihoods," Daugaard said. "The current beetle infestation threatens those business owners as well as their employees and families. It also threatens to damage the very nature and character of the Black Hills."

Daugaard thus pledged $1 million a year for three years to an expanded effort to slow the beetle's advance. He also committed South Dakota state government to a collaborative effort involving the Forest Service and private businesses in the Black Hills. "We will not wait for the fire to rage before mobilizing our response," he said. "The mountain pine beetle epidemic is an emergency situation – a disaster we can see coming."

In 2015, Thom's Black Hills Mountain Pine Beetle Working Group published its Black Hills Regional Mountain Pine Beetle Strategy, a five-year umbrella plan that addressed not just beetles but also invasive species, habitat diversity, healthy and productive forests, public safety and fire risk and hazard.

"The useful role wildfire can play in ponderosa pine ecosystems was well understood," Thom said. "But it had to be balanced against the importance of protecting communities and local economies from increasingly destructive fires."

The balance point was reflected in two of the strategy's four goals: maintain wood processing infrastructure and increase natural resiliency by reducing forest density to a point where it can fend off beetle epidemics. Minus private markets, the federal government could not afford the cost of removing beetle-infested trees from the Black Hills National Forest.

Citizen volunteer groups and advisory boards like those formed in the Black Hills are just that: volunteers and advisors. They have no authority over the decisions and actions of the federal government, especially the U.S. Forest Service, which has functioned with great autonomy since its founding in 1905.

Not so with Cooperating Agency Status [CA], a not well understood federal regulation imbedded in the 1969 National Environmental Policy Act [NEPA] and the 1976 Federal Lands Policy Management Act [FLPMA].

CA Status acknowledges and accepts the government-to-government relationship that exists between the federal government and state and county governments. The federal obligation extends well beyond simply checking to see which way the political winds are blowing.

A working network is formed that runs from the Forest Service through congressional delegations, state legislatures, state and county agencies and county commissioners and mayors. State and county representatives typically serve as members of interdisciplinary teams responsible for crafting land use plans or projects requiring NEPA analysis.

"It was huge for the states and counties," recalled Craig Bobzien, Black Hills Forest Supervisor from 2005 until his retirement in 2016. "The county commissioners really engaged at the grass roots level. We had to be strategic and tactical in the same stroke but it was very satisfying for me to watch people come together around a set of common ideas and goals. You've heard of the Civilian Conservation Corps – the 3C's. We had three new C's working for us: collaboration, cooperation and coordination. You can't beat it."

David Thom concurred with Bobzien's assessment of the significance of Cooperating Agency Status. "I sat in on many interdisciplinary team meetings and can confirm that the roles played by the governors, their resource management agencies, counties, municipalities and ordinary local citizens were significant."

The lead CA authority in South Dakota is the State Department of Agriculture and, more specifically, State Forester Greg Josten. He is tasked with administering and enforcing state laws relevant to public and private forests and woodlands

Fallen logs are removed from a Black Hills National Forest restoration project.

in the Mount Rushmore State.

"My job was to herd all of our cooperators including the counties and our conservation districts," Josten said. "It was four years out of my life but I learned a great deal about the NEPA process and what the U.S. Forest Service goes through to comply with the laws and regulations governing their work."

Josten says the state is as cemented to the Forest Service in every way possible.

"The immediate risk is wildfire," he explains.

"The longer-term risk is the mountain pine beetle and the goal is to reduce the risks posed by fires and beetles by thinning ponderosa pines which reseed themselves naturally and grow quickly in our forests. The management goals are structural and age-class diversity – maintaining trees of varying ages randomly spaced across the landscape – not too thick and not too thin."

Wyoming State Forester, Bill Crapser, echoed Josten's comments. "The State of Wyoming and Weston and Crook Counties acted as Cooperating Agencies during completion of the amended Black Hills National Forest Plan. Our Wyoming State Forestry Division took their lead, but their work was invaluable in our efforts to reaffirm the fact that beetle and wildfire control are primary management strategies in the Black Hills National Forest.

The man in charge of the "not too thick and not too thin" balancing act in the Black Hills is Forest Supervisor Mark Van Every, a graceful leader who looks like he just stepped out of central casting.

"It is a balancing act," he says of the pressing need to keep pine beetles in check by removing sufficient timber to slow their advance."
Beyond strong public support, Van Every agrees that he is blessed by the convergence of three economic and environmental factors.

- Ponderosa pine responds exceptionally well to periodic thinnings that yield park-like visual results tourists enjoy.
- Black Hills terrain is gentle enough to safely allow for balloon-tired logging equipment that registers fewer pounds per square inch than horses.
- The industry that resides in the Black Hills is heavily dependent on timber harvested from the Black Hills National Forest.

"It also helps that ponderosa reseeds itself naturally," Van Every grins. "If you stand in one place long enough, a ponderosa seedling will grow up your pant leg."

Not really, but the fact that ponderosa regenerates naturally and quickly is both a blessing and a curse. There are age gaps in the Black Hills: too many old trees with too many young trees growing beneath them and too few middle-aged trees. The imbalance necessitates working from both ends, creating space in which some young trees can grow old. The goal is to fill in the gaps before the next beetle infestation occurs 20 to 30 years from now.

It isn't possible to completely eliminate the risks posed by wildfire, but the Forest Service aggressively attacks the 100 or so fires that break out in The Hills annually. It helps that the region has a well-maintained road system and that loggers in the area have sufficient heavy equipment to corral most fires in their early stages.

"We work hard to minimize risk," Van Every says. "Interagency cooperation between states, counties and private landowners is a big plus for us. When fires are spotted we jump on them immediately. Fire is a great tool for clearing away woody debris and brush that can fuel bigger fires, but we are very careful about when and where we use it. I'd like to get back to the era when there were more frequent low intensity fires in the Black Hills, but that will take time and lots of public education. People don't like fire in their forests."

It took a monumental "all hands on deck" effort to rescue the Black Hills National Forest from its worst mountain pine beetle epidemic in more than 120 years. At least 1.3 million infested trees required one of two treatments:

- Dead and infested trees with commercial value were removed from 187,050 acres and smaller trees on 87,430 acres were precommercially thinned so that the healthy trees that remained could grow again.
- Non-commercial treatments were initiated on other acres defined by one of three criteria:
- Acres politically or physically inaccessible.
- Trees still too small to be made into a wood product.
- Trees still needed to be treated to keep beetles from flying.

Appropriated funds provided by the states of South Dakota and Wyoming paid crews to individually mark, cut down insect-infested trees that could not be commercially harvested, then cut them into 24-inch lengths. As they dried in the sun, beetle larvae died.

The State of South Dakota also provided private landowners in the Black Hills with technical assistance at a per landowner cost-share capped at $10,000 for treating green-infested trees in some areas. Wyoming did much the same.

County-level weed and pest boards in the Black Hills also swung into action. Crews were trained to work with their respective states and municipalities and to assist industry and Forest Service crews in identifying and mapping infested areas within active timber sale boundaries.

Some private landowners also bought and paid for federally registered insecticides that proved effective in warding off beetle attacks in individual, high-value trees. Others hired loggers to rescue their healthy trees by harvesting dead or infested trees.

None of this rescue work would have been possible had it not been for the presence of a vibrant logging and sawmilling industry – a robust and imaginative culture well equipped with log processing and wood manufacturing technologies capable of profitably handling trees that would have been considered worthless when the beetles struck in the 1970s. Such are the remarkable technological advances that drive logging and forest products manufacturing today.

In its current configuration, the Black Hills wood complex includes about 50 logging contractors, possibly twice as many log haulers, sawmills at Spearfish, Hill City and Rapid City in South Dakota and nearby Hulett, Wyoming and pellet mills in Spearfish and Rapid City. Also in Rockerville, a particle board manufacturer and a remanufacturing plant that makes everything from fence posts to faux barnwood in six stains.

The largest piece of the Black Hills wood processing complex belongs to Neiman Enterprises. Credit the nearly invisible hand of Jim Neiman, a quiet and congenial man who is quick to share credit for the Black Hills recovery with the three collaborative groups that formed and a supporting cast that included hundreds of volunteers. Neiman went to work in his family's mill at Hulett when he was six years old. Now 66, his mind still runs at warp speed.

Neiman and his management team have assembled a milling complex that includes facilities at Spearfish and Hill City, South Dakota, Hulett, Wyoming and Montrose, Colorado. He is also immersed in a campaign to diversify Hulett's economy by expanding recreational opportunities that already include a spectacular 18-hole golf course with club house, restaurant, homesites and a 5,500-foot paved runway overlooking the town. Next on his list: a research hospital.

"When you are the largest employer in your hometown, you bear a responsibility for doing your best to make things better for your community," Neiman said. "All boats rise on a rising tide."

The tide is definitely rising in the Black Hills. The region has become a magnet for families and businesses wanting to escape more crowded cities in the Midwest. A remarkably diverse economy, educational opportunity and great natural beauty are the magnets.

Neiman sees his family's company as but one of the keepers of the flame that attracts new people and new opportunity. He senses potentials far greater than what most can see in the Black Hills today and he fears the loss of what he calls "a wider sense of perpetuity," that can capture the symbiotic human and natural rhythms that make the Black Hills such a special place.

"The kind of thinking we need here can't be done in five or 10-year increments," he says, referencing the Forest Service's regulatory timetables. "You have to think 100 years down the road because that's how long it takes to grow a forest here, and it is the forest that brings people here to vacation or put down roots. If your investment horizon is shorter than the life cycle of our Black Hills forests, you should probably invest your money in something different."

Neiman keeps a Bible on the credenza next to his desk. When asked about it he explains that his faith has helped him come to grips with his own limitations.

"I'm a numbers guy and not very good with the spoken or written word," he says. "It took time for me to realize that it takes all kinds of people to make the world go around. Ephesians 4:11 set me straight: 'Now these are the gifts Christ gave to the church: the apostles, the prophets, the evangelists and the pastors and teachers.' We are fortunate to have all of these here in The Hills."

You need look no further than the complementary variety of wood processing facilities in the Black Hills to see what Neiman is talking about – everything from a glistening circle saw that cuts rough sawn log facing to a machine that molds highly absorbent pellets used in North Dakota's natural gas fracking wells.

Forest Products Distributors [FPD] at Rapid City sells the pellets to gas drillers probing the Bakken shale formation in western North Dakota. The company is also the largest post manufacturer in the nation. But the list of products it makes from ponderosa is long: countertops, butcher blocks, flooring, livestock bedding, faux barnwood in six different stains – and pellets.

It takes great ingenuity and an independent streak to make a wood products complex hum. Both can be found in abundance at Baker Timber Products south of Rapid City. The company's motto is routed in a steel plate fastened above the office door: It reads, "You should see what we saw."

What the Bakers – Bill, Bob and Bob's son, Jack – can squeeze from the logs they buy in the Black Hills is amazing considering that the sawing is done with a circle saw their late father, Clayton, installed in 1961. There have been upgrades, but there isn't much you can add to a sawing technology that dates from 1813.

The Bakers have turned their aging saw into a marketing advantage by being exceptionally good at reading customer preferences.

"Our customers like the rustic look," brother Bill Baker explains. "We make lumber and beams, plus tongue and groove lumber siding and flooring. What we can't cut we grind into livestock bedding and landscaping bark and chips."

Bakers customers include people who make the 20-minute drive from Rapid City to their mill and those who prefer not to shop at any number of building supply stores in the region.

"We all do a little bit of everything around here," Baker explains. "The products you see here plus some logging and roadbuilding. We do our own logging, some on private land but also for the Forest Service and we grind a lot of brush that would otherwise burn up in a fire. You have to be versatile to stay alive in our ever-changing business."

No word in the English dictionary more accurately or completely describes the forest products industry's manufacturing complex in the Black Hills than the word "versatile." A word whose synonyms include "adaptable, flexible, multifaceted, multitalented, multiskilled, protean, convertible and resourceful."

Versatility and its synonyms have been central to the industry's drive to convert as much wood fiber into useful, everyday consumer products. Advancing milling technologies have helped but there are no substitutes for entrepreneurship and a keen grasp of ever-changing market conditions.

The symbiotic relationships – the ties that bind timber, tourism, mining, agriculture and the U.S. Forest Service – have been the key economic drivers in the Black Hills since Case No. 1 was sold to the Homestake Mining Company 120 years ago.

The forest products industry that thrives here is between 70 and 80 percent dependent on timber it harvests from the Black Hills National Forest. Pinchot's vision had been spot on: show lumbermen that they had a future here and they would put down roots. Then show his young foresters how ponderosa in The Hills could be managed in perpetuity.

Black Hills tourism is totally dependent on ponderosa. Mount Rushmore, Crazy Horse and Black Elk look down on a sea of green surrounded by grasslands that run for hundreds of miles in all directions. They remind us that this sea must be navigated and navigation takes patience, skill and endurance. Skills that were at the core of Gifford Pinchot's long game.

Keeping this sea green has been the responsibility of the U.S. Forest Service since its founding in 1905. It's a big job. Beetles, wildfires and political headwinds have buffeted the agency's course from Day 1. But it enjoys something in the Black Hills that is rare today: a reservoir of public support from South Dakota and Wyoming residents who are comfortable with logging and forestry because they know that managing ponderosa is key to keeping beetles and wildfire from roiling their beautiful green sea.

CHAPTER 15

In harm's way

If you have not read *Young Men and Fire*, please do so. You can snag an e-book copy on Amazon for $10.49.

Young Men was Norman Maclean's second book. It is a page-turner for sure, gripping, tragic and easily as well-written as *A River Runs Through It.*

I read *Young Men* cover to cover in one night. The subject is the August 5, 1949 Mann Gulch Fire. The gulch rises high above the Missouri River about 25 miles northeast of Helena, Montana's capital.

Twelve Forest Service smokejumpers – the agency's elite – died in Mann Gulch in a murderous firestorm that could not have lasted longer than a minute or two. Wind-driven flames moving at 300 feet per minute – the length of a football field - swept over them as they frantically scrambled up a grassy 18 percent slope. Most of their bodies were burned beyond recognition.

Maclean called Mann Gulch "their Calvary," a reference to the hill on which Christ died. He likened the places where they fell to the 14 Stations of the Cross, and their last terrifying moments to those Christ must have felt. "Eloi, Eloi, lama sabachthani?" "My God, My God, why hath thou forsaken me?"

The hands on James Harrison's watch were cemented by searing heat at 5:55, 5:56 or 5:57 p.m. It hardly mattered. He had passed by the Twelfth Station at around 5:50 p.m.

Mann Gulch puzzled Maclean for years. Despite the help of several Forest Service researchers, he was never able to locate the original investigative report and he died before he completed the book. Old age and illness overcame him when he was 87 years old. His son, John, also a fire writer, finished it.

The loss of life was the worst the Forest Service had endured since 87 died in the Great 1910 Fire. It shook the agency to its core. Not a single smokejumper had died in the line of duty since the elite corps was established a decade earlier. The Intermountain Fire Sciences Laboratory was established at Missoula soon after.

Maclean would have made little headway in his forensic investigation had it not been for the help of Dick Rothermel, an Intermountain fire behavior analyst and the late Laird Robinson, a former smokejumper who took Maclean to Mann Gulch so he could see the area through his own curious eyes.

Rothermel, an aeronautical engineer who had worked on a federal project looking for ways to build an atomic-powered airplane, joined the Missoula lab in 1961. He had initially been reluctant to meet with Maclean because the 1949 tragedy had so deeply wounded the Forest Service.

Rothermel's colleague, Frank Albini, a Hughes Aircraft veteran, laconically told Maclean that it would be easier to predict the speed of missiles than the speed of a wildfire. Using wind tunnels and combustion chambers, the two former rocket scientists would subsequently build a computer model that allows modern day fire behavior analysts to predict wildfire spread. Although their basic model remains the most reliable means for analyzing wildfires, it has been revised several times to reflect new knowledge. That's how good science works.

Prescribed burns like this one are key to reducing the risk of catastrophic wildfires in western forests. Prescribed burns work best in combination with tree thinnings.

In a sense, 14 of the Forest Service's finest died at Mann Gulch: 12 jumpers, one ranger stationed nearby and Harry Gisborne, a fine young forester hired by the Forest Service on April 1, 1922 to be the first Forest Examiner at the agency's Priest Lake Forest Experiment Station in the far recesses of northern Idaho. His salary: $1,920 per year.

In Young Men and Fire, Maclean's artistry for words is at its best in his description of Gisborne's keen and enthusiastic eye for new information that could only be found in the woods. "To Gisborne," Maclean wrote, "science started and ended in observation and a theory should always be endangered by it."

Fire "research" was a much-discussed topic in the Forest Service following the Great 1910 Fire. but more funding was needed and it did not arrive until 1921. Upon his hiring, the 29-year-old Gisborne was dispatched to Priest Lake.

When Gisborne arrived at the station, he found an impressive body of climatic and metorological data dating from 1913. It had been assembled by the station's earliest employees. I suspect they were looking for clues to the hurricane-force winds that appeared out of nowhere on a sunny August afternoon and drove the 1910 Fire into a killing firestorm.

The science of "fire behavior analysis" did not exist in 1922. Gisborne patiently and methodically invented it after coming face to face with the fact that no single variable related to weather or forest conditions was an accurate predictor of the size or frequency of wildfire.

Gisborne's considerable analytical skill led him to suspect that moisture content in the "duff layer" of soil was a good place to start. It made sense given that seeds sprout in nutrient-rich duff that accumulates atop sub-surface mineral soil over long periods of time.

To understand Gisborne's remarkable instincts, you need only know that there are still wind-blown places where wildfire-impacted soils eroded to such an extent that only the hardiest of plants can grow in areas where the 1910 Fire crossed the Idaho-Montana border. It may be another century before sufficient duff has enriched the soil to a point where it will again support tree growth.

On November 9, 1949, three months after Gisborne and Bob Jansson, the ranger on whose Forest Service district the Mann Gulch Fire had burned, hiked into the gulch. Although Gisborne's heart was weak, he had insisted that Jansson take him there so he could study the fire's behavior first-hand. Though reluctant, Jansson agreed on Gisborne's promise to stop and rest every 100 yards.

On their return walk, Gisborne stopped one last time to rest his legs.

"Here's a nice rock to sit on and watch the river," Gisborne told Jansson. "I made it good. My legs might ache a little tomorrow though."

After a pause, Gisborne half-rose, started to say, "Let's go," gasped twice and pitched forward as his heart beat its last two or three beats. He died in seconds. Jansson put his glasses back on his face and piled rocks around his body so it could not roll off the trail into the Missouri River a hundred feet below.

> Of the macabre scene, Maclean wrote:
>
> "When Jansson knew Gisborne was dead, he stretched him out straight on the trail, built the rocks around him higher, closed his eyes, and then put his glasses back on him so, just in case he woke up, he could see where he was.
>
> Then Jansson ran for help. The stars came out. Nothing moved on the game trail. The great Missouri passing below repeated the same succession of chords it probably will play for a million years to come. The only other motion was the moon floating across the lenses of Gisborne's glasses, which at last were unobservant."

To understand the godawful killing power of wildfire – and the enormous contributions Gisborne, Rothermel, Albini and many others have made to our greater understanding of its behavior – read *Young Men and Fire*. Then you will understand why so many have died in the 70 years since Mann Gulch, and why we cannot allow the West's murderous wildfires to continue killing us.

Body count

Near midnight on September 1, 1967, Luther Rodarte, a Forest Service firefighter from Santa Maria, California and Lee Collins, a heavy equipment operator from Thompson Falls, Montana, took shelter beneath Collin's bulldozer in hopes that the fast approaching Sundance firestorm would pass over them.

I watched the flames top Sundance Mountain from a dock in Luby Bay on the west side of Priest Lake, not realizing that I was witnessing the deaths of two men who were literally roasted alive by the radiating heat of 1,000-degree flames.

Fanned by 95-mile-an-hour winds, the Sundance Fire blew through a 16-miles of old growth timber in only nine hours. Once it crested the spectacular Selkirk Divide, a wall of flames four miles wide burned across the entire Pack River Drainage and over Apache Ridge – another 10 miles – in three hours.

On the west side of Roman Nose, near 450-foot tall Chimney Rock, radiating heat ignited the forest below so violently that entire trees were ripped from the ground and hurled over Roman Nose into forests below.

John Wood, a young logger on the fire lines, watched it all from a logging road that crossed Pack River. He had been sent there by a Forest Service dispatcher to see what he could do to slow the fire's advance.

I spoke at the 50th Annual Remembrance Ceremony in 2017, and heard Wood say that he saw old growth trees ripped from the ground by their roots, then tossed above his head and across the river, where gravity brought them crashing back to earth near a steel bridge. Radiating heat melted the bridge into a twisted mass.

56,000 acres of beautiful forest gone, most of it in 24 hours. Bonner County coroner Bud Moon traveled to the still smoldering top of Sundance Mountain to gather the remains of Rodarte and Collins.

"It was an awesome sight," Moon told a reporter. "Like a lava hot springs. Everything was denuded. Pack River Bridge was just a mass of twisted steel. The heat must have been tremendous."

It was. Sundance and the nearby Trapper Peak Fire took out two of my favorite fishing spots – Harrison Lake at the foot of Chimney Rock, where Dad and I fished every summer for years – and Soldier Creek on the east side of Priest Lake, where countless thousands of native cutthroat trout were boiled alive.

The summer before, I had perfected my short casts with a six-foot No. 5 Hardy flyrod beneath fallen cedars that spanned the creek and made it impossible to fish from above. You had to wade up the creek beneath huge limbs that touched the water and made casting upstream very difficult. Those limbs and the tree trunks that shaded Soldier Creek also formed a perfect oven for roasting trout. Their upside down bodies were everywhere I looked.

I'm going to get a little off track here for a couple of paragraphs, but for years, fisheries biologists believed that debris in stream channels impeded fish passage. Loggers were required to removed everything – even limbs – from streams.

Then, maybe 25 years ago, fisheries biologists changed their minds. Debris was a good thing – so good in fact that loggers were hired to build log jams and place boulders in streams to create [wait for it] spawning habitat for trout. I know two loggers who were hired to "restore" the same stream channels they had been required to clean out years earlier.

Any boy or girl who chased trout as I did could have told the biologists that fish hide beneath logs and around root wads, but no one asked us. Still, you have to admire the fisheries folks for owning up to their error. New science. New ideas. Now it turns out that too much shade along a stream channel isn't a good thing either. The water cools to a point where aquatic life – the stuff fish eat – has a hard time surviving. I've seen this in small streams in western Oregon that have legally required buffers as wide as a football field is long. Not good if you are a trout hunting for something to eat.

Back on track.

Fourteen wrongly positioned firefighters perished on Storm King Mountain in Colorado's 1994 South Canyon Fire, a tragedy of compounding errors chronicled in John Maclean's *Fire on The Mountain*. It was the first of four books involving fatal fires written by Maclean.

Maclean also finished *Young Men and Fire*, his father's gripping account of the 1949 Mann Gulch Fire referenced in Chapter 12. Read Norman Maclean's *A River Runs Through It* for its artistry and majesty. Read Young Men and Fire to see how art and majesty can be reduced to ash and death in mere moments.

Nineteen died June 30, 2013 in their heat-resistant shelters on Yarnell Hill, a brushy hardwood savannah near Yarnell, about 80 miles northwest of Phoenix, Arizona. The story of the freakish lightning-caused blaze that threatened tiny Yarnell has been told in two riveting books: *Fire Line*, by Fernanda Santos and *Granite Mountain* by Brendan McDonough, the only survivor and a fire lookout whose position was run over as he fled. His crewmates all perished in 2,000-degree flames that turned their heat-resistant shelters into ovens.

My wife, Julia, and I were vacationing on the Oregon coast, the day the 19, all Prescott, Arizona firefighters and members of the Granite Mountain Hotshots, perished. My visual is of the funeral procession – 19 white hearses passing single file through Yarnell.

Julia is still in touch with two women left behind on Yarnell Hill: a mother who lost a son and a wife who lost her husband. Those left behind often develop their own ways to account for the unexplainable – a son or daughter here, an entire crew over there. After Yarnell, the National Fire Protection Association weighed in to say that the loss of firefighter life at Yarnell was the greatest since the 1933 Griffith Park Fire in Los Angeles. Twenty-three impromptu civilian firefighters died trying to stop the advancing flames.

I traveled to New York City in April 2002 so that I could peer into the gaping hole created at the corner of Liberty and Church streets by clean-up crews attempting to erase all evidence of what happened there on September 11, 2001. I thus have no trouble adding the 343 New York City firefighters who perished at the World Trade Center in their futile attempt to rescue 2,634 innocents who crashed to earth with the Twin Towers.

For firefighters the world over, this remains the darkest day.

Eighty-six died in northern California's 2018 Camp Fire – the greatest loss of life since 78 died in the 1910 Fire. Most of picturesque Paradise, 85 miles north of Sacramento was leveled by the Camp Fire. Fifteen thousand homes were lost.

These Camp Fire 911 call notes, from a January 18, 2019 San Francisco Chronicle report, tell the tale of a firestorm that at one point was consuming the equivalent of one football field per second:

"I live on Dean road in Paradise…We're getting engulfed in smoke," one caller reported at 7:40 a.m.

"Yes, ma'am, I know," a dispatcher replied. "But the fire's not here in Paradise. It's north of Concow on Highway 70," naming a small town a few miles away.

At least 132 calls to 911 were answered between 6:30 a.m., when the flames were first reported about 10 miles northwest of town, and 8:20 a.m., when the center rerouted all calls to nearby Chico because of overwhelming volume.

"There's a fire up north of Concow, up near Highway 70," dispatchers told dozens of callers who reported heavy smoke and ash in Paradise between 7:10 and 7:40 a.m. One caller was told, "There is no threat to Paradise."

By 7:48 a.m., people were reporting new spot fires ignited by embers blown ahead of the main conflagration – over a large section of Paradise's east side.

"The fire has come over the top of Sawmill Peak," one caller said at about 7:50 a.m., referring to a mountaintop a mile northeast of Paradise. "There are spot fires all over and the wind is blowing like hell, and nobody notified us of anything."

Wildfires are relatively common in the Concow area," Jim Broshears, Paradise's emergency operations center coordinator and former fire chief said later. "Many previous blazes have threatened to spread to Paradise, but that day the shift was so fast."

In a matter of five minutes, the flames in Concow shot to the west flank of sawmill Peak, just across the Feather River.

"It was a game-changing moment," Broshears said.

By then, many of those calling 911 were clustered in certain locations. Some were at the Ridgewood Mobile Home Park, a 100-space senior living community nestled in the foothills just west of the Feather River.

"I have no way to evacuate," one Ridgewood resident told a dispatcher at 8:06 a.m. "I don't have a car."

The dispatcher transferred the person to Cal Fire. Two minutes later, an unidentified person reached the Paradise dispatch center, making what was already a futile request.

"Hey, do you have someone you can send out to Ridgewood Mobile Home Park?" the caller asked. "We have multiple calls from there with people saying they don't have any way to get out."

"No," the dispatcher replied. "We don't have anybody available."

Of the 86 people who died in the Camp Fire, at least three were discovered inside residences at Ridgewood. Throughout Paradise, many of those killed were older, hand physical disabilities or were unable or unwilling to flee.

William Richards, 71, said that as he fed his backyard chickens around 7 a.m., he noticed a growing ball of yellow and black smoke on the horizon. He called 911 and was told there was a wind-driven fire in Concow, still far from his home on Pentz Road.

Richards said that, within 10 minutes, embers were falling into his yard. Richards left before receiving an evacuation order, then got stuck in traffic on one of the town's few escape routes as flames surrounded him.

Aftermath of the 1967 Sundance Fire in northern Idaho. Searing heat killed firefighter, Luther Rodarte and bulldozer operator, Lee Collins, after they took shelter beneath this bulldozer.
Spokesman Review photo

"I don't think there's a fire department in the world that could have gotten ahead of the fire as fast as it was moving," Richards said.

Three months earlier, the Carr Fire, near Redding, California destroyed more than 1,000 homes and killed eight, including a firefighter whose pickup was sucked into a 143 mile-an-hour fire whirl and tossed 100 yards into a grove of burning trees. Some 230,000 acres of forest and rangeland were blackened.

Near where his pickup was found, his firefighting brothers and sisters erected a small memorial complete with a tattered American flag, a ball cap and beer cans that forced me to again remember my three trips to the Vietnam Wall to visit boyhood friends who today would be grandfathers.

Pacific Gas and Electric [PG&E] has admitted that faulty equipment probably sparked the Camp Fire. The company – California's largest public utility – has filed for bankruptcy, taken an $11.5 billion charge for fires over the last two years, and now says it might not stay in business.

I know a lot of people who wish the lights would go out permanently in California, but that's not going to happen, so let's get serious for a minute. Every public and private electric utility in the West faces the same level of risk where transmission lines pass through national forests or cross miles of federally-owned grasslands. No one is immune. No one.

I don't believe PG&E should be forced to shoulder all of the blame for wildfires that start beneath its transmission lines. Tree mortality in California's national forests runs into the millions annually. No one knows for sure how many trees have died over the last 10 years, but I'd hazard a guess that we are nearing one billion. Shouldn't the federal government bear some responsibility here?

The heartache seems to be everywhere. Heather Furnas, a Santa Rosa, California woman, wrote to the Wall Street Journal on March 9, 2019 to say that she'd lost everything in the October 2017 Tubbs Fire when it raced down the pastoral Napa Valley, killing 22 and incinerating some 5,700 homes, schools, stores, churches, assisted living and health care facilities and wineries.

Ms. Furnas wrote the Journal in response to another writer who had observed that, "The bareness is partly a result of having lost everything in the fire and realizing stuff isn't important."

> "My small, temporary home is also bare," Ms. Furnas began. "Nothing hangs on the walls, not because my old stuff wasn't important, but because I can't replace the cherished paintings I'd created throughout my life. I have no fire safe like the ones that housed my 35 journals, the first one written when I was 14. I preserved my children's antics and conversations on those pages, sometimes writing bleary-eyed before the details faded.
>
> When my children could write, I requested the same birthday and Mother's Day presents every year: a journal entry from each child. Their awkward lettering, simple thoughts and childish drawings evolved into the deeper perceptions of young adults.
>
> On October 9, 2017, the fire melted metal and transformed my safes to ashes. My vibrant past, previously brought to life through my journal readings, has been reduced to the shadows and whispers of my own fallible, incomplete memory.
>
> The destruction has left a form of permanent amnesia. Sometimes things are pieces of ourselves."

One thousand one hundred and twenty-eight wildland firefighters have been killed in the line of duty since 1910. An astonishing 313 have been killed since 2000 – a 60 percent increase in the per year average.

Thousands more – townspeople fleeing flames – have perished in wildfires since the counting began following Wisconsin's 1871 Peshtigo Fire.

This ever-increasing death toll gives rise to two thus far unanswerable questions:

> Why are we sending wildland firefighters into harm's way in forests that federal resource management agencies have not thinned or cannot thin without running afoul of ambiguous and conflicting environmental rules and regulations that make restoring natural resiliency nearly impossible?
>
> And why has Congress refused to rescind laws it passed that have transformed federal forest management into a vast and very lucrative feeding ground for environmental litigants and their lawyers?

I don't think this carnage is the outcome Americans who love their forests are expecting and I'm damn sure this isn't what my Bronx cabdriver sees in his mind's eye when he dreams about coming West – someday.

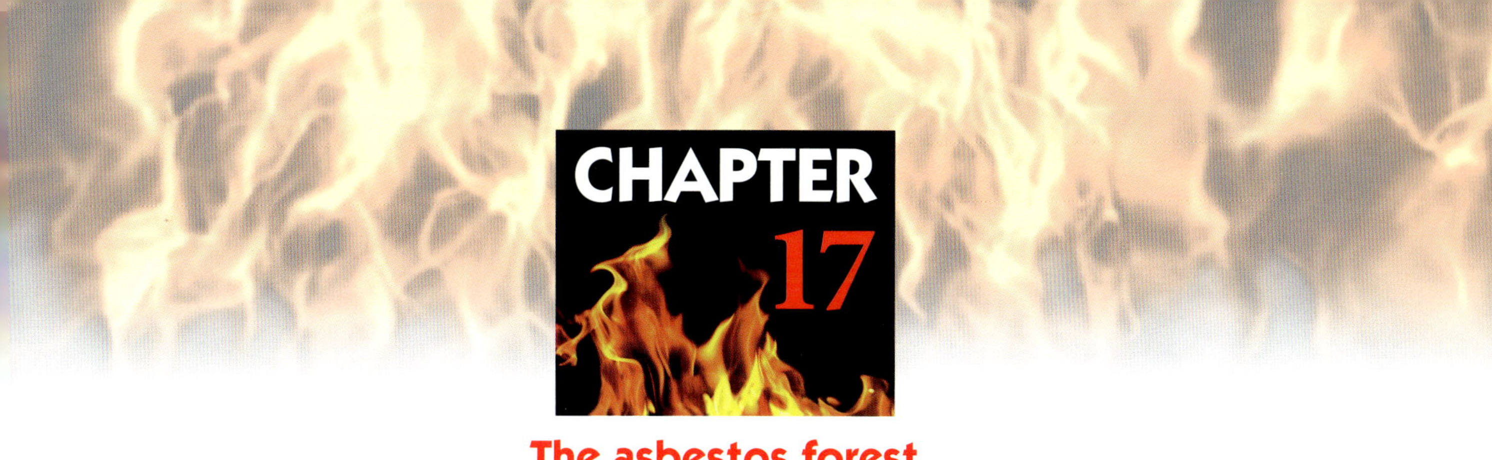

The asbestos forest

Foresters who toil in the coastal rainforests of western Oregon and Washington have an apropos name for them. They call them "asbestos forests." It is apropos given how difficult it is for wildfires to do much damage in forests that get as much as 200 inches of rain annually. Like asbestos, they seem almost fireproof.

But it does happen. I have two old black and white photographs taken in 1935 following a massive wildfire that swept through the upper Sol Duc River Valley on Washington's Olympic Peninsula in 1907. Although 28 growing seasons had come and gone, black sticks and white ash still stretched for miles. Forest Service records indicate 12,800 acres of old growth Douglas-fir were lost.

I sent my photographer friend, Mike McMurray to the Sol Duc's Kloshe Nanitch Lookout in 1994 to re-photograph the devastation that was recorded in August 1935. He had the map coordinates for the old lookout, but it's gone now, so he had to hike to a nearby overlook to re-photograph the valley. It is again a sea of green. Good soil, sunlight and 200 inches of rain a year will do wonders. It just takes a little time.

A different and far more dangerous asbestos forest blankets northwest Montana. Its origin is an old vermiculite mine a few miles north of Libby. No one knows how far microscopic particles of toxic asbestos spread, but the mine operated from 1919 until 1990 – long enough to kill 400 townspeople who have been inhaling the fibers for decades. Another 3,000 are struggling with deadly asbestosis, mesothelioma and emphysema.

Libby has been a Super Fund site for nearly 20 years – the kiss of death in a community already reeling from thc collapse of its once robust timber industry. Whatever hopes the town had held for diversifying its struggling economy were dashed as word of the unfolding tragedy spread on the pages of every major news magazine in the nation.

One reporter called the Libby's asbestosis crisis "the worst environmental disaster since Love Canal," a reference to the first Super Fund site, created by the federal government at Niagara Falls, New York. It took 21 years and 400 million taxpayer dollars to remove 21,800 tons of toxics that the Hooker Chemical Company had dumped into abandoned Love Canal before it sold the property to a local school district in 1953. Entire neighborhoods were subsequently built atop the dump site.

Thus far, the EPA has spent more than $500 million cleaning up and disposing of toxic asbestos the mine's most recent owner was giving to locals who used it as home insulation or a soil amendment in their gardens. It was everywhere: yards, gardens, roads, playgrounds and in the walls of hundreds of homes.

In a 2009 interview with Guardian reporter, Joanna Walters, Dean Herreid, a former wildland firefighter, described what inhaling felt like. "If you took a hot knife and stabbed me through the chest, that's what the pain feels like. Sometimes I can barely breathe."

Like most of the boys who grew up in Libby, Herreid played baseball on diamonds covered with asbestos. He also worked with his father, a local plumber whose jobs often included drilling into asbestos-filled walls. "It would rain down on us," Herreid recalls. At last report, he was teaching in an alternative school in Libby, still deter-

The gin clear waters of the Kootenai River near the Canoe Gulch Ranger Station, and Julia Petersen with Dave Blackburn and a nice Kootenai Rainbow above the mouth of the Fisher River, a heavily logged drainage will a well-protected fishery.

mined to live his life to its fullest.

In its most recent report, the EPA estimated that the amount of toxic asbestos present in the air in downtown Libby has been reduced by a factor of 100,000. That's the good news. The bad news is that many doubt Libby will ever regain its reputation as a hunting and fishing paradise.

Widely known but rarely discussed is the worrisome fact that non-flammable asbestos is lodged in the organic soil layer in the surrounding Kootenai National Forest. It also clings to the branches of hundreds of thousands of trees within a 73-mile danger zone that surrounds the old mine.

The EPA has contributed $300,000 to a fund to train firefighters to work in asbestos but the Forest Service had difficulty finding volunteers willing to enter the training program. Fortunately, the 10-member Chloeta crew showed up from Oklahoma in time to battle a never officially named wildfire that burned within 1.5 miles of the mine site in July 2018.

Donned in full-face respirators and for ritualistic reasons involving their own safety, crewmembers began their workdays listening as one of their own recited the ancient *Rainbow Passage*:

> *When the sunlight strikes raindrops in the air, they act like a prism and form a rainbow. The rainbow is a division of white light into many beautiful colors. These take the shape of a long, round arch, with its path high above and its two ends apparently beyond the horizon. There is, according to legend, a boiling pot of gold at one end.*
>
> *People look, but no one ever finds it. When a man looks for something beyond his reach, his friends say he is looking for the pot of gold at the end of the rainbow.*
>
> *Throughout the centuries, men have explained the rainbow in various ways. Some have accepted it as a miracle without physical explanation. The Greeks used to imagine that it was a sign from the gods to foretell war or heavy rain.*
>
> *The Norsemen considered the rainbow as a bridge over which the gods passed from earth to their home in the sky. Other men have tried to explain the phenomenon physically. Aristotle thought that the rainbow was caused by reflection of the sun's rays by the rain.*
>
> *Since then, physicists have found that it is not reflection, but refraction by the raindrops, which causes the rainbow. Many complicated ideas about the rainbow have been formed.*
>
> *The difference in the rainbow depends considerably upon the size of the water drops, where the width of the colored band increases as the size of the drops increase. The actual primary rainbow observed is said to be the effect of super-position of a number of bows.*
>
> *If the red of the second bow falls upon the green of the first, the result is to give a bow with an abnormally wide yellow band, since red and green lights when mixed form yellow. This is a very common type of bow, one showing mainly red and yellow, with little or no green or blue.*

"Once we make a commitment to don those masks, a time clock starts," explained Nolan Buckingham, superintendent of the Chloeta crew, noting that the required respirators limit air intake to 60 or 70 percent of normal. "It takes twice as long to complete normal tasks like digging a handline or sawing a snag."

The afterwork cleanup process is equally ritualistic: two showers in a trailer in the woods. Everything is washed: bodies, masks, hand tools, cell phones, clothes, even dollar bills in their wallets. Then a decontamination crew power-washes their hoses, pumps and chainsaws.

Because the Chloeta crew works alone – and isn't part of other line crews working the same fire – they are heavily dependent on aerial support. Columbia Helicopter crews from Aurora, Oregon dropped more than 220,000 gallons of water, siphoned from the Kootenai River, on the fire.

I shudder to think what might have happened in 1994. As a worrisome wildfire season grew worse, the Forest Service railed fire trucks from Cleveland, Ohio to Libby because it feared shifting winds might drive a big wildfire burning east of Libby through the town of 2,700. Had it happened, the fire would have also overrun the old vermiculite mine site.

Cleveland's spare fire trucks sat on flatcars on a rail siding near the Burlington Northern train station in downtown Libby for two weeks.

Once-thriving Libby lost its last major sawmill in 1999. Stimson Lumber, the mill's last owner tried in vain to convince the Kootenai National Forest to provide the 14 million board feet of timber needed to close the mill's annual supply gap. Perhaps fearing litigation, the Forest Service said it could not comply with the request. This in spite of the fact that the Kootenai easily holds twice as many trees as growing conditions there can sustain.

Some 30 percent of Libby's retail storefronts are now boarded up. The ill-advised hope had been that tourists would flock to northwest Montana once the timber industry was silenced, but it hasn't happened despite the fact that the Kootenai, one of Montana's finest trout rivers flows through town. The nearest destination resorts are two hours distant in the Flathead Valley.

Julia and I love the Kootenai and would joyfully spend our summers on the river but for the near-absence of Internet service. Many homes in the area still have dial-up service. Rural China has faster Internet speeds than much of the rural West. *Twenty million* Americans still don't have broadband service, but Tongguan, a village in mountainous China has 4G service! What's up with that? No business can afford to relocate to an area that doesn't have broadband service. You can't eat the scenery.

Adding to our challenge, there are few places along the Kootenai River where you can park a trailer except in Corps of Engineers campgrounds that have no electric, water or septic services. The "recreational" vehicle parks along the river are filled with people who can't afford to buy or rent a house.

Libby's Super Fund designation created quite an uproar among environmentalists, but not for the reasons you'd expect. In late 2004, Michael Shellenberger and Ted Nordhaus traveled to Hawaii to present an essay to several hundred representatives of foundations that support environmental causes.

Their 37-page essay, titled The Death of Environmentalism, accused the nation's leading environmental groups of being narrow, self-interested and too focused on grizzly bears and wilderness to care about human needs.

"Most of the movement's leading thinkers, funders and advocates do not question their most basic assumptions about who we are, what we stand for or what it is that we should be doing," Shellenberger and Nordhaus wrote. "What the environmental movement needs more than anything else right now is to take a collective step back to rethink everything."

It was harsh criticism coming from two men who had worked for a decade on campaigns concerning water, land-use planning and other issues. Especially harsh given the fact that Love Canal had played a significant role in environmentalism's rise in the early 1970s. How, then, could those gathered in Hawaii in 2004 have missed what had happened in Libby?

Although Sierra Club Director, Carl Pope, was enraged by their report, which he labeled as "rubbish…unfair, unclear and divisive" on the club's website. But former Sierra Club President, Adam Werbach, sided with Shellenberger and Nordhaus in remarks he later made at a Commonwealth Club meeting in San Francisco.

"We speak in terms of technical problems, not vision and values," he said. "We are failing to attract young people…we are failing to attract the disenfranchised, the disempowered, the dispossessed and the disengaged."

In February 2005, *High Country News* essayist, Ray Ring, suggested that Libby would be a good place to test the ideas Shellenberger and Nordhaus advanced in their 2004 report. It would be, but so would hundreds of once vibrant logging towns scattered across the West – close knit communities brought low by public worries about logging in national forests – worries that politically powerful environmental grant makers fanned for decades without regard to the senseless social, cultural and economic damage that groups they were funding were doing to the very people Werbach had described in his Commonwealth Club remarks.

By the time Shellenberger and Nordhaus sounded the alarm in Hawaii in 2004, two kinds of fire were raging in the West – one political and other literal. Both seemed unstoppable.

How did we miss this?

You can be forgiven for wondering how so many smart people missed the signs that should have told us all hell was about to break loose in the West's forests.

- Every major environmental group in the nation employs foresters.
- Every major conservation group employs foresters.
- The Forest Service employs hundreds of them.
- The timber industry employs hundreds more. States have foresters.
- Some counties have them.

But only *one* forester seems to have seen this coming and he saw it approaching in 1943 – at least 50 years before anyone else.

His name was Harold Weaver and he was the Forest Supervisor on the Colville Indian Reservation in eastern Washington. He raised the red flag in a Journal of Forestry article in which he wrote the following:

> *Complete prevention of forest fires has certain undesirable ecological and silvicultural effects. Conditions are already deplorable and becoming increasingly serious. Fires, when they do occur, are exceedingly hot and destructive and are turning extensive areas of forests into brush fields.*

Weaver's warning was met with dead silence, which I find astonishing given the fact that the Journal of Forestry was America's most prestigious forestry journal, read by the nation's most influential foresters, those in the employ of the nation's most powerful and prestigious public and private forestry organizations.

How could so many professionals who purport to care about forests miss what Weaver's warning? It wasn't that he was any smarter than them. I hate to say it, but I think Weaver's warning fell on deaf ears in 1943 because he was a Bureau of Indian Affairs forester in a world in which the BIA had little cache.

But lord almighty, the plain-as-day evidence could be seen in Intermountain forests that stretched the spine of the Rockies from Canada to Mexico. And the evidence said that a wildfire paradox would soon emerge and the paradox could tell us that the harder we fought to stuff the Wildfire Genie back in her bottle, the more times she would escape and the more damage she would do. Wildfires would get bigger, hotter, more dangerous and more destructive.

What caught Weaver's eye that no one else apparently saw – or perhaps cared to see – was the steady encroachment of shade-tolerant white fir in forests that had historically been dominated by sun-loving ponderosa pine.

Frequent, low intensity wildfires – often set by Indians to clear growing space for crops, create habitat for deer and elk, or defensible perimeters – also stimulated growth in thick-barked and fire-resistant ponderosa.

Low-intensity burns also renewed nutritious huckleberry patches. The abundance of Vitamin C in Indian diets prevented scurvy, a fatal disorder characterized by poor wound healing and infections.

Removing Indian fire and extinguishing natural wildfires before they could complete their good work gave thin-barked and fire-sensitive white fir the opportunity to slowly overtake ponderosa.

To slow white fir's advance Weaver recom-

A borate bomber swoops down on a fire above the Rogue River near Shady Cove, Oregon.

The 1910 fire burn area

mended that federal forest managers de-emphasize clearcutting and re-emphasize selective harvesting methods that would give ponderosa the opportunity it needed to recolonize favored sites.

Weaver's name came up at a wildfire conference I attended in Spokane, Washington in September 1994. Wildfire experts from all over the country offered their opinions on what might be done to regain the upper hand in what was becoming a losing battle against the West's increasingly frequent and deadly forest fires.

Not to be sidelined, the Land's Council, a Spokane-based environmental group, ran a full-page ad in the *Spokesman Review* that bore a bold headline befitting the group's hostility:

Where There's Smoke, There's Liars!
"Forest Health" Scare Tactic Is A Public Rip-off!!

I don't know if the Council had been invited to attend, or if they had refused an invitation, but the scraggly band of placard-carrying protestors assembled on the sidewalks outside got lots of press. Too bad they didn't come inside to talk about Weaver's 1943 warning.

Thanks to Bob Mutch, one of the conference's headline speakers, the wildfire paradox Weaver described in 1943 got a good airing in Spokane. Mutch, a former smokejumper turned fire behavior analyst at the Forest Service's Fire Science Lab at Missoula, Montana, used his time at the podium to describe the paradox that now – 25 years later – still continues to confuse so many of us.

"Fire suppression is not, by itself, the problem," Mutch told some 300 conference attendees. "Let it be remembered that the Forest Service has been suppressing wildfires for 84 years for a very important reason: to protect property and lives."

I interviewed Mutch at length following the conference. I wanted to know more about what he knew and I was on the hunt for a fire behavior expert's take on the Great 1910 Fire, which was front and center at the Missoula lab because of the wildfire bullet Libby had dodged that summer.

"Fires like the 1910 fire and the Tillamook burns of the 1930s, 40s and 50s, focused our attention on a single-minded approach based on the idea that all fires were bad," Mutch said. "We thus concluded that we would do everything in our power to exclude fire from the landscape. We would manage our forests through various timber harvesting practices. It's taken us a long time to accept the fact that it was the wrong approach."

And what was the right approach?

"What we have failed to do is balance our fire suppression program with an equally ambitious prescribed fire program," Mutch explained. "Periodic use of intentionally set fires will make the big firefighting job easier by reducing the fuel buildups that lead to very large, very dangerous fires like the ones we are seeing across the West today."

"Today" was 25 years ago and the other tool Mutch referenced – timber harvesting – has all but disappeared from national forests, adding to the woody buildup that fuels our godawful wildfires.

"You look back and you wonder, my God, why did it take five decades for folks to wise up," Mutch asked me. Several answers came immediately to mind and they all began with what we politely refer to as "the light burning episode," a vigorous debate among foresters working in northern California in the early 1900s.

Light burning – also known as "Piute Forestry" among those who observed that Indians systematically burned their lands – did not gain even a smidgeon of traction with professional forests until 1920. C.E. Ogle defended the practice in a 1920 essay published by The Timberman, an industry trade journal of the time. Ogle noted that fire suppression had only been the nation's accepted forest policy for about 10 years. Until then, ground fires had regularly swept the forest clean of debris and the forests were still there and the trees were growing and properly spaced to make prevent fires from reaching into treetops.

Other foresters scoffed at Ogle's claims. None more resolutely that Bill Greeley, who was named Forest Service Chief in 1920. Greeley had been a Forest Service ranger in northern California early in his career. His puritan roots in New England did not comport with waste for any perceived reason.

"Let us recognize frankly that light burning is simply part of the game of timber mining," Greeley wrote in *The Timberman* less than a month before he was named Chief in April 1920.

"To the gutting of heavy cutting it adds the gutting of a total destruction of young growth," he said. "To cheapen the protection and utilization of old timber, it deliberately transforms the forest into a brush patch."

No Chief would dare speak so frankly today, but Greeley had been District One Forester in Missoula during the 1910 Fire and the task of burying the 78 poorly equipped firefighters – most of the skid row bums recruited from the streets of Spokane – had fallen to him. No doubt he had read many of the news accounts assembled by sensationalist reporters of that era. Among them this one by David Bailey describing the loss of seven members of his crew who fled into a small cave in hopes of escaping flames and searing heat.

> "It was while holding a covering over my head that I burned my hands. We were in the creek for about two hours and we were all shaking from the cold as though we were suffering from the fever when we piled out.
>
> Our comrades who fled into the cave were cooked alive. They tried to get at the very end of a small hole and they were piled up in an awful heap, fists composed only of powdery bones, fists clenched and legs locked, the bodies were braced in a fight to the death. It was impossible to recover their bodies because they would have fallen to pieces."

Greeley later conceded that the carnage put him on a road he never left in his eight years as Forest Service Chief or the subsequent 27 years that he ran the now long- gone West Coast Lumbermen's Association.

"I was out to get converts," he said of his commitment to forest conservation as he saw it. It was Greeley who envisioned and founded the American Tree Farm System. Today, millions of green and white Tree Farm signs mark the locations of the best managed forests in America.

Over the last 30 years, we described the wildfire paradox-turned-conundrum and its associated white fir epidemic in six special *Evergreen* reports, the first being *Grey Ghosts in the Blue Mountains*,[47] our largely ignored 1989 warning of what lay ahead in beetle-infested national forests in eastern Oregon's Blue Mountains.

The West is Burning Up,[48] which we published in December 1994 was our most comprehensive report. Parts of my interview with Bob Mutch can be found there along with a good look at Bill Greeley's influence on our nation's shifting wildfire policies and priorities.

And so we return to Bob Mutch's rhetorical question. Why has it taken us so long to see the West's wildfire crisis for that it has become? The unfortunate answer to this mostly rhetorical question is that rather than accept personal responsibility for the conservation and management of our forests, we've chosen to blame everyone but ourselves. What we have here is as much a moral and ethical crisis as it is an environmental disaster.

Is logging to blame? Partly, though it's hard to blame individual loggers who were only doing what the Forest Service told them to do. Besides, conventional logging as it was done following World War II hasn't occurred on a national forest in the West in more than 30 years.

Photo courtesy of the Forestry History Society

Third Forest Service Chief, W.B. Greeley, abruptly resigned in 1928 to become executive vice president of the West Coast Lumbermen's Association.

Is the environmental movement to blame? Partly, though many environmental groups are now active participants in local collaborative groups that represent a broad cross-section of outdoor and community interests. They are working with the Forest Service on projects designed to restore natural resiliency in forests that are diseased and dying – but not too far gone to be saved from wildfire.

Historically, human nature has also been a factor. The process we call "science" gave us an early and rudimentary understanding of how trees grow and what we needed to do to make them grow better to meet our needs. Early forestry texts,

47 

48 

some written more than 200 years ago, stressed our utilitarian need for wood.

Though correct in their understanding of tree growth, our earliest foresters saw no need to pursue a further understanding of forest ecosystem function or the roles played by invisible organisms and processes. Our agriculture systems suffered from the same selective knowledge base. Eating, building and heating were the main societal concerns.

Europe's regimented forestry model did not transfer to U.S. forests as well as hoped. Countless millions were invested in tree improvement cooperatives that developed genetically superior, disease-resistant seedlings. Millions more were invested in fertilizers to speed tree growth and herbicides and insecticides that could slow the advance of forest diseases and insects.

All well and good, but these investments in "industrial" forestry required that forests not be killed by wildfire before the trees were ready for harvest – and it took decades longer than expected to stuff the Bad Wildfire Genie back in her bottle. But by the mid-1950s the job was largely completed.

What no one understood was the wildfire conundrum. It warns that the harder we fight to stuff the Bad Genie back in her bottle, the angrier she gets and the more frequently she escapes.

Industry's investments in forestry were predicated on a desire to meet growing public demand for forest products – everything from lumber to paper to the sugar in candy bars and edible torula yeast that grows on wood alcohol and is used in medicines and as a food additive.

What wasn't fully appreciated was that the European concept of a fully-regulated forest was unworkable in steep western mountains, especially in areas where soil productivity, moisture – even sunlight – vary widely. European forestry is great in Europe and it works pretty well in privately owned forests in the Southeast and the Pacific Northwest, but not very well in national forests in the Interior West. It's that old cookie cutter thing again. It's trying to jam square pegs in round holes. The devil is always in the details.

Climate is unquestionably a driver in most Rocky Mountain forests. And we've learned a great deal about climate fluctuations since the whole idea of human-caused climate change was first suggested. We know that climate and weather, its microscale representation, have varied greatly at time and geographic scales.

Here in the Pacific Northwest, which is pretty much the cradle of our national forest system, the Pacific Decadal Oscillation [the long-lived El Nino-like climate pattern] gave us a cool and wetter than normal period that lasted for 40 years following the dreadful wildfire seasons that dominated the 1910-1930s period.

Some have argued that it was this cool, wet period – and not the Forest Service's massive wildfire suppression campaign – that led to a false belief that our efforts to stuff the Bad Wildfire Genie back in her bottle were working.

You could make the same argument about the seeming "friendliness" of grizzly bears that fed daily for decades in garbage dumps in Yellowstone and Glacier National Park. Both arguments played to our arrogant belief that humans are masters of nature. We aren't. Now – fortunately – we are learning how to live within nature's boundaries. Where wildfire is concerned, this involves learning how to use fire – how to help the Good Genie clean up our forestry messes.

Peter Kolb frequently reminds me that hope is not a strategy and science is a process, not a religion. There is a big difference between applied science – the real stuff – and normative science – our list of usually unattainable wishes. For more on normative science read Normative Science Essay,[49] Bob Lackey and Normative and Ethical Foundaitons of Ecological Forestry in the United Sates,[50] V. Alaric Sample.

The bottom line: Science is most helpful when it is applied in an unbiased process that invites skepticism and constructive criticism. But science falls flat on its face when it is misused to prove a point, and skepticism and criticism must necessarily be silenced before the point made is disproven. Self-serving environmentalists are currently cherry-picking science in hopes of steering us away from

49 

50 

a wide variety of forestry tools we should be using to help the Good Genie clean up our mess.

Collaboration – patterned after the old New England Town Hall meetings – is the pathway forward. Everyone gets to weigh in on possible solutions. No one gets to argue that there isn't a solution. That's good but the pace and scale of restoration work currently underway in at-risk national forest is too slow and small. We aren't doing everything we should be doing to help the Good Genie. Congress needs to allow the Forest Service and its local collaborative groups to work at a much faster pace on much larger landscapes.

Again, do the math. The Forest Service estimates we have 80-90 million acres of forest and rangeland in Condition Class 3 [ready to burn] or Condition Class 2 [will soon be ready to burn]. Fire ecologists tell us we have 30 years at the outside to restore what can be restored before wildfire takes the rest.

90 million = 3 million acres per year for 30 years

We aren't restoring more than 15 percent of what we should be restoring annually. Wildfires aren't constrained by rules and regulations that limit their destructive paths. And they don't respect property lines so other public and private lands are also in harm's way.

Why are we limiting our restoration efforts? Human intervention – hands-on forestry in sick and dying forests is the only safe or reliable strategy for getting our wants and needs met. Nature doesn't give a damn.

The public discourse is infested with hocus-pocus designed to reassure you that all is well in our national forests. "A little of this here and a little of that there and everything will be fine." Nonsense. We aren't even close to fine. The timid path forward Congress has us on is a prescription for environmental disaster.

Many of us lack the practical understanding necessary to understand what's happening and why in our national forests. We were born in cities or suburbs two or three generations removed from rural roots put down by our self-sufficient grandparents and great grandparents.

Most of us have no idea where our everyday comforts and conveniences come from. We drive to Whole Foods, The Home Depot or Nordstrom and shop amid jaw-dropping abundance. This doesn't just happen. Farmers, ranchers, miners, oilfield wildcatters, loggers and sawmill workers deliver this abundance to us 24/7.

Not too long ago, more of us – including school kids - understood this. Uniformed Forest Rangers visited our classrooms and many of us were the sons or daughters of men and women who got their hands dirty every day.

Had you suggested a "let Nature" management approach to forests that were vital to our country's 1940s-1950s transition from wartime to peacetime footing, you would have been laughed out of town.

Bob Mulch

Had you recommended that a forest ravaged by wildfire be left "to Nature," because "salvaging fire-killed timber was like mugging a burn victim" you might have been run out of town.

In a cultural sense, the world the Greatest Generation built up began to crumble under the weight of swiftly changing social and cultural values. Opposition to the war in Vietnam jump-started a new era in American conservation history that began April 22, 1970 with the first Earth Day celebration.

The revolution continues though it hasn't done enough to build on our common understanding of how Nature works or what we must do to protect

Photo courtesy of Eli Shotola

A timber faller takes his measure of a giant on Freres land.

Bicycling amid red pine in the George Washington National Forest near bucolic Grand Marais, Minnesota.

and conserve our forests while enjoying the economic, social and cultural benefits that flow from them. Again, our failure to take responsibility for earth's bounty.

Our colleague, Jim Bowyer, a PhD Professor Emeritus from the University of Minnesota Department of Bioproducts and Biosystems Engineering, and Director of the Responsible Materials Program with Dovetail Partners, has written a great book about all this that you should read.

The Irresponsible Pursuit of Paradise challenges us to rethink ethically bankrupt environmental policies that require us to import our natural resources [minerals, chemicals, wood and oil] from less affluent nation's that need our money but lack our regulatory safeguards.

Dr. Bowyer challenges our selfish "not in my backyard, out-of-sight-out of mind" declaration, asserting that we should tap our own natural resource bounty to fulfill our own consumptive lifestyle needs. I wholeheartedly agree.

Misplaced environmental worries and ineffective and often politically-inspired federal forest management policies are the major reasons why our forests are dying and burning in wildfires for which there are no ecological precedents in our nation's history. Climate change has certainly become a factor in recent years, but it took us decades to dig the hole we are in now.

The six-second sound bite: We have too many trees in our national forests – the ones you own – for the natural carrying capacity of the land: the aggregate of soil fertility, annual rain and snowfall, elevation, sunlight and the cyclical influences of climatic warming and cooling cycles.

These cycles, which look like sine waves, reveal themselves in soil and pollen samples and tree ring counts. Scientists have collected samples from lake bottoms that date back tens of thousands of years. Muskeg samples reveal that Earth was once warm enough to support redwood trees inside the Arctic Circle.

Are we entering such a warming period again? Possibly. No one knows for sure.

What we do know is that our western national forests are overstressed by prolonged drought. They have become magnets for insect and diseases that can detect stress in trees. Our forests are in a death spiral. Our trees are killing each other in their fight for growing space, sunlight, moisture and soil nutrients.

So which is it: Nature? or Us?

Analysis paralysis

If you answered "Us" to the "Nature or Us" question I asked in the last sentence in Chapter 16, you are correct. Hands-on forest management is our best tool for reducing the risk of catastrophic wildfire in our national forests. It will take many years, but the tangible rewards are plainly visible in forests that have already been thinned. The photographic record here dates from 1905.

And so my question: rather than letting Nature clean up our mess, why don't we do it ourselves by removing all those dead and dying trees from our overcrowded forests before they burn. We can then store all that carbon-laced smoke in the useful wood products rather than our lungs.

If this was easy, I think we would have done it long ago. But nothing is ever as easy as it seems and the backstory here is an instructive reminder that the road to hell is almost always paved with good intentions. Who could have predicted that every well-intended environmental law Congress has passed since 1970 could be twisted into impossible-to-meet standards established by federal judges and federal agencies that wrote the rules in the first place!

Cynics in the Forest Service complain about "analysis paralysis" and "the process predicament." They say forest planning staffs spend most of their time analyzing possible environmental problems and almost no time solving these problems.

Analysis paralysis has become so pervasive inside the Forest Service that the agency belatedly commissioned a study in 2002 titled "The Process Predicament: How Statutory, Regulatory and Administrative Factors Affect National Forest Management."

Not surprisingly the commission's key finding was that the thousands and thousands of pages of environmental regulation written by federal agencies since 1970 – including the Forest Service – are making it very difficult to get any "boots-on-the-ground" work done.

Why does the Forest Service spend so much time and money analyzing and analyzing? Three reasons. First because the agency prides itself on crossing all the "T's" and dotting all the "I's" in Environmental Assessments and Environmental Impact Statements that sometimes take years to prepare. Second because agency leaders are risk-adverse because they fear they will make career-ending mistakes. Third because they hate being sued by the leave it to Nature crowd. Meritless lawsuits generate bad press.

Ours is an unnecessarily litigious society. We sue each other at the drop of a hat. An entire industry was born of character flaw though an old lawyer friend often reminded me that we sue one another because it beats settling our differences with guns and knives. At times, I'm not so sure.

In the forestry world, lawyers who repeatedly sue the Forest Service are called "serial litigators." They sue on "process" – their interpretation of conflicting laws, rules and regulations Congress and regulators have written. Win or lose, the Equal Access to Justice Act requires taxpayers – that's most of us – to pay their legal bills.

Meantime our western national forests are falling apart and the Forest Service now spends half its taxpayer-funded budget putting out fires.

This needs to change. The sooner the better. We're running out of time and "Nature" doesn't give a rip what we want or need from our forests. Either we clean up the mess we've made or "Nature" will keep right on burning and burning until there's nothing left to burn. Is this what we want? I don't think so.

Sally Fairfax, a PhD Professor of Forest Policy at the University of California Berkley, predicted this regulatory morass more than 30 years ago. Here is what she wrote about the mostly unanticipated impacts of just two well-intended federal laws – the 1974 Resources Planning Act and the 1976 National Forest Management Act.

> *"Far from achieving a rational decision-making process, RPA and NFMA may well result in stalemate and indecision as the Forest Service turns from managing land to simply overseeing a convoluted, ever more complex set of congressionally mandated procedures. The tradition of land stewardship, if indeed it survived the 1950s and 1960s, may have died in the 1970s. RPA and NFMA take the initiative from experienced land managers – those revered people on the ground, the folks who have lived with the land and their mistakes long enough to have developed wisdom and a capacity for judgment – and gives it to lawyers, computers, economists and politically active special interest groups seeking to protect and enhance their own diverse positions.*
>
> *This shift in initiative will result from layers of legally binding procedure that RPA and NFMA foist on top of an already complex and overly rigid planning process. Constant procedural tinkering does not, I fear, lead to efficiency or simplicity. Rather it promises a proliferation of steps, sub-steps, appendices and diverticula that makes the Forest Service susceptible to the ultimate lawyer's malaise: the reification of process over substance."*

A lawyer's malaise – disquiet turned hostility – and ashen ruin for the rest of us.

Aftermath of the 2003 B&B Complex fire on the Santiam Pass west of Sisters, Oregon. Amid political controversy, standing dead timber was not salvaged. Parts of this fire have since reburned. President George W. Bush flew over burned area and call it "a holocaust."

Three fires burning

A newspaper reporter recently asked me if I could summarize my thinking on our wildfire pandemic "in just a sentence or two."

"I can," I quickly replied. "This isn't the forest legacy we should be leaving our children and grandchildren. We look like childish fools."

My off-hand reply opened the door to a much longer conversation in which I said I thought there were three very different fires burning in America today.

"How so?" she asked.

Paraphrasing, here is the rest of my answer.

Of our three fires, two are literal, one is figurative.

On the literal side, we have Bad Fires we need to attack quickly and work like crazy to extinguish them before they become uncontrollable firestorms.

We also need to accept the fact that not all fires are Bad. We can use Good Fires, what foresters call "prescribed fire" to clean up woody debris that otherwise fuels large and very destructive wildfires.

Aggressive risk management – thinning trees from forests that have become too dense, then using prescribed fire to clean up the debris – is the key to ridding our forests of uncontrollable fire storms.

So remember, there are Good Fires and there are Bad Fires. Frequent use of Good Fire can help us reduce the frequency of very destructive Bad Fires.

On the figurative side, we need to tone down the fiery rhetoric!

There is plenty of blame to go around so let's dump the scape-goats, stop the name-calling and forget the serial litigators. They've marginalized themselves in their refusal to join other citizens at the collaborative table where our most vexing and controversial issues are being resolved using a model that bears remarkable similarities to the old New England town hall meetings.

My late friend, Jack Ward Thomas, the Forest Service's thirteenth Chief, said it best. "We need to stop fighting the last war and quit wasting our time walking old battlefields, bayonetting the wounded again and again."

Jack was right. We aren't going to turn the corner in this crisis if we don't start working together, learn how to say please and thank you, listen more carefully to one another's points of view and show some respect for differing opinions and values. In short, adopt the old New England town hall model.

We must overcome the sum of our fears. Many of us believe the Forest Service is in bed with the big bad timber industry. That romance ended 30 years ago. Others are pretty sure the Forest Service is in bed with the anti-forestry crowd. I doubt it. The Forest Service figures that if half of us are mad at them they must be doing something right. None of this is helpful.

Can we make a short list of things we might agree on? Too much wildfire smoke blankets urban centers out west? Too much wildfire smoke in and around rural communities out west? Fish and wildlife habitat turned to ash and ruin? Hiking trails and campgrounds obliterated? Watersheds that supply drinking water to almost every western city and town turned to mud? The loss of billions of trees? We can see them standing dead in aerial and satellite images. Does anyone care?

I'm guessing that my cabdriver friend would be mad as hell about the loss of so many trees. But we'd need to explain wildfire smoke to him – bearing in mind that he drives in New York's five boroughs where the air is rarely something people brag about.

I think Danny O'Neill would also be dismayed by the loss of so much habitat but, again, we'd have to explain to him that the post-fire recovery process can take hundreds of years. To get started, I'd show him some still barren areas where the Great 1910 Fire crossed from northern Idaho into western Montana. The fire was so hot it melted the soil into a waxy paste that water could not penetrate for a long time. The wind blows hard most days in this area so it might be several hundred years before there is sufficient organic soil to support plant life.

Danny would also be upset about the loss of so much beauty. Remember, this is a guy who thought he'd like to come west someday to check on all the trees I'd told him are still here. Maybe the 2,500-mile trek from the Bronx to Wallace, Idaho isn't a big deal if you are a cab driver.

Where does this leave us? I'd say it leaves us with some very fertile common ground and quite a bit to talk about.

Seeing is believing so pictures will help. Lord knows we have countless thousands of pictures of beautiful green forests, forests burning to the ground and thinned forests that look a lot like city parks. We also have hours of video shot from drones that show what the actually thinning process looks like.

Several years ago, I was involved in some focus group work that took several of us to four cities east of the Mississippi to test public reaction to some thinning projects that had been done in western national forests.

For comparison sake, we held up pictures of thinned forests and pictures of burnt forests. No one in any of the groups liked the look of burnt trees. One woman in Memphis pointed her finger at the photo of the thinned forest and said, "That's the one I like. Why aren't we doing more of that?"

We explained that national forests belong to all of us and that there wasn't much public support for thinning in major urban centers where most voters reside. She shook her head in amazement. My Irish cabdriver friend would have added a few choice adjectives. He had a very colorful way with words.

If there was ever a time for us to rely on the safety and reliability of repeatable time-tested forest science, the time is now. And for heaven's sake, let's include local folks with historic and cultural knowledge in this discussion. Don't buy all the nonsense about rural people being too stupid or greedy to make good choices. These are the same folks who deliver a lot of your "stuff" to you every day.

Most people living in the rural west know that they live in a post-industrial society. They accept the fact that outdoor recreation has replaced timber management as the main economic activity in our national forests. But they also know that outdoor recreation and forest management are not mutually exclusive. Indeed, forestry – removing diseased, dying, dead and undesirable tree species from at-risk national forests that have grown too dense – is key to protecting recreational areas from the increasing risks posed by insect and disease infestations and inevitable catastrophic wildfire.

The "Man or Nature?" question is the wrong question! The right question is what must we do to restore lost resiliency in national forests that are teetering on the brink of ecological collapse? It's the question I ask in the Chapter 1 title: What do you want from your forest? I don't think you're looking for more black sticks.

We are blessed with marvelous quantitative tools – remote sensing probes and satellites that can read license plates from miles above earth – technologies that allow us to peer deeply into our forests, to see far beyond anything that Gifford Pinchot, Teddy Roosevelt or George Perkins Marsh could have conceived in their wildest dreams.

With so many marvelous tools at our fingertips, why are we are so conflicted where our choices between Man and Nature are concerned? We need both. And right now we're losing both.

John McColgan's iconic picture of elk taking refuge in the East Fork of the Bitterroot River south of Missoula, Montana in August 2000 amid the Bitterroot National Forest's 365,000-acre Sula Complex Fire. Prescribed burns help reduce the ecological risks posed by stand-replacing wildfires.

The new normal

We hear lots of chatter these days about the West's big wildfires being "the new normal." This mischaracterization is being advanced by people who would have us believe there is nothing we can do to turn back the walls of flames we see on the nightly news all summer long.

It is also a convenient excuse offered by some in Forest Service leadership positions in Washington D.C. And it's not truee. The truth is there is much we can do to reduce the size, frequency and destructive power of the wildfires we are witnessing. We just aren't doing it.

Remember, the only constant in nature is change. There is no equilibrium, no steady state in which all the forces of nature exist in harmony with one another and no tooth fairy. The natural processes that drive life and death in our forests are complex and in constant motion. We cannot simplify them by legislative fiat, but we can help these natural processes right themselves.

Some examples to consider:

Was it normal when a thousand feet of ice covered the one-acre plot where our house sits today in Dalton Gardens, Idaho?

Was it normal when buffalo roamed New Jersey, and Manhattan was pretty much a rattlesnake infested swamp?

Was it "normal" when redwoods grew inside the Arctic Circle or when 1,000-foot-deep Lake Missoula covered most of western Montana? You can see numerous lateral high-water marks above the white "M" at Washington Grizzly Stadium in Missoula.

Was it "normal" when North America's first inhabitants walked here across the Bering Sea on a land bridge that once joined Asia and Alaska? That bridge is long gone but our so-called "First Nations" are still with us.

Things happen, sometimes in sudden and startling ways that are beyond human control: Earthquakes, hurricanes, volcanic eruptions, and Jokulhloup, an Icelandic word meaning "glacier bursts." The Lake Missoula ice dam collapse near Noxon, Montana some 10,000 years ago is a great example.

The ensuing floodwaters helped carve the spectacular Columbia Gorge that separates western Oregon and Washington. Floodwaters in downtown Portland were 600 feet deep, 54 feet taller than the 40-story Wells Fargo Center, Rose City's' tallest building. Who living in Portland today would think this normal?

Northern Idaho's glacially-carved Pend Oreille Lake is thought to have been partially shaped by the Missoula Flood at about the same time that the first north American inhabitants arrived from Asia. Did any of them see it? What must they have thought about what they saw and heard?

Can you imagine a 600-foot tall wall of rushing water, soil and rock crashing onto the flatlands of eastern Oregon and Washington? From 30,000 feet, the alluvial fans are still visible, and truck-sized boulders still litter the flood's path. You can see them along the state highway that runs between George and Levenworth, Washington and on the road that runs south of Coulee City.

Deep blue Crater Lake in southern Oregon's Crater Lake National Park – the deepest lake in the United States – was created by a violent volcanic eruption some 7,700 years ago. Prevailing northeasterly winds carried white ash from the collapsing 2,148-feet deep caldera all the way to Idaho and Montana.

The 1980 eruption of southwest Washington's Mount St. Helens generated winds that exceeded the speed of sound, snapping old growth trees like tooth picks. I have pictures of salvage loggers picking their way through jack-strawed piles of Weyerhaeuser trees three and four feet in diameter that were snapped in two by 600 mile-an-hour volcanic winds.

The blast force of the May 18, 1980 Mount St. Helens eruption killed 57 people, 1,500 elk, 5,000 deer and 12 million salmon. Four billion board feet of timber were laid flat by winds that exceeded the speed of sound.

The August 26-27, 1883 eruptions of Indonesia's Krakatoa was heard 2,200 miles distant in Alice Springs, Australia. The force of the blast was 13,000 times greater than the bomb that destroyed Hiroshima in 1945. The explosion's pressure wave encircled the globe 3.5 times. Average global temperatures fell 2.2 degrees Fahrenheit, creating chaotic weather patterns that lasted until 1890.

But Krakatoa seems insignificant when compared to what the Yucatan Peninsula's Chicxulub Crater reveals. The crater 93 miles in diameter and 12 miles deep was created when a comet between seven and 50 miles wide slammed into our earth about 66 million years ago. The ensuing climate disruption is thought to have caused the extinction of 75 percent of all earth's plant and animal species, including all non-avian dinosaurs.

Could it happen again? No one knows but Wyoming's Yellowstone Caldera – also known as the Yellowstone Supervolcano – is all the rage with volcanologists who enjoy thinking about the possibility that we'll all be blown to smithereens.

Calderas are basically dome-like groundswells. This one formed after the last big eruption some 640,000 years ago. It spans about 1,750 square miles and is rising 1.5 centimeters per year. Go anyway. The geysers, deep blue pools and boiling mud pots formed by the caldera are beautiful.

The aftermath of the 1988 Yellowstone fires are also worth a look. The 793,880- acre conflagration began as several fires driven by high winds. At its peak in early September, 9,000 firefighters worked day and night to slow the fire's advance.

The greatest losses were in 250-year-old lodgepole pines, very old for a tree species that grows in dense stands and rarely lives more than 80 or 90 years before succumbing to insects and fire. Fast growing aspen trees quickly claimed some of the turf lodgepole had occupied, but where lodgepole cones found fertile soil, the trees are again growing in stands so dense that walking is difficult.

Swing past Quake Lake while you're in the neighborhood. It was formed on the night of August 17, 1959 by an earthquake that triggered an enormous landslide that blocked the northerly flow of the Madison River.

Twenty-eight unfortunate souls died when 50 million cubic feet of careening rocks and mud buried their campground. The force of the slide generated winds strong enough to toss cars off the highway. Around 11:40 p.m. lampshades in our living room in Kellogg, Idaho – 383 miles west – swayed back and forth. Now that's an earthquake!

But Quake was small potatoes compared to Valdivia, at 9.6 the largest earthquake ever recorded on the Richter scale. The May 22, 1960 Chilean monster unleashed a tsunami that raced across the Pacific Ocean at several hundred miles per hour. Hilo, on the Island of Hawaii, was devastated by 35-foot waves. Sixty-one died. Estimates of the Chilean death toll run as high as 7,000.

Astronomer Bob Berman has written an entertaining book about the natural calamities that have shaped our earth. *Earth-Shattering* recounts several cosmic calamities including our collision with Theia, a Mars-sized planet that crashed head on into us. Debris from the collision gave us our moon and stabilized our axial tilt. We got four

A Weyerhaeuser forester gazes at the devastation on company lands following the May 1980 eruption of Mount St. Helens. The company salvaged 850 million board feet of its timber and replanted some 68,000 acres. Not so 22 years later on southern Oregon's Siskiyou National Forest. Writer Dave Skinner took this selfie in following the 2002 Biscuit Fire, a lightning-caused colossus that scorched 500,000 acres. Amid political controversy, little salvage or clean-up work was done.

lovely seasons – spring, summer, fall and winter – and 12 full moons a year in the deal. Nice!

The worst day in earth's history – the day the dinosaurs died – is chronicled minute-by-minute in rock samples removed from the Mexico's Chicxulub crater. The city-sized asteroid that struck us some 65 million years ago blasted a hole 100 miles wide and 12 miles deep, wiping out three-fourths of all life on earth. In the first seconds after impact, the asteroid punched a hole 25 miles deep in earth's crust sending a plume of molten rock more than five miles into the sky. An entire mountain range was created in minutes. Global temperatures dropped 30 some degrees and stayed there for decades.

Yup, big stuff happens in Nature and there is nothing we can do about it, but we can do a much better job of controlling the little things that influence our destiny by doing a better job of taking care of our stuff: the air we breathe, the water we drink, the soil from which all life springs and the forests we love.

If you want to see how much "*normal*" has changed in western forests over the last 150 years, there are several books featuring photographs that document the changes that occurred in western forests as our firefighting capacity and skill increased. A century ago our western forests held far fewer trees than they do today. "Exclusion of fire" allowed tree species that are more sensitive to fire to grow in places normally dominated by fire resistant species. We made the problem worse by harvesting too many of the best seed trees.

I'll have more to say about our "wildfire paradox" in the next chapter but know this: the visible and anecdotal evidence of the West that once was is on parade in dozens and dozens of books but one of the best is the beautiful coffee table book I mentioned in Chapter 13: *Exploring with Custer: The 1874 Black Hills Expedition.* If you enjoy outdoor photography, make a trip to the Black Hills sometime and try to retake the photographs William Illingworth took in 1874. You can't – and our wildfire paradox is the reason why.

Illingworth's photos are among countless thousands taken by pioneers who ventured west as early wagon roads were opened in the 1840s and 1850s. They reveal forests that were far sparser than they are today. Fewer trees, different tree species, more meadows and grasslands.

Other books and reports worth exploring:

- *Seventy Years of Vegetative Change in a Managed Ponderosa Pine Forest in Western Montana*, published by the Forest Service's Intermountain Forest and Range Experiment Station in 1982
- *Historic Increases in Woody Vegetation in Lincoln County New Mexico*, by E. Hollis Fuchs, VanGuard Printing, Albuquerque, New Mexico, 2002
- *A Study In Repeat Photography: Long-Term Vegetation Change on Utah's Fishlake National Forest*, by Charles Kay, University of Utah, 2003
- *Yellow Ore, Yellow Hair, Yellow Pine*, by Donald Progulske and Richard Sowell, Agriculture Experiment Station, South Dakota State University, 1974
- *Fire and Vegetative Trends in the Northern Rockies: Interpretations from 1871-1982 Photographs*, by George Gruell, Intermountain Forest and Range Experiment Station, U.S. Forest Service, 1983
- *Snapshot in Time: Repeat Photography on the Boise National Forest, 1870-1992, Boise National Forest, Intermountain Region, 1993*
- *Fire in Sierra Nevada Forests: A Photographic Interpretation of Ecological Change Since 1849*, by George Gruell, Mountain Press Publishing, Missoula, Montana, 2001.

I encourage you to hunt up these books on the Internet. One of the first things you will discover is that the "vast sea of old growth" that environmentalists champion never existed. Only in Hollywood has it ever been possible for a squirrel to cross the Great Plains by jumping from one tree to the next.

The repeat photography displayed in these books is supported by anecdotal accounts in the diaries of pioneers who emigrated to Oregon Territory. From one wagon train, Miss. Rebecca Ketcham described what she saw in September 1853 from a plateau overlooking the Grand Ronde River near present day La Grande.

> *"I can almost say I never saw anything more beautiful, the river winding about through ravines, the forests so different from anything I*

have ever seen before. The country all through is burnt over, so often there is not the least underbrush, but the grass grows thick and beautiful. It is now ripe and yellow, and the spaces between the groves, which are large and many, look like fields of grain ripened, ready for harvest."

What Miss. Ketchum was describing was the natural result of wildfires that burned so frequently the mountain air was blue all summer and fall, so blue in fact that the pioneers that crossed eastern Oregon called their westerly route "the blue mountains." Now we call the mountains west of La Grande the Blue Mountains, capital "B," "M."

Pioneers who settled in the Southwest described grass "as tall as a horse's belly" in parts of New Mexico and Arizona. Scattered throughout these grassy savannahs were large ponderosa pines, often in clusters of three. Thick-barked ponderosa easily survived the frequent low-intensity burns fires that kept thin-barked fir in check. I've photographed similar scenes in forests near Flagstaff, Arizona.

"Excluding fire" [a forester's term for the quest that began following the 1902 Yacolt Burn] dramatically changed the species composition in the Intermountain West. Ponderosa trees, which thrive in full sunlight, gradually gave way to shade-tolerant fir species that, while beautiful, don't handle prolonged drought, insects or diseases as well as ponderosa. Early loggers made things worse by removing the high-quality ponderosa, which created more growing space for fir.

William "Bush" Osborne, Jr. built his first Osborne "fire finder" in 1911, two years after he went to work for the U.S. Forest Service in the Mount Hood area of what was then the Oregon National Forest. The device integrated a sighting mechanism with a transit and a map of the surrounding forest. Installed in a lookout tower, it proved to be remarkably accurate at locating wildfires when they weren't much larger than campfires.

Osborne took his fire finder to Leopold and Volpel, a Beaverton, Oregon instrument manufacturer in 1913. They built the first commercially produced version and the Forest Service bought 100 of them. The company built about 3,000 Osbornes before ceasing production in 1989.

To prove his invention's accuracy, Osborne installed one in 1914 at a Mount Hood lookout manned by Elijah Coalman. In one month, Colman spotted 131 fires with it. Osborne added a camera to his invention in 1917, making it possible to shoot 360-degree photographs of forests.

I have several Osborne originals that were shot from fire lookouts in western Oregon and Washington in the 1920s and 1930s. My photographer friend, Mike McMurray, has attempted to reshoot many of the old photo points but it is very difficult. Trees 50 to 100-feet tall block the view.

These photographs – the old and the new – give lie to the claim that western Oregon and Washington was once "a vast sea of old growth." Never happened. Huge wildfires saw to it that no "sea" ever developed. The Oregon Department of Forestry reports that the three largest for which evidence can be found were the 1849 Siletz fire, 800,000 acres, the 1853 Yaquina fire, 480,000 acres and the 1865 Silverton Fire, 988,000 acres – about one-third the size of the three million-acre Great 1910 Fire that swept over northern Idaho and western Montana.

Today, satellites, aircraft equipped with infrared cameras and remote sensing technologies do the work done by Butch Osborne's fabled fire finders, but you can still enjoy an unforgettable few days in one of the old Forest Service lookouts or fire cabins.[51]

The views are fabulous. Bring your binoculars and camera, wear good walking shoes and bring warm clothes. It gets chilly after sundown. Fly rods optional.

If you are in the neighborhood, you should also plan to visit the Weyerhaeuser Company's Mount Saint Helens Museum at Toutle, Washington – one of the world's finest displays of the visible power of forestry set against the natural recovery occurring within the St. Helens National Volcanic Monument.

The address is 17000 Spirit Lake Road. Google maps will take you there. You won't be sorry. The "Eruption Chamber" rocks!

51 

500,000 Northern Arizona acres were lost in the 2002 Rodeo-Chediski Fire and 18,000 acres in five major watersheds were lost in Colorado's 2012 Waldo Canyon Fire. It killed two and destroyed 346 homes northwest of Colorado Springs.

Our great wilfire conundrum

Our Great Wildfire Conundrum harbors the supposedly self-evident idea that fighting wildfires leads to larger, more frequent and more destructive wildfires.

This isn't true. What is true is that when we purposefully allow forests to grow too dense bad things can happen. Specifically, the cascading environmental impacts of insects and diseases and inevitable wildfire. We love trees, so why not have more? And many of us are very suspicious of the motives and environmental impacts of logging, so let's not do that. Fine. Let's not.

And when we don't? Well, Nature takes over where we left – and we stopped logging on a commercial scale after the federal government listed the northern spotted owl as a threatened species in 1990. So now we have this 30-year buildup of fuel created by Nature: dead trees, dying trees and billions of tons of woody debris on the ground.

We have two choices. We can continue to allow Nature to do the cleanup work or we can clean up the mess ourselves. We're seeing how nature does this in the news every day during our longer and longer wildfire seasons. Do we like it? Some do. Most don't.

What's involved in cleaning up the mess ourselves? The surprising answer to this question is the subject of this chapter. Know this for openers. We have a really good partner in Nature if we learn how to merge our tools with hers. Working together, we reverse the very alarming wildfire trends we're observing.

What we have here is forestry's Rubik's Cube. To solve it before the clock runs out, we must deal with the current assertion that fighting wildfires only leads to bigger, more frequent and more destructive wildfires.

At first blush this appears to be true. But remember, we haven't done much about the increase in forest density for 30 years. Our challenge is to get the red, white, blue, orange, green and yellow cubes back into alignment in the 30 some years that remain before uncontrollable wildfires destroy what remains of our treasured western national forests.

Plainly stated, we want to help the Good Wildfire Genie stuff the Bad Wildfire Genie back in her bottle. But this will be easier said than done because the Bad Genie has a 30-year head start in our race against the clock. Good luck to all of us.

Some background: Currently, about half the Forest Service's current $5.8 billion annual budget is spent fighting wildfires – and that doesn't include the cost of replanting or repairing damaged watersheds. The story here is long, with many twists and turns, but the short version goes like this:

The 1988 Yellowstone Fire marked the beginning point in a slow evolution in the way federal resource management agencies, including the Forest Service, handle wildfires. Although the official Forest Service policy is to put them out as quickly as possible, some wildfires are now allowed to burn themselves out when and where favorable conditions are present.

The Yellowstone situation was made more complicated by the fact that the fire started inside the park and the National Park Service wildland fire policy is very different from the Forest Service policy. Park Service officials allow wildfires to burn naturally because that's nature's way, so by the time they figured out it had a tiger by the tail in 1988, it was too late. The fire – actually there were four fires in the park burning at the same time – burned into surrounding national forests before it was finally contained. Some 1.2 million acres were blackened including about 794,000 acres inside Yellowstone.

Public safety remains the top priority for the Forest Service within the "Wooey." That's Forest Service-ese for "wildland urban interface." But there is a decision space in which fire managers are permitted to let wildfires run where they would otherwise be fought. Although unwritten, this policy shift has triggered a fierce debate between fire ecologists who hold diametrically opposed positions where wildfires are concerned.

One contingent sees these big fires as the solution to the insect and disease infestations that are killing the trees that are fueling big fires.

The other group sees our insect and disease infestations as a symptom of problems that begin with the presence of too many trees for the natural carrying capacity of the land – the sum total of soil nutrients, sunlight, moisture, elevation and whether the forest faces north, south, east or west.

This latter group believes the solution lies in removing some trees from these overcrowded forests before they burn, reducing the environmental and health-related risks to people, watersheds, wildlife habitat and fish-bearing streams.

Caught betwixt and between are people whose communities and homes lay in harm's way. Many of these communities were economically shattered by federal endangered species listings that idled thousands of loggers and sawmill workers in the 1980s and 1990s. Anger overflows when federal agencies allow wildfires to run in no-harvest habitat reserves that were the source of lost timber and jobs.

No matter where you live in these United States, you have an ownership stake in the outcome of this wildfire debate and the fateful question it invites. Do we turn to Forestry for answers, or do we leave our national forests in Nature's hands?

Here's my thought. We Americans own 193 million acres of forestland in need of infinitely better care than Nature is providing. Why can't Nature deliver what we need? Because Nature is reactive and doesn't give a damn what we want or need. Forestry is proactive and very capable of seeing to it that we get what we want and need in perpetuity.

So, which is it? Good Fire or Bad Wildfire? Proactive or reactive? Let Nature or Helping hands-on?

Again, Peter Kolb offers what seems to be the most rational starting point. "Fire is a tool, not a solution. Indians used fire for eons to create habitat for deer and elk they hunted, clear cropland, keep trails open and create defensible space around their villages."

In Kolb's opinion, the best one-two management option for forests that have grown too dense is thinning first, then prescribed fire – intentionally ignited to clear away remaining woody debris, the first fuel to burn when wildfires start.

"Thinning works beautifully in Intermountain dry-site forests dominated by mixed conifer tree species," he says.

Unfortunately, thinning has become a lightning rod among environmentalists who favor allowing big wildfires to run their course without regard to the economic or environmental damage done. In hopes of delaying proposed thinnings until the trees rot or burn, opponents routinely sue the Forest Service in federal court. The goals are always the same: delay the project until its trees have no commercial value. Block all efforts to use thinning and prescribed fire to restore natural resiliency in at-risk national forests.

We'll have much more to say about this in subsequent chapters. For now, it is enough for you to know that the oft-quoted notion that our wildfire pandemic is "the new normal" is ridiculous on its face. If anything, what we have here is the "new abnormal," a set of forest conditions far outside what forest ecologists call "the range of natural variability."

Forestry's many disciplines provide the tools we need to nudge our national forests back into their range of natural variability by restarting the self-correcting processes that encourage a natural genetic resistance to the insects and diseases that are devouring our national forests. Thinning and prescribed fire are two of the most important tools Forestry offers.

And why aren't we using these tools? Because getting re-elected is more important to many members of Congress than rescuing the West's national forests from their fiery deaths. They fund

their campaigns with contributions from special interest groups whose wealthy anti-forestry donors cling to a celestial belief that Nature knows best. The environmental and economic losses that accompany killing wildfires simply don't matter to them.

Thankfully, Congress has taken a more informed approach to the many communicable diseases that killed millions of Americans before life-saving vaccines were developed for: diphtheria, smallpox, malaria, polio, whooping cough, measles, typhoid fever, Spanish flu, tuberculosis and pneumonia.

Of course, the vaccine miracle hasn't stopped the anti-vaxxers from slandering pharmaceutical companies who manufacture these drugs or doctors and public health officials who administer them. Do you see a life-threatening pattern here? You will in due course, and you will learn more about the health threats posed by carcinogenic wildfire smoke that fills our lungs for months every summer.

Conservationist Brian Cotton stands beneath several old growth ponderosa pines that were protected from wildfire by removing hundreds of small diameter pines that surrounded them.

How many cigarettes in a burning tree?

I had a hissy fit one morning last spring – 2018 – just as we were heading into yet another godawful wildfire season in northern Idaho. So, I did something I rarely do. I posted my tirade on our website. It was titled "How many cigarettes in a burning tree."[52]

This morning I reread it. I still like what I said – enough so that I've cut and pasted it here. See what you think:

A cigarette is what, three inches long?

A burning tree is anywhere from 100 to 250 feet tall.

How many cigarettes in a burning tree?

No one knows…

Not the American Cancer Society.

Not the American Lung Association.

Not the Centers for Disease Control.

Not even the U.S. Forest Service, which will soon be sending young men and women into harm's way to fight the country's godawful forest fires.

In fact, none of these organizations has anything to say about the risks of cancer-causing chemicals found in the wildfire smoke that will be invading young lungs during the 2018 fire season. So far as I know, we here at *Evergreen* are the only ones thus far willing to pin the bell on this cat. We hope to change that this year.

The American Cancer Society and the American Lung Association both have lots to say about cigarettes and air pollution. And they should. It's their job.

Shouldn't they also be waving red flags about wildfire smoke?

They don't seem to think so.

52 

I'll give my friends at the Forest Service a pass on this one. They are funding research aimed at identifying the long list of deadly chemicals found in wildfire smoke. Google "smoke from wildland fires" and you'll be led to scads of studies dealing with wildfire smoke and how wildland firefighters are prepared for risking their lives and health on fire lines.

Now that Congress and most of the West's state legislatures are back in session, all sorts of ideas for combating "climate change" are being run up flagpoles. Climate change is pretty much the default position for gasbags who are "concerned" about air polluted by wildfire smoke.

The state legislatures in Oregon and Washington are pretty sure that raising energy taxes will improve air quality. No mention of economic impacts or – inexplicably – the health and economic losses associated with enduring months of wildfire smoke.

Most legislators in these states seem determined to whistle past the wildfire graveyard. Why? Don't they breathe the same air we breathe? Meanwhile, California Assemblyman, Tim Grayson, a Bay Area Democrat, has introduced legislation that would make it harder for litigators to stop the construction of roads and transit projects that have already passed muster with state climate regulators.

We sympathize with Mr. Grayson's frustration with slow moving or derailed transit projects. Serial litigators are destroying our national forests – to say nothing of our rural timber economies – faster than we can grow new ones.

Litigators don't need to prove environmental

harm. Simply showing that confusing regulations have not been followed – a crap shoot at best – is sufficient. Just ask the leadership in any federal resource management agency. I doubt Assemblyman Grayson knows this. Likewise, urban legislators anywhere in our nation.

California has long been a political petri dish, much to the dread of voters in "flyover" country – the vast expanse that lies between west of the Great Smokey Mountains and east of the Cascade Range. I wonder what great public inconvenience will finally force legislators in California, Oregon and Washington to get serious about the environmental and health risks posed by these enormous wildfires and the cancerous smoke they generate.

Tom Bonnicksen's analysis of one 1990s California wildfire included an estimate that every car in California needed to be garaged for an entire year to mitigate the fire's emissions.

No one blinked. The PhD fire ecologist's report landed with a dead-cat bounce on the state legislature's front porch in Sacramento.

When will well-choreographed, fake concern for public health, safety and welfare give way to legislation that reflects genuine concern for people and the environment?

"You're lucky," a dying and disgusted forester friend told me 15 years ago. "I won't live long enough to see blood in the streets, but you will."

I hope he was wrong about the blood part.

Here's an idea ripe for California's petri dish: The federal government can't be sued without its permission. But Congress already cleared the way for such suits when it ratified the Equal Access to Justice Act. Serial litigators routinely use its provisions to help stymie Forest Service plans for reducing the risk of wildfire in National Forests.

It's time for state legislators to test the veracity of the Act by suing the federal government for sponsoring and paying serial litigators who are poisoning our air, water and citizens.

States could lose this lawsuit, but if they do there will be a citizen uprising unlike any in our country's long history. To save themselves, members of Congress who routinely cast their free environmental votes will be forced to join beleaguered rural delegations that have been trying for years to fix this damned mess.

To help set the stage, we're going to find someone who can help us figure out how many cigarettes it takes to equal the cancer-causing chemical release from a single 100-foot-tall burning tree.

A year has passed since I posted my temper tantrum and I still can't tell you have many cigarettes there are in a burning tree, but I've read dozens of reports [53] that warn about the chemical composition of wildfire smoke.

Although no one has confirmed my assertion that inhaling wildfire smoke all day the same as smoking a pack of cigarettes, every report I've read affirms my long-held belief that breathing wildfire smoke for months on end can cause lung cancer, heart disease and many lesser respiratory diseases.

And so my question: why hasn't the federal government gone after wildfire smoke culprits with the same vengeance it directed at cigarette makers? The answer is simple: *Our federal government is the culprit!* It alone holds the power to reduce the amount of wildfire smoke we inhale summer after summer. Yet the government refuses to hold itself to the same legally enforceable air quality standards it holds American industry.

A few weeks after I had my hissy fit, a friend sent me a copy of the *Montana/Idaho Wildfire Carbon Emissions Inventory for 2013-2017*. I was so astonished by the report's findings that I posted them on our website with the following editor's note:

> *I never cease to be amazed by the stuff that comes over the transom here at Evergreen. Just when I thought I'd said all that need be said for now about the cancerous risks of wildfire smoke.*
>
> *We owe a debt to the Forest Service's Shawn Urbanski for assembling this data, and the data that appears in my earlier temper tantrum, "The Pack-a-Day Club," in which I assert that the choking wildfire smoke that hung over much of the West for more than two months last summer was the easy equivalent of smoking a pack of cigarettes a day.*

Thus far, no one has contested my claim. I don't think anyone will, and the data sets that appear below help explain why.

Apart from the deadly health risks associated with wildfire

53 

smoke, there is the matter of its contribution to atmospheric pollution and, of course, climate change itself. Note the record 15,129,539 tons of carbon dioxide that Montana's wildfires generated in 2017 – more even than the 13,925,262 million tons of CO_2 that Idaho's wildfires generated in 2015.

The governors of Washington and Oregon are proposing new taxes on industrial polluters in their states, but there is no mention of the biggest air polluter of all: The West's federal lands wildfire crisis and, by extension, the United States Government. In a word: Congress.

I have no idea how many million tons of CO_2 wildfires in Oregon, Washington and California dumped into the atmosphere in 2013-2017, but I intend to find out. I do recall PhD forest ecologist, Tom Bonnicksen, telling me a few years ago about one northern California firestorm that released more pollution into the state's airsheds than all the cars in California had released in the same year.

We're going to be treated to lots of election-year posturing from the usual gasbags in the coming months, but I don't see much evidence that the West's state and federal delegations are serious about curbing the economic and environmental impacts of climate change, to say nothing of the carcinogenic risks associated with breathing wildfire smoke for months on end. If any of you think I'm wrong, tell me what I'm missing.

Meantime, here are some of the data sets Shawn Urbanski assembled.

Montana/Idaho Wildfire Carbon Emissions Inventory

Wildfire carbon emissions were calculated for Idaho and Montana for 2013 through 2017. The results are shown in the Table 1 and Figure 1. To allow further context a graph is provided of acres burned over the last 13 years compared to the number of wildfire data flags for the same year (Figure 2). The method used to calculate emissions is on page 124.

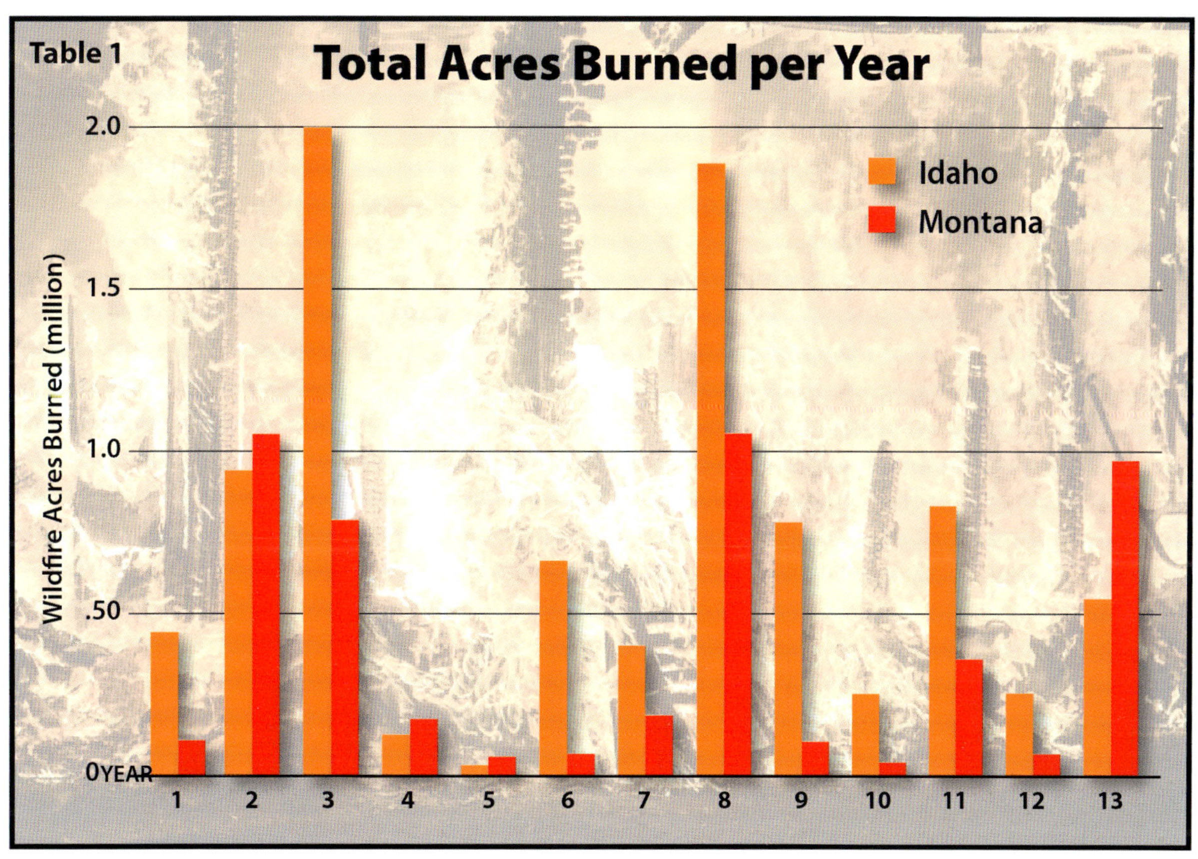

Figure 1

Parameter	Year	Montana	Idaho
Area Burned (acres)			
	2013	89,923	752,455
	2014	24,762	232,597
	2015	337,572	793,410
	2016	52,431	231,686
	2017	922,038	512,023
CO_2 Emissions (tons)			
	2013	2,443,791	10,830,746
	2014	260,911	2,648,319
	2015	8,327,930	13,925,262
	2016	1,033,597	4,907,299
	2017	15,129,539	6,590,812
CO Emissions (tons)			
	2013	230,116	1,021,286
	2014	17,060	251,012
	2015	825,666	1,369,736
	2016	86,156	403,165
	2017	1,252,740	517,325
$PM_{2.5}$ Emissions (tons)			
	2013	37,216	165,237
	2014	2,666	40,261
	2015	134,042	222,276
	2016	14,752	68,726
	2017	214,06	486,914
CH_4 Emissions (tons)			
	2013	11,128	49,651
	2014	754	12,206
	2015	40,291	66,991
	2016	4,660	21,743
	2017	67,669	27,632
Hg Emissions (tons)			
	2013	0.21	0.93
	2014	0.02	0.23
	2015	0.72	1.21
	2016	0.09	0.41
	2017	1.26	0.55

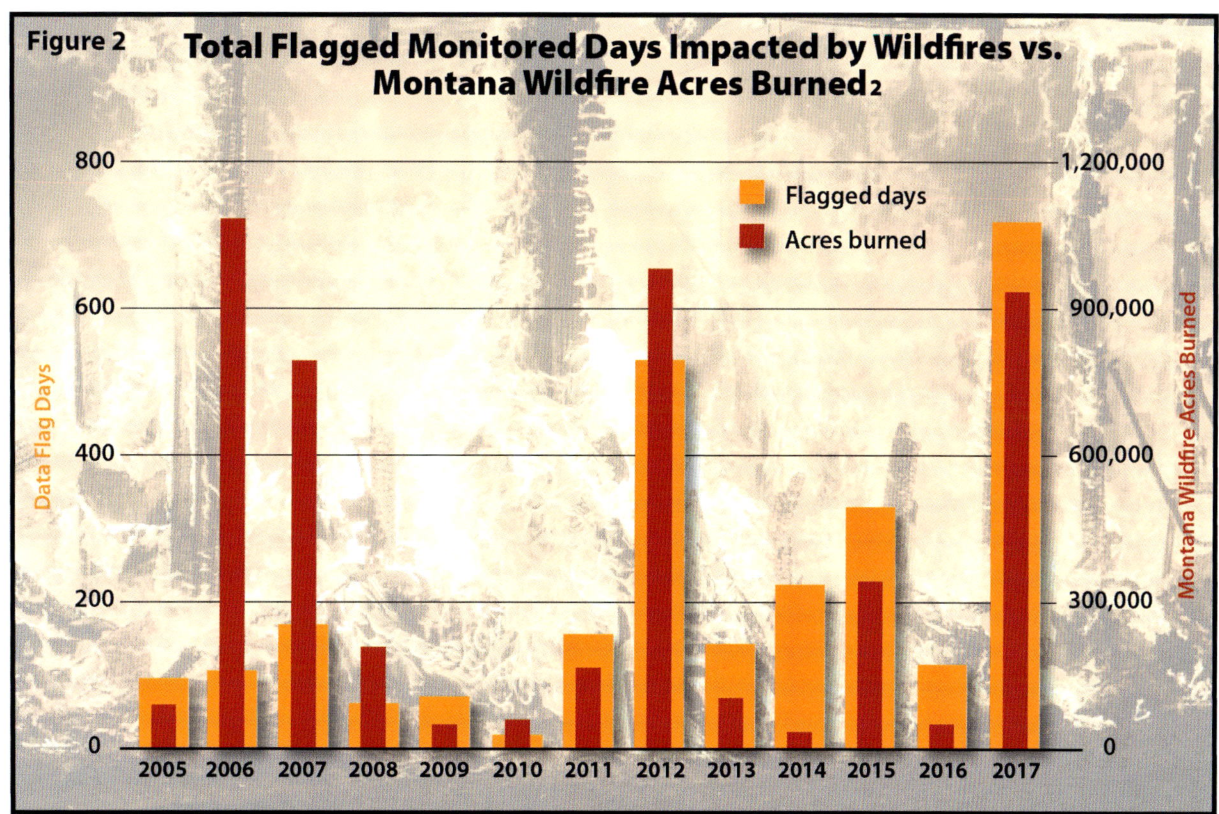

Number of monitored days that were flagged by Montana DEQ staff as having been impacted by wildfires during a year shown along with the number of wildfire acres burned during that year. 2

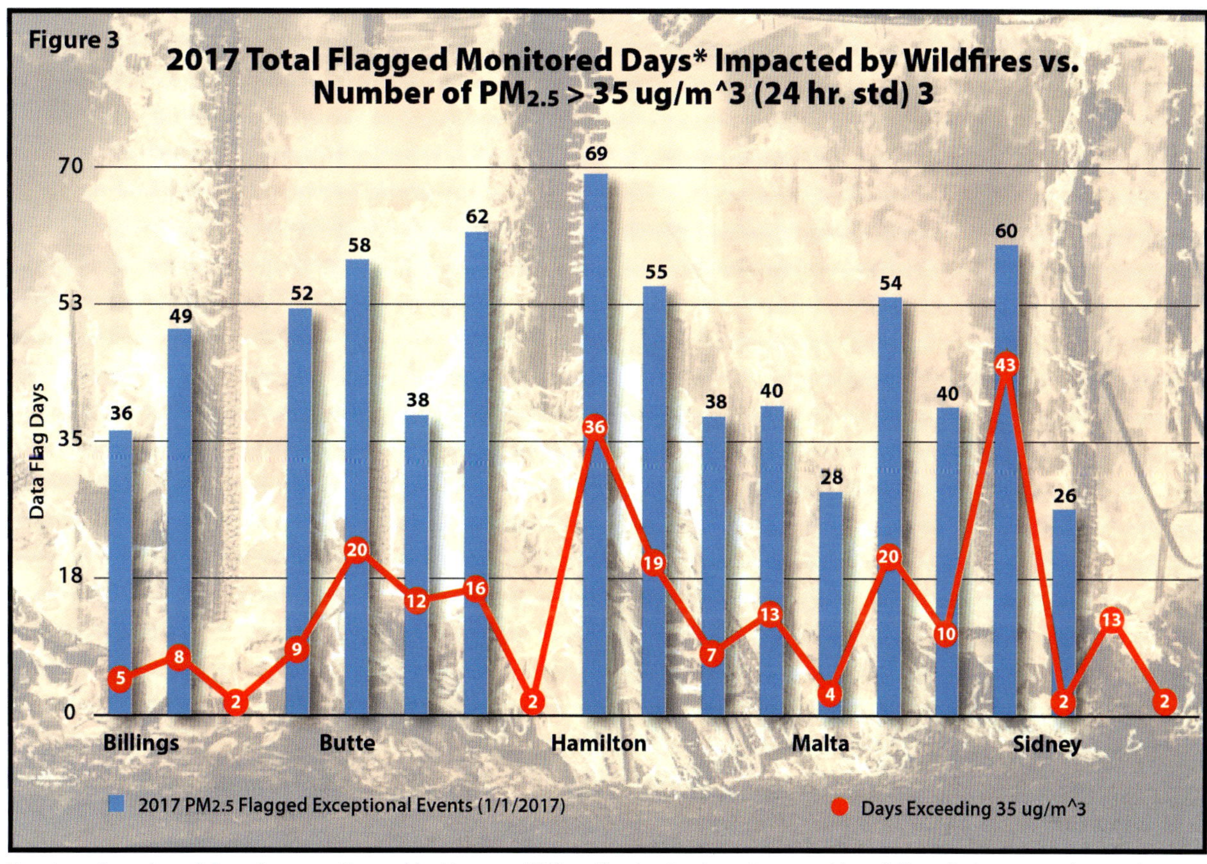

Number of monitored days that were flagged by Montana DEQ staff as having been impacted by wildfires during a year shown along with the number of times that the 24 -hour average ambient fine particulate matter ($PM_{2.5}$) concentration exceeded the corresponding National Ambient Air Quality Standard (NAAQS) level of 35 micrograms per cubic meter (ug/m^3).

Year to Date Wildfire Emission Inventory

2013 through 2017 carbon dioxide (CO_2), carbon monoxide (CO), methane (CH_4), particulate matter with an aerodynamic diameter of 2.5 microns or less ($PM_{2.5}$), and mercury (Hg) emission estimates for wildfires in Montana and Idaho have been estimated by Shawn Urbanski, United States Forest Service. This describes the methodology used to derive the emission estimates.

Methodology

Fire emission of pollutant X (EX) may be estimated as the product of area burned (A; m2), fuel load (F; kg-dry vegetation m-2), combustion completeness (C; unitless), and specific emission factor for X (EFX; [g-compound X] [kg-dry vegetation burned-1]) (Urbanski et al., 2011 and references therein):

$$EX = A \times F \times C \times 0.001 \times EFX \qquad (1)$$

Equation (1) was used to estimate annual fire emissions of CO2, CO, CH4, PM2.5, and Hg from wildfires in Montana and Idaho. The methods and data sources used to estimate EX are described in the following sections.

Area Burned, A

Burned area polygons were compiled using four burned area/fire activity datasets: Monitoring Trends in Burn Severity (MTBS) fire boundaries (https://www.mtbs.gov\/direct-download; last access August 18, 2017), the Moderate Resolution Imaging Spectroradiometer (MODIS) active-fire based Direct Broadcast Monthly Burned Area Product, the incident fire perimeters from the Geospatial Multi-Agency Coordination Wildland Fire Support archive (GEOMAC - http://www.geomac.gov/index.shtml) and a spatial wildfire occurrence database (FOD).

Fuel Load, F

The fuel load for the area burned was estimated from an overlay of the fire perimeters with vegetation and fuel loading maps. Forest vegetation type and fuel loading was assigned using an expanded version of the Fuels Type Group (FTG) fuel classification system [Keane 2013], which used recently available Forest Inventory and Analysis (FIA - https://www.fia.fs.fed.us/library/database-documentation/index.php fuels data. The forest surface fuel loading was augmented with fuel loading estimates of understory fuels [Wilson et al., 2013] and canopy fuels, the latter which was derived from FIA plot Treelist tables. Rangeland fuels were estimated using the Rangeland Vegetation Simulator (RVS) [Reeves, 2016]. Woody and herbaceous fuel loading was quantified using the inputs from LANDFIRE (https://www.landfire.gov), in addition to using the normalized difference vegetation index (NDVI) from MODIS for herbaceous material.

Fuel Consumption, C

Fuel consumption for forest surface, understory, shrub and herbaceous fuels was estimated from simulations using the fire effects models CONSUME [Prichard et al., 2006] and First Order Fire Effects Model (FOFEM; http://www.firelab.org/science-applications/fire-fuel/111-fofem) [Lutes, 2016a].

Emission Factors, EFX

Emission factors for CO_2, CO, $PM_{2.5}$, and CH_4 used modified combustion efficiency (MCE) values, fire types and emissions factors for western forests [Urbanski 2017]. Emission factor for Hg was based on Wiedinmyer and Friedli (2007) Environ. Sci. Technol., 2007, 41 (23), pp 8092-8098.

References

Forest Inventory and Analysis (FIA), Data and Tools: https://www.fia.fs.fed.us/tools-data/, last access: 10 April 2017, 2015.

Forest Inventory and Analysis (FIA): The Forest Inventory and Analysis Database: Database description and user guide version 6.0.1 for Phase 3, U.S. Department of Agriculture, Forest Service, 182 pp., available at: https://www.fia.fs.fed.us/library/database-documentation/index.php, last access: 27 April 2017, 2014.

GEOMAC: Geospatial Multi-Agency Coordination Group, Wildland Fire Support, Services and Data: https://www.geomac.gov/, last access: 12 November 2012, 2012.

Keane, R. E., Herynk, J. M., Toney, C., Urbanski, S. P., Lutes, D. C., Ottmar, R. D.: Evaluating the performance and mapping of three fuel classification systems using Forest Inventory and Analysis surface fuel measurements, Forest Ecology and Management, 305, 248-263, https://doi.org/10.1016/j.foreco.2013.06.001, last access: 27 April 2017, 2013.

LANDFIRE, LANDFIRE Project, U.S. Department of Interior, Geological Survey: https://www.landfire.gov/ , last access: 28 April 2017, 2017.

Lutes, D.C.: FOFEM: First Order Fire Effects Model v6.3 User Guide, available at: https://www.firelab.org/project/fofem, last access: 27 April 2017, 2016a.

Prichard, S. J., Ottmar, R. D., and Anderson, G. K.: Consume 3.0 user's guide, Pacific Northwest Research Station, Corvallis, Oregon, 234 pp., available at: https://www.fs.fed.us/pnw/fera/research/smoke/consume/consume30_users_guide.pdf , last access:27 April 2017, 2006.

Reeves, M.C.: Development of the Rangeland Vegetation Simulator: A module of the Forest Vegetation Simulator, A Final Report to the Joint Fire Sciences Program, Project ID:12-1-02-15, 129 p., 2016.

Urbanski, S, Hao, WM, and Nordgren, B (2011) The wildland fire emission inventory: western United States emission estimates and an evaluation of uncertainty. Atmospheric Chemistry and Physics, 11, 12973 – 13000.

Urbanski, S.P., 2013. Combustion efficiency and emission factors for wildfire-season fires in mixed conifer forests of the northern Rocky Mountains, US. Atmos Chem Phys 13, 7241–7262. doi:10.5194/acp-13-7241-2013

Wilson, B. T., C. W. Woodall, and D. M. Griffith (2013), Imputing forest carbon stock estimates from inventory plots to a nationally continuous coverage, Carbon Balance and Management, 8, doi:10.1186/1750-0680-8-1.

I know reports like this one are more than a little daunting, but it is very important that you know that the health risks associated with exposure to wildfire smoke are real and that this isn't some scary story that I made up to sensationalize *First, put out the Fire!* Far from it.

I admit that I was tempted to title this chapter "Smoke Deniers," because there is a lot of hokum swirling around the "climate change" debate that can easily divert your attention from the fact that there is much we can do to significantly reduce the amount of carcinogenic smoke our wildfires belch into the atmosphere every summer. We simply aren't doing it – thanks to the political influence of people who distrust science and see nothing morally or ethically wrong with allowing nature to burn our western national forests to the ground.

Last week, I sat in on a Forest Service-sponsored webinar titled *Wildfire Fighter Smoke Exposure and Risk of Lung Cancer and Cardiovascular Disease Mortality.*

It was as close to an actual autopsy as I hope to ever get.

Host Kathleen Navarro, a PhD at the University of California Berkeley, ran us through some of the latest field research involving wildland firefighters. These are tough-as-nails men and women who spend long months on torturous fire lines every summer. There is an esprit de corps in their DNA that merits our respect and thanks, but I wonder if they know that among career firefighters the risk of lung cancer increases 43 percent and the risk of heart disease 25 percent. Or do they know that the heart attacks kill more wildland firefighters than fire.

And, again, I wonder why our government is sending young men and women into harm's way when there is so much we could and should be doing to reduce the size, frequency and destructiveness of these wildfires. Why aren't we doing it? How many innocents must die in wildfires like the one that leveled Paradise, California last summer? *This will happen again – and again.*

Here are the links to dozens of studies that help define and quantify the health hazards associated with wildfire smoke. You decide, but first do your homework.

How many cigarettes in a burning tree?

Part of your assignment is to sign up for a nifty "citizen science" project developed by the EPA. It's called "Smoke Sense," [54] and its purpose is to give you the opportunity to report what you are experiencing when you can't see a half-block down your street for all the damned wildfire smoke.

The app is amazing. Works for Android and iOS. Among its features:

- Current and forecasted air quality information
- Maps showing current fire locations and plumes
- A log for reporting personal health symptoms and smoke observations
- A learning module about air pollution, wildland fire and health impacts
- Reward badges for completing tasks

I'm not much for reward badges at my age, but I'm signing up and reporting what I experience. I don't know if it will do any good but after what we experienced in northern Idaho and western Montana in July, August and September I'll try anything that might help awaken our conflicted federal government.

More on that in the next chapters.

54

CHAPTER 24

Thanks Smokey!

I have been packing flyrods with me since I was eight years old – 67 years. I fish for all of the same reasons cited by Michigan Supreme Court, John Voelker, in *The Testament of a Fisherman*, a small act of rebellion he assembled in 1964 under the pen name, Robert Travers. He also wrote the best-selling *Anatomy of a Murder* under the same pen name. Here's his *Testament:*

> *I fish because I love to;*
> *Because I love the environs where trout are found, which are invariably beautiful, and hate the environs where crowds of people are found, which are invariably ugly;*
> *Because of all the television commercials, cocktail parties, and assorted social posturing I thus escape;*
> *Because, in a world where most men seem to spend their lives doing things they hate, my fishing is at once an endless source of delight and an act of small rebellion;*
> *Because trout do not lie or cheat and cannot be bought or bribed or impressed by power, but respond only to quietude and humility and endless patience;*
> *Because I suspect that men are going along this way for the last time, and I for one don't want to waste the trip; because mercifully there are no telephones on trout waters;*
> *Because only in the woods can I find solitude without loneliness;*
> *Because bourbon out of an old tin cup always tastes better out there;*
> *Because maybe one day I will catch a mermaid;*
> *And, finally, not because I regard fishing as being so terribly important but because I suspect that so many of the other concerns of men are equally unimportant – and not nearly so much fun.*

I bought my first flyrod – a three-piece, eight-and-a-half foot seven-weight – when I was still in high school. Joe Inama, an old Italian rod maker who emigrated from Italy to my hometown in the 1950s built it as a thank-you gift for Mayo Rinaldi, a friend who sold Joe's dry flies out of the back of his pickup on the North Fork of the Coeur d'Alene River.

I bought hundreds of Joe's flies from Mayo, whom I also knew well because we were neighbors on Mission Avenue and I had worked with him in a blacksmith shop in the summer of 1963. Mayo let me use the rod a couple of times so I knew what a fabulous find it was. I pestered him all summer about buying the rod and he finally caved in just before I headed off to the University of Idaho.

It turned out to be the last rod Joe ever built. He gave up rod building because he was going blind. As the darkness closed in he slowly lost the ability to slice Tonkin cane into equilateral triangles to a tolerance of one thousandth of an inch. The rod's smooth-as-glass finish hides the fact that the triangular slices are glued together to form a hexagonal square.

I still use Joe's Last Rod at least once a year, usually on the same day I haul out my two-piece five-weight Hardy Palakona, built in England in the early 1950s, and a gorgeous two-piece six-weight Dennis Burenak rod, a gift from my stepson.

Glen Brackett, who owned the Winston Rod Company in Twin Bridges, Montana rewrapped and refinished Joe's rod and the Hardy maybe 20 years ago. When he found out I was still using the rods he politely suggested that they belonged in a display case on the wall in my office. I thanked him for his suggestion and still use the rods because the waters of memory run deep over both rods.

What does my long-winded fish tale have to do with wildfires?

Just this. Smoke from at least a dozen wildfires – two in Canada – drove my wife and me off the Kootenai River in the summer of 2017 at the height of what my guide friend, Dave Blackburn, calls "hopper-mania," a two-week period in August when the grassy banks along the Kootenai are alive with big juicy grasshoppers.

Rainbows in the six-pound range prowl the shallows in hopes that an exhausted hopper will tumble into the river. Sometimes they get so close to the bank that their dorsal fins break the surface. They look like sharks cruising the shoreline.

Dave calls these moments "hoppertunities." Yeah, I know, way too corny, but what can I say? Dave and I have been friends for 30 years. Two other pals who fished with us for years are both gone now. Leigh Johnson last November and Bill Closs in June 2011. My pal Larry – my oldest friend – never made it. Cancer killed him 18 years ago. But he gave me his drift boat about a month before he died. Now he travels the Kootenai with us in spirit.

Speaking of hoppertunities, I'm still mad about the ones Julia and I missed during our lost summer on the Kootenai. It was so smoky on the river that you couldn't see more than a hundred feet in any direction. The air took on a brownish hue that turned the warm summer sun into an orange ball the size of a quarter.

While we packed up our rods and kayaks, Dave busied himself cancelling more than $20,000 in cabin rentals and guided float trips. My friend might be a cornball at times, but he's honest to a fault. You can't fish when you can't breathe.

We were hardly alone. Millions were forced indoors at the peak of the summer vacation season: anglers, bicyclists, four-wheelers, golfers, hikers, boaters and campers of all kinds, berry pickers, wildlife lovers, you name it. All indoors and not spending money in the great outdoors.

According to the Outdoor Industry Association, tourism is a $254 *billion* a year industry in the 11 western states. I don't know how much tourists spend during the summer travel season, but during our lost summer, western Montana, all of northern Idaho and most of Oregon, Washington and northern California – an area larger than the state of Texas plus Maryland and Massachusetts – was shrouded in acrid wildfire smoke so thick you could chew it.

You could have fired a cannon across the Coeur d'Alene Resort's world-famous golf course – with its equally famous floating green – and not hit anyone. Ditto any other golf course in the region. Downtown Spokane was nearly invisible from the freeway – three blocks distant. The waterside deck at the Edgewater in Sandpoint, one of our favorite summer watering holes, was inhabitable. Likewise, every other outdoor venue in northern Idaho and eastern Washington.

At Beyond Hope Resort on Pend Oreille Lake, 40 minutes east of Sandpoint, you could not see Memaloose Island, no more than a quarter-mile distant. The aptly named resort shut down its restaurant – one of northern Idaho's best – cancelled its Labor Day weekend Music on the Lawn festival and told its 100 or so RV guests to go home. We were the last to leave. In no more than two hours, the lakeshore park became a ghost town.

Three hours east, at Seeley Lake, Montana, carcinogenic smoke from the Rice Ridge Fire was the worst since air quality monitoring began in Big Sky Country in 1967. You could not see any of the 30 or so mountain peaks that rise more than a mile into the sky east and west of town. On the worst days, visibility fell to less than 100 feet. Townspeople stayed indoors and tourists stayed away.

Small wonder. When the sky above sylvan Seeley Lake is blue, this is one of the prettiest places on earth. Look west into the Swan Range and 11,000-foot Swan Peak. Look east into the Rockies and 9,300-foot Holland Peak, gateway to the 1.5 million-acre Bob Marshall Wilderness Complex.

Hiking, climbing, elk hunting and fly fishing. Minutes north of town, the Swan River begins its northbound journey to Flathead Lake. East, the South Fork of the Flathead River drains much of the Bob Marshall. Both rivers offer spectacular fishing for stunningly beautiful West Slope cutthroat trout.

East and west of Seeley Lake, more than a dozen peaks hold snow for most of the year. Sometimes all year. State-owned monitoring stations generally record about 35 micrograms of particulate matter per cubic foot per hour around Seeley Lake. But in one 24-hour period in early September billowing Rice Ridge smoke pushed monitors beyond their maximum 1,000 micrograms per cubic foot, 20 times the norm. It was as though the Missions and the Rockies and all the beauty they hold had disappeared from the face of the earth.

If this Story of Smoke seems a bit like overkill to you, imagine what it is like for those of us who breathe it for seemingly endless months summer after summer. Imagine watching your summer disappear from view. Welcome to Sisters, a pretty little enclave east of Oregon's Cascades, about three hours southeast of Portland.

Wealthy Portlanders own palatial vacation homes here. Some come for the skiing at nearby Mt. Bachelor. Others come to fish the legendary Metolius River. Most everyone makes the same thing for dinner: reservations at any of several toney restaurants in downtown Sisters.

Putrid smoke from the August-September 2017 Milli Fire shut down Sisters at the height of its Labor Day tourist season. Although comparatively small by present day standards – a mere 25,000 acres – Milli forced Sisters to cancel its annual $150 per ticket Folk Music Festival. The town's art galleries, restaurants and motels lost more than $1 million over the long weekend.

By August 17, six days after the fire was spotted, 650 homes stood in harm's way and the Forest Service advised the town's 1,600 residents to prepare to evacuate. What began as a "look see" by a seven-member helitack crew that rappelled into the area on August 13, ended with 673 on fire lines, backed by bulldozers, air tankers and helicopters. Milli was finally controlled September 24.

Julia and I sat in on a webinar last fall in which the Forest Service attempted to explain its apparent decision to allow Milli to run for several days before realizing that it was headed straight toward Sisters. I don't think anyone on the call bought it. There was too much humming and hawing and too little accountability from several nervous voices on the other end of our cell phones.

Never mentioned was the fact that the lightning-caused fire had burned its way through unsalvaged standing dead timber killed by the 2006 Black Crater Fire. Nor was there any mention of the brush fields that quickly recolonized the Black Crater site following the site.

Had dead timber and woody debris been removed following the 2006 fire, Milli might have been slowed or stopped there, but with so much bone-dry debris still present, the fire had more than enough fuel to continue its run toward Sisters.

Nothing like this would have happened had the 2006 Black Crater Fire burned on state, tribal or private timberland. Burnt trees would have been quickly removed and the area replanted. Not so in national forests. Salvage is routinely ruled out by the Forest Service because hard-core environmentalists claim salvaging dead timber is "like mugging a burn victim."

A half-century of post-fire salvage logging in western Oregon proves this isn't the case. Millions of acres are green and growing today because needed salvage and replanting work was promptly completed by landowners – including the Forest Service before it lost sight of its own mission statement: caring for the land, serving people. I wish.

It wasn't as bad on the Kootenai River last summer, but we did get to share the canyon below Kootenai falls with two giant twin-rotor Chinooks from Columbia Helicopters. The Aurora, Oregon company provides aerial firefighting services for the Forest Service, and on the day in question, the big machine was assigned to a wildfire burning in timber near the top of the rocky canyon, so the airship's pilots were round-tripping the fire every four minutes.

Columbia's Chinooks are all business. Behind the pilot and co-pilot there is an internal tank that holds 2,000 gallons of water. Onboard pumps can fill the tank in about two minutes via an umbilical hose that sucks water from its source – on this morning the depths of the Kootenai River.

I know the Columbia story well because my late friend, Wes Lematta, was the company's founder, and because Wes asked me some years ago to assemble the history of the Columbia's first

Choking wildfire smoke killed tourism in western Montana and northern Idaho for most of July and August in the summers of 2017 and 2018.

50 years. Flying Finns remains one of the most uplifting stories I've ever written.

On the morning in question, with rotor mist showering our drift boat, I got to thinking about how Wes and Jack Erickson had pioneered helicopter logging for the Forest Service in the early 1970s. In 1971, I wrote several newspaper stories about the experimental sale Wes and Jack completed near Lobster Creek on the lower end of southern Oregon's Rogue River. I spent two days photographing an S-64 at work. I can still call up visuals from memory.

Over the years that followed, Wes frequently lamented the Forest Service's reluctance to thin fire-prone forests. He would have gladly traded the $10,000 an hour the government pays for Columbia Chinooks on fire-lines for less profitable logs that weren't burnt to a crisp. But that was just Wes.

I got well acquainted with wildfires the year after I started *Evergreen* Magazine. The 1987 Silver Fire pumped so damned much smoke into the Rogue Valley that we all drove around for two weeks with our headlights on, day and night.

The smoke was so thick that birds were disoriented. One morning I awoke to the sounds of geese honking in our yard. I walked outside to see where they were and found them sitting on the limbs of big oak trees in the front yard. When I turned around to walk back in the house I counted 25 sitting on the ridgeline. How they managed to keep their balance on webbed feet is beyond me.

We are now engulfed in fill-in-the-blank wildfire seasons. The world-renowned Shakespeare Festival at Ashland, Oregon booked a $2 million loss for its 2018 season after wildfire smoke forced the cancellation of 26 outdoor shows. The nearby Britt Festival at Jacksonville fared better but still had to cancel several of its evening concerts. Smoke forced cancellation of high school athletic events all over the West in late August and early September.

The 2017 Eagle Fire in the Columbia Gorge east of Portland scorched 50,000 acres and shut down dozens of tourist-dependent businesses in the Hood River-Cascade Locks area. It was started by foolish teenage boys tossing firecrackers from a trail overlooking the Gorge. Portland was engulfed in smoke and winds drove sparks across the mile-wide Columbia River into dry timber on the Washington side.

Blessedly, the fire's advance was slowed by towering basalt cliffs but it took heavy fall rain to extinguish the last embers. Two years later, rehabilitation crews were still picking up the pieces along landslide-prone Interstate 84. On May 21, 2018, Seventh Circuit Court Judge, John Olson, Portland, handed the family of one 15-year-old Vancouver, Washington boy a firefighting bill for $36 million.

Since 2000, our nation has lost 135 million acres of mostly publicly-owned forest and rangeland to wildfire. Here in the West, we lost 6.6 million acres in 2018, the greatest losses occurring in California, where 1.8 million acres were burned and 86 perished when the Camp Fire incinerated otherworldly named Paradise.

And still there are hard-core environmentalists who believe we should let these godawful fires burn out on their own. "It's natural," they declare from what they perceive to be the moral high ground. There is nothing more about the ground they occupy or the words they utter.

On and on it goes. Where does it end? Who will end it – and how?

The minimalist approach that Congress and the Forest Service have taken isn't working – and it won't. You can't conquer a 90-million acre forest health crisis a few thousand acres at a time. Yet that is the crippling restriction placed on "forest restoration" projects by politically influential hard-core environmentalists who favor allowing killing wildfires to burn out on their own. No firefighters. Just wildfire, no matter the environmental or economic losses.

Why such a senseless approach? Because they are luddites who hate the free enterprise system that provides the technology and boots-on-the-ground know how needed to reduce the risk of catastrophic wildfire in forests the rest of us love and need – before they burn.

Where are the big picture thinkers who invented Smokey Bear? Legendary illustrator, Albert Staehle, who also gave us Borden's Elsie the Cow, drew Smokey for the Forest Service in October of 1944. He was pouring a bucket of water on a campfire, reminding campers to be sure to douse their fires.

The story of Smokey is historically and environmentally significant, so much so that it bears repeating, if only for the fact that his federally protected image is the most recognized advertising symbol on earth.

Moreover, Smokey's sonorous six-word admonition - "Only YOU Can Prevent Forest Fires" - now recited on radio by actor, Sam Elliot, embodies the longest running public service campaign in American in history. Who in American cannot recite it from memory?

Smokey's story begins not long after the Japanese bombed Pearl Harbor in December of 1941. Many feared the Japanese were capable of bombing the U.S. mainland and, in fact, they did at least three times from small airplanes launched from submarines moored off the Pacific Coast.

Although no damage was done, the bombings underscored the fact that west coast Douglas-fir and redwood forests might be set afire by incendiary bombs. And with millions of able-bodied young men marching off to war, who would fight any forest fires the attacks might cause in timber that was urgently needed to support the war effort?

In hopes of transforming public fear into pubic action, the Forest Service quickly organized the Cooperative Forest Fire Prevention Program with the help of the War Advertising Council and the Association of State Foresters.

The triumvirate created a series of posters and slogans that supported war preparedness: "Forest Fires Aid the Enemy" and "Our Carelessness, Their Secret Weapon." Their big break came in 1944 when The Walt Disney Company loaned its Bambi characters to the campaign for one year. Albert Staehle's first Smokey poster followed in October of 1944.

The "real" Smokey did not arrive on the scene until 1950, when firefighters rescued a frightened black bear cub from a tree scorched by wildfire on New Mexico's Lincoln National Forest. His paws and legs had been singed. His burns treated, he was soon given to the National Zoo in Washington, D.C., where he lived until he died in 1976.

It did not take long for Cooperative Fire Prevention Program leaders to realize that in "Hotfoot Teddy" they had the living symbol they needed to replace the Bambi characters Disney had loaned the campaign.

In 1952, the renamed Smokey got his own song, the Ballad of Smokey The Bear, written by Steve Nelson and Jack Rollins and sung by country music legend, Eddie Arnold. Nelson and Rollins added "the" to Smokey's name to keep their musical score in rhythm. Which is why most folks call him Smokey The Bear.

I am well acquainted with Smokey because we use him in the annual Christmas Parade here in Coeur d' Alene, Idaho. He comes complete with a 17-page rule book describing what he can and cannot do, a bear costume purchased from a Forest Service authorized manufacturer and a list of do's and don'ts concerning the costume's handling. His jeans are always blue, his eyes dark brown and his belt buckle gold. And he carries a round-point shovel, not a square-point.

Our Smokey works on fire crews for the Idaho Department of Lands, which also loans us a beautifully restored 1948 fire truck that is permanently assigned to parade duty, though it does have a fully operational pumping system.

Trust me when I tell you Santa Claus does not possess Smokey's magnetism with children. I think it is because Santa can be seen anywhere and everywhere during the Christmas holidays, but during Coeur d' Alene's sparkling holiday season, Smokey will only be found in our Christmas parade.

Julia and I walk the three-mile parade route beside a loaded log truck that we decorate with colorful lights. Fitting because this is an evening parade and our Sherman Avenue route reminds me of that unforgettable scene from "It's A Wonderful Life." There is Jimmy Stewart running through the snow looking frantically for anything that looks like the Bedford Falls he knew before he wished himself dead and Potter turned his hometown into Sodom and Gomorrah.

Smokey rides behind us on the fire truck waving to thousands who line the curbs. Kids love the Olsen Logging truck because it's big and it has an ear-shattering air horn that Dusty Howerton, our 75-year-old driver, loves to blow. Actually, his grandkids who ride with him in the cab take turns blowing the horn.

Children that line the parade route also love Smokey for who he is and what he represents in their young lives. They all look to be five, six, seven, maybe 10 years old. We can hear them yelling, "Smokey, Smokey, Smokey." How do they know this bear that waves at them from the back of an old fire truck?

They are much too young to know anything about our tiresome and self-defeating wildfire debate, but they know all about Smokey and his tireless efforts to protect them and all the animals in the forest from wildfire.

What is Smokey's power and where do we find more of it? When do we stop whistling past the graveyards our forests are becoming? When do we stop storing carbon in our lungs? When will we again speak of economic and environmental wellbeing in the same sentence? Why is this taboo an either-or proposition?

Some say Smokey is to blame for our wildfire mess because he symbolizes our nation's post-war obsession with putting out forest fires as quickly as possible.

I say we need to stop this banal debate before it's too late. Banal as in trite, hackneyed, cliched, platitudinous, vapid, tired, hoary, unimaginative and humdrum. Pick your adjective but stop now!

Let's ask Smokey to lead us out of our burning forests. Let's implore him to explain the difference between Good Fire and Bad Fire. Let's put him in the cab of a mechanical harvester and show us how to carefully thin a ready-to-burn forest. Let's team him up with a logger and a conservationist with big personalities and even bigger ideas. Add a lumberman and a carpenter to show where the logs go.

God only knows how much forestland Smokey has protected from smoldering campfires and glowing cigarettes tossed from car windows over the last 75 years, but it must run into the millions of acres. His friendly reminder to be careful with fire is as timely as it ever was – and it still resonates with unmatched power and simplicity: Only YOU Can Prevent Forest Fires.

Where is this genius today? Where are our leaders? Where is our courage?

Thanks Smokey, for reminding us that all of us share a moral and ethical responsibility to protect and care for our forests.

How do you want your smoke?

The worst place on earth to store carbon is in our lungs!

The best places to store it is in trees or wood products.

Paul Hessburg, a well-respected landscape ecologist with the U.S. Forest Service frames the carbon discussion in a bluntly-asked question that speaks to the inevitability of fire in forests: How do you want your smoke?

I love the question because it forces the debate about our wildfire pandemic into the open in a way that can't be ignored by loopy people who believe we should allow our killing wildfires to burn themselves out "naturally."

This silly idea makes no sense to me. Remember the Big Five: clean air, clean water, abundant fish and wildlife habitat, a wealth of year-round outdoor recreation opportunity and beautiful forests.

You won't find much of the Big Five amid the black sticks and rubble left behind by big wildfires that burn everything in sight.

Hessburg's question begs the obvious: what to do about the billions of tons of nasty smoke that wildfires are pumping into the air we breathe?

If forest fires are inevitable – and they are – what might we do to reduce their size and frequency and thus amount of smoke they are depositing in our lungs?

Hessburg – among many – contends that increasing the use of "prescribed fire" [Good Fire] will reduce the number and size of our wildfires [Bad Fire]. I agree.

Hessburg also advocates for something called "managed fire." Allowing big wildfires to run if they pose little or no risk to community safety. I understand the premise, but I struggle mightily with the whole idea of allowing wildfires to do the clean-up work Congress refuses to do in our forests.

Why does Congress refuse? Because most in the House and Senate represent urban and metropolitan constituencies on the east and west coasts. Folks like my Bronx cabdriver friend who asked me if there were any trees left out West.

Danny O'Neill's big fear was that "greedy" loggers and lumbermen were destroying the West's national forests. He'd never been out of New York's five boroughs, which was why he asked me if there were any trees left out west. He thought maybe he'd drive west sometime for a closer look.

Danny and millions more like him are easy prey for the "let burn" crowd that sees logging as capitalism run wild – the absolute worst thing that Congress should ever permit in our national forests.

For the record, industrial-scale logging hasn't occurred in a western national forest in close to 40 years. Nor is it likely to ever occur again. Yes, some thinning is occurring in national forests, but not nearly enough to reduce the size, frequency and destructive power of our wildfire crisis.

How does thinning help reduce the risk of wildfire? By removing diseased, dying and dead trees that are the primary ignition sources on about 100 million national forest acres in the West. This is an area larger than all but our three largest states: Alaska, Texas and California.

The wildfire-smoke issue matters to westerners for many reasons, none more important than the environmental and economic losses we are suffering. Almost 75 percent of all forestland in the West – some 120 million acres – is held in 84 of

Research Landscape Ecologist, Paul Hessburg, PhD., U.S. Forest Service, is the driving force behind Era of Megafires, a spectacular one-hour presentation that explains the roots of the West's wildfire pandemic. This link leads to his research. https://scholar.google.com/scholar?q=paul+hessburg+wildfires&hl=en&as_sdt=0&as_vis=1&oi=scholart

our country's 154 federally-owned national forests. What happens in the forests, which form the cornerstone of our much-admired outdoor lifestyle matters to millions of westerners.

Acrid smoke generated by our wildfire pandemic poses enormous health risks because of its long-term impacts on our hearts and lungs. This is why the answer to Paul Hessburg's question has become so important, especially in western cities where wildfire smoke has not historically been as much of a problem as it is in the rural west. Now it is – and as a result many city-dwellers are asking a question that was unthinkable a decade ago: Can thinning help reduce wildfire smoke?

It absolutely can.

It turns out that the best way to reduce the size, frequency and destructive power of big wildfires is first thin forests that hold too many trees, then clean up the mess by purposefully setting prescribed fires when it is safe to burn.

Every possible impact of this one-two combination has been studied throughout the western hemisphere. State and private forestland owners in the U.S. routinely use prescribed fire to clean up logging debris, retard growth in undesirable brush and tree species, promote growth in desirable trees and improve wildlife habitat.

Federal and state air quality regulations restrict prescribed burning to such a narrow window that in some areas, particularly here in the West, landowners find it difficult to complete their burn plans. The counter-intuitive result is that we are subjected to much longer periods of much heavier wildfire smoke than we would experience were more prescribed burning permitted.

As much as is humanly possible, prescribed fire imitates the more frequent natural fire cycle that dominated the West for eons before white settlement began following the Civil War. It also imitates Indian fires that were the subject of much controversy among early western foresters who believed the fires Indians were deliberately setting annually lead to the loss of productive forestland in northern California's lowlands.

Indians didn't have cross-cut saws or chain saws, so they used fire to clear land, create defensible space around their villages and create habitat for game animals, herbs and fruits they harvested from lands they kept clear with fire.

Indians were also America's first farmers – a fact well documented in the first written account of our "New World," written in 1575 by Hernando D'Escalante Fontaneda. His memoir describes Indian-grown palms, palmetto, vine grapes, truffles, coontie and maize. Diarists with DeSoto's army noted that the further north they marched into the Florida Panhandle, the more maize they found.

Indians all along the 2,000-mile eastern seaboard, from Plymouth, Massachusetts to the Gulf Coast taught starving white settlers how to grow crops: maize, beans, squash, peas, lettuce, chard, onions, radishes, pumpkins, wheat, barley, oats, peas and more in well-tended gardens.

Fire served many useful purposes in everyday Indian life: cooking, heating, hollowing logs for canoes, clearing land for gardens, keeping meadows and prairies open, firing pottery, as a mosquito repellant and in religious ceremonies.

The Puritan ethic white settlers brought from Europe more than 400 years ago has never allowed us to embrace fire in the same way Indians did – and still do. But prescribed fire, which certainly has its roots in Indian culture, has recaptured the public's attention, especially here in the West where many are beginning to see it as a safe and socially acceptable alternative to our wildfire crisis.

Kudos to the Forest Service's Paul Hessburg for orchestrating this long overdue transformation in public sentiment. His riveting "Era of Mega Fires" multi-media presentation, which he narrates for his audiences, has awakened thousands to the deadly consequences of ignoring the West's wildfire pandemic.

Hessburg's presentation and his research are laced with "before and after" photographs that reveal how dense our forests have become in the years since "running smoke out of the woods" became the cornerstone of the nation's forest policy. Millions of acres across the West now hold 10 to 20 times more trees than they held a century ago. It is the enormity of this unintended transformation that has Hessburg advocating for managed fire.

Apart from the ecological upheaval Hessburg describes, he cites a serious lack of capacity – the human and financial capital needed to restore natural resiliency in western forests in the 30 or so years remaining before wildfire claims whatever portion of 100 million acres that has not been restored.

Here, restoration means removing diseased, dying and dead trees from forests, then returning fire to the land – either small-scale prescribed fire or large-scale managed fire. Basically allowing wildfire to run where it doesn't pose a risk to people or communities.

I admire and respect Paul Hessburg, and I understand why he advocates for managed fire, but I struggle with what his advocacy signifies in our social order:

- It means we aren't caring for our forests the way we should.
- It reveals society's vulnerability to a lot of loopy ideas about what forest conservation means.
- It defines decades of neglect by forest product manufacturers who should have funded forestry's public relations offense but too damned cheap to do it.
- Neglect that has created a vast and lucrative feeding ground for lawyers who represent social malcontents and luddites who could not care less if the entire West burns to the ground.
- Neglect that has fostered so much upheaval inside federal resource management agencies that it is next to impossible for the Forest Service to honor its time-honored mission: caring for the land, serving the people.
- Upheaval that has forced the Forest Service to redirect more than half its $5.14 billion budget to firefighting.

Wildfire now soaks up billions of taxpayer dollars and millions of hours of staff time that should be invested in restoring resiliency in collapsing national forests. Of necessity we have created a vast and very sophisticated fire-fighting industry that now includes retrofitted 747s, 737s, Sikorsky-64 Skycranes and twin-rotor Boeing 107s and 234s.

All very impressive – but all very unnecessary had we managed our forests in ways that accommodated the frequent, low-intensity burns that were central to the West's fire-adapted forests for eons.

My use of the term "fire-adapted" comes courtesy of our Peter Kolb. His 23-year research track traces ecosystem function, soil characteristics, forest succession dynamics, tree root diseases, woody debris, wildfire and plant community recovery following wildfires, and salvage logging.

Kolb reminds me that *fire-dependent* ecosystems can't function without fire. But *fire-adapted* forests can. The northern Rockies – Montana, Wyoming, Colorado and Idaho – hold mixed conifer forests that are fire-adapted. It doesn't matter whether the disturbance is human or natural, so long as there is some form of disturbance to re-energize the system.

Kolb leads forestry tours to Germany and Austria every summer. Forests there have functioned nicely without fire for centuries because they are well-managed. Harvest-related disturbance is constant and dire predictions of nutrient depletion in forest soils has yet to occur. So much for "unsustainable forest practices."

Kolb frets constantly about what he calls "the politicization of forest science" by scientists "with big egos" who troll constantly for federal research dollars that invariably come with strings attached that pre-judge the outcome.

"There are lots of camp followers out there," Kolb laments. "People who are willing to repeat false equivalencies until they take on an air of unproven truth. It's disheartening and morally corrupt."

"And what might one of these false equivalencies be," I ask.

"Species richness would be one," Kolb answers. "Richness plays to the long-ago debunked idea that nature exists in some steady state equilibrium, so if we just leave nature alone richness is retained and the system will right itself."

"Not true?" I ask.

"Not even close," Kolb says. *"Read Discordant Harmonies,* Daniel Botkin's marvelous book about the myths and metaphors that impede our use of science to solve environmental problems."

"Yup, I've read the book," I reply. "And I've talked with Botkin at length about the string of well-funded attempts to corrupt science for nefarious political purposes by first bringing the narrative into alignment with myth. Kolb's greatest concern has been for the attempt to miscast the role of fire in forests.

"We need fire," Kolb says firmly. "But when scientists and policymakers advocate for allowing wildfires to take their own course, what we're really doing is dumbing down complex forest ecosystems in the same way we dumbed them down with blanket logging systems. We are losing the very complexity they say they are trying to reintroduce."

"And the solution?" I ask.

"Forest management should be site specific," Kolb replies. "Every drainage is different. Every change in soil composition, elevation, moisture, aspect or tree species connotes fine scale differences in management techniques. Remember, nature is reactive, not proactive. It reacts to stimuli. For example, the presence of too many trees stressed by prolonged drought. Human beings constitute the only proactive force in nature. The decisions we make determine what nature delivers. It's that simple."

Ah, but that it were truly that simple. Unfortunately, it isn't. Human behavior is easily as complex as the forest ecosystems Kolb has been studying for nearly 40 years. Congress is slowly relaxing its grip on its cookie-cutter approach to forest conservation, but our proactive approach to national forest management doesn't even come close to nature's reactions. Shouldn't a 500,000 acre forest fire be met with a proactive 500,000 acre recovery plan? The federal government doesn't do this after a flood or a tornado or an earthquake. We pick up all the pieces and start over – the goal being to rebuild what was lost. Why not in our forests?

A segment of the A-to-Z thinning project on the Colville National Forest in northeast Washington is designed to reduce the risk of catastrophic wildfire. Environmentalists sued to block this thinning but the project was upheld by a federal court in San Francisco.

The 1988 Stafford Disaster Relief and Emergency Assistance Act provides the Forest Service with all the latitude it needs to move swiftly following big wildfires. It even enlists the Federal Emergency Management Agency [FEMA] to assist with physical and financial aid.

All it takes to get the ball rolling is a presidential disaster declaration. Lots of those during hurricane season. The president can also establish and fund disaster preparedness programs. Isn't that what forest restoration is all about? Averting disaster? But the Forest Service won't budge on the big stuff. Why? Should we only repair two percent of a town flattened by a tornado?

Why are we so afraid to fix that which is broken in our forests? Nature isn't going to do this for us because – again – nature doesn't give a damn about our wants and needs. Nature is responsive, not proactive.

Kolb explains. "Our role – the role of proactivity – is to re-create as much resilience and as many functions in forest ecosystems as we possibly can. These successional patterns that drive forest growth are snapshots in time. If you are a careful observer, you can see them at work in the visible changes that occur year after year."

The successional patterns that Kolb references can be seen in the multitude of plant and tree species that colonize areas where human or natural disturbance has occurred. As trees grow taller, less sunlight reaches the ground and plants that require full sunlight give way to plants that can grow in shade.

Low intensity fire – be it prescribed or natural – performs the same function. Trees with thin bark – white fir for example – rarely survive, but trees with thicker bark – ponderosa and larch for example – can take the heat and they grow well in the sunlit openings disturbance provides.

When fearful Americans decided 90-some years ago to "exclude fire" from forests, they opened the door to a natural response they did not understand. Trees that thrive in shade, most notably white fir, soon crowded out ponderosa and larch. Lodgepole pine can't reproduce because its cones are opened by the heat that fire generates. No fire, no lodgepole in the succession parade.

We can see the plain-as-day result in thousands of photos that compare "the look" of forests today to their look before fire was excluded. I challenge you to repeat any of the glass plate photos shot by George Illingworth in the Castle Creek Valley in 1874. Compare his photos with the ones we attempted in August 2018. They're in *Black Hills Green* on our *Evergreen* website.

To see what we should be doing in our national forests to reduce tree density, pick up a copy of *Mimicking Nature's Fire: Restoring Fire-Prone Forests* in the West, a marvelous book written by Steve Arno and Carl Fiedler, two of the finest forest ecologists I know. Their research at Lick Creek, a Forest Service research site in the Bitterroot Valley south of Missoula, Montana is exceptional. Google either one of these guys on the Internet. Their body of work is very impressive.

Paul Hessburg's Mega Fire presentation from North 40 Productions is also very informative. Since 2016, more than 53,000 people in 100-plus western communities have seen it. His well-researched message is sobering, though as I've already said, managed fire is a poor substitute for a more enlightened approach to conserving our national forests.

You can see "the look" of this more learned approach in thousands of "before and after" photographs of areas where thinning and prescribed fire have been used to reduce forest density and the risk of wildfire. There is also an excellent series of photos in the earlier referenced Arno-Fiedler book.

You'll also find some informative videos on the Vaagen Brothers Lumber Company [55] website. The company's second-generation owner, Duane Vaagen, has invested millions in small-diameter log processing technologies that allow the company to mill an impressive array of products from small diameter trees contract loggers are removing from the Colville National Forest.

I've known Duane for many years and admire his courage and willingness to try new ideas. When the Colville's timber sale program cratered several years ago, he invited Mike Petersen, executive director of the Lands Council in Spokane, to tour his Colville, Washington sawmill. It was a daring decision given the Council's preference for litigating most Forest Service restoration projects.

Mike hadn't been with the Council long before he realized that litigation wasn't delivering

55

what the Council members wanted most: more designated Wilderness and an approach to logging that favored conserving what remains of the Colville's old growth forest.

Long story short, the friendship Duane and Mike developed led to the formation of NEWFC – the Northeast Washington Forest Coalition – a diverse collaborative group that now works at the project level with Colville forest planners. Diverse in the sense that its members form a working template that looks very much like a mirror image of America writ large.

Writ large in the sense that every forest value is represented in the suggestions and recommendations that the coalition makes to the Forest Service: air quality, water quality, fish and wildlife habitat, old growth conservation, wilderness and a wide variety of year-round recreation activity. Agreement isn't always easy, but it always comes eventually because coalition members have formed bonds of respect and trust that did not exist before Duane and Mike got together.

Of NEWFC's many successes, none is more remarkable than A-to-Z, a 53,000 acre restoration project that was unsuccessfully litigated by the Alliance for the Wild Rockies [AWR], a long-time serial litigant based in Helena, Montana.

AWR was uncomfortable with the fact that the Forest Service allowed NEWFC members to help craft the restoration plan. Worst, the agency had agreed to let Duane Vaagen pay for the necessary NEPA [National Environmental Policy Act] work necessitated by the size and complexity of the project.

Under terms of the contract, Vaagen paid more than $1 million for third-party NEPA work, but had no say in the outcome. This fact did not deter AWR's Mike Garrity from suggesting that Vaagen had his hands in the Forest Service cookie jar. Fortunately, a three-judge panel of the Ninth Circuit Court of Appeals saw through Garrity's accusations and his refusal to participate in A-to-Z's collaborative design.

Not many lumbermen in the Pacific Northwest have embraced collaboration as enthusiastically as Duane Vaagen, who sees the small diameter logs he processes as byproducts of collaborative projects that account for the values and viewpoints of diverse stakeholder groups like NEWFC. Support for his thinking dwindles west of the Cascades in Oregon and Washington where distrust runs as deep today as it did during the Spotted Owl Wars some 30 years ago.

Collaboration has its roots in the congressionally ratified 2014 Farm Bill, which provided the Forest Service with many of the innovative regulatory tools needed to speed the pace and scale of forest restoration. I suspect more tools are coming as soon as Congress sees measurable progress from the agency.

Some Forest Service staffers wince at my suggestion that locally-based collaboratives are providing the get-out-of-jail free card the agency has needed for a long time. But I think they provide both the Forest Service and Congress with a long-missing social license to do necessary forest restoration work on physical scales that may someday match the scale of the West's wildfire crisis. In just two years, this license has enabled the Colville National Forest to increase its harvest of small-diameter trees from 70 million to 120 million board feet, and A-to-Z has spawned a new project closer to Spokane, near a popular ski area.

Paul Hessburg's very timely question may find its answer in the work forest collaboratives are doing in several western states, most notably states that have also embraced Good Neighbor Authority [GNA], another nifty tool embedded in the 2014 Farm Bill. GNA allows the short-handed and under-budgeted U.S. Forest Service to contract with state forestry departments to get more on-the-ground work done sooner. Idaho was the first to embrace it after then Governor Butch Otter asked the state's forest collaboratives to identify top priority restoration projects. Montana and Washington followed, then Utah, California, Michigan, Wisconsin and Mississippi.

How do most westerners want their wildfire smoke? Anywhere but their lungs and preferably in the much smaller and carefully controlled amounts emitted by prescribed burns.

Hands down, the two best places to store carbon are in trees and the thousands of everyday products made from trees. But even here there is some debate as to which is the better place – trees or the useful products they yield – so keep turning the pages. We're closing in on several practical, honest-to-goodness answers to Paul Hessburg's nagging question. How do we want our smoke?

A Columbia Helicopters airship in the Kootenai Canyon. It was dropping its water on a nearby wildfire in August 2018. These helicopters are exceptionally effective firefighting tools, but they cost north of $8,000 an hour to fly.

Dave and Turtle

My friend, Dave Ehrmantrout, has been logging for a living since he got out of high school more than 30 years ago, probably closer to 40. He grew up in Bonners Ferry, the last Idaho town before you cross the border into Canada. Logging has been a way of life there for close to a hundred years.

The fabled Kootenai River – our fly-fishing haven – passes through Bonners Ferry on its way back to Canada. Before Kootenai Dam was completed in the late 1960s, downtown Bonners Ferry was flooded most springs. Floodwaters four feet deep on Bonner and Kootenai streets were commonplace.

I'm not sure what Dave's dad did for a living, but I'd guess it had a lot to do with logging since there isn't much else to do in Bonners Ferry, unless you work for the Indians at their Kootenai River Inn and Casino or in the Budweiser hop yards south of town. The soil here is deep and rich. Practically everyone has a garden.

Bonners Ferry made big news in September of 1974, when the Kootenai Tribe declared war on the United States Government. They posted guards at both ends of town and asked folks passing through to pay a toll to cross tribal lands. They used the money to house and care for elderly tribal members, which was fine with most who were waylaid. Many of us are a little suspicious of the federal government, so we understood when the Kootenai's declared war.

Most Indian tribes are forbidden by treaty to declare war on the federal government, but the Kootenai's never signed the deal, so the war went on until the feds gave them about 10 acres of land on which the tribal offices now sit. Most of us think highly of the tribe because their casino operation donates a ton of money to charities in northern Idaho. They're also significant participants in one of northern Idaho's most successful forest collaborations.

Anyway, my friend, Dave, lives in Priest River now, another big logging and sawmilling town west of Sandpoint. If you live in either Priest River or Bonners Ferry you probably do your big shopping in Sandpoint – another timber town – or further south in Coeur d'Alene, where we live. It had seven or eight big sawmills when I was a youngster. One was then the largest in the world. It ran 24/7.

I last saw Dave about a year ago. He was doing some thinning work for the Forest Service about 10 minutes northeast of Bonners Ferry. Another good friend, Barry Wynsma, suggested that we photograph the work Dave and his son, Mackie, were doing on a small timber sale that Barry had designed the year before he retired from the Forest Service. That's where we met Turtle, who is an important character in this story.

Turtle is a forwarder, and a forwarder is half of what we call a "mechanical harvesting system." Turtle hauls small logs that have been cut by the harvester. Dave's son runs the harvester. Dave runs Turtle.

Mechanical harvesting systems are very much in vogue in the world of forest restoration. They come in many different sizes and weights, but Turtle and his nameless counterpart – we'll call him Bob – are so light they don't compact the soil beneath their tracks. Soil compaction is a big deal with the Forest Service, so if you have a mechanical harvesting system that doesn't compact the soil, you're much in demand in northern Idaho.

Bob cuts small trees at ground level, turns them horizontally, delimbs them, cuts them into the right lengths and drops them on the ground. Turtle picks them up and loads them on a rack behind the cab. Dave runs Turtle from inside a cab filled with levers and gauges. Not as many as there are in Mackie's cab, but things can get really busy in a hurry when Turtle and Bob get close to one another.

The Forest Service usually marks the trees it wants harvested, or the trees it wants left behind, but this stand was such an unholy mess when Dave and Mackie started that Barry let them pick the harvest trees based on diameter limits. I think the limit was eight or nine inches. Anything larger had to be left. Mechanical harvesting systems are perfect for this kind of work.

Photographing Bob and Turtle was a real joy. Once you get into the rhythm of their movements you can get pretty close to them without fear of getting hurt. Maybe a little too close, but up close you develop a real appreciation for how talented Dave and Mackie are and how much pride they take in their work.

Barry had told them to be on the lookout for any western white pines they found hidden in the clutter of lodgepole and white fir. There aren't many left in our part of the world, so the Forest Service likes to protect them.

Sure enough, Dave found one maybe 14 or 15 inches in diameter hidden in a lodgepole thicket. Mackie cleared away the lodgepole, then Dave delimbed it with his chainsaw as far up as he could reach so that no ground fire could ever crawl up the tree trunk. He was pretty proud of himself and, honestly, so was I. Loggers are often the brunt of jokes about how their knuckles drag on the ground and they're stupid and greedy. Trust me when I tell you I don't know any stupid loggers. This is tough and dangerous work done by woods savvy men and women.

As for greed, a new mechanical harvesting system will set you back a couple million dollars, which reminds me to tell you that Turtle is 20-plus years old and still runs like a Swiss watch. No need to buy a new Turtle yet, but the day will come that Dave heads downtown to deliver the bad news to his banker. Turtle is done. RIP. Bob will soon be headed to the boneyard too.

Dave and Mackie are real artists in the brave new world of restoration forestry. Just for fun, we'll drive up to Bonners Ferry this spring to see what their thinning job looks like, but I can already tell you that save for the park-like setting and the wildflowers blooming in the sun, we won't see any evidence that Turtle and Bob were ever there. That's the beauty of restoration forestry done right by loggers who take pride in their work.

As you might imagine, not everyone is pleased to see how good this stuff looks, and they're even more unhappy with my constant reminders that what loggers and the Forest Service are doing is restoring the natural functions that promote resiliency – the ability of a forest to fend off insect epidemics or survive a fire that might otherwise burn the whole place to the ground. Removing enough trees to allow residual trees to grow again is Step 1. Step 2 is to clean up the woody debris, tree limbs, log butts and rotting wood on the ground.

Mechanical harvesting systems are used globally today. Most are larger and more expensive than Turtle and Bob, which Dave and Mackie purposefully modified for Forest Service thinning jobs in North Idaho, northeast Washington and northwest Montana. On steeper slopes, they don't do as well as conventional cable logging systems, but on more gentle terrain they're unbeatable.

Serial litigators hate these restoration projects because they unmask their fraudulent claims about "greedy loggers" and "logging without laws," bullshit assertions that imply that loggers run wild in the woods whenever and wherever they want. Not true. The whole process is carefully planned and regulated. Turtle and Bob are model citizens in the big woods of northern Idaho.

Most conservation groups including the Nature Conservancy, the Rocky Mountain Elk Foundation, the Theodore Roosevelt Conservation Partnership, the Wilderness Society and the Lands Council – are strong supporters of both forest restoration and citizen collaboration with the Forest Service.

In fact, the Nature Conservancy is actively seeking a partner willing to help it build and operate a high-speed, small-diameter sawmill somewhere near Wenatchee, Washington. Minus such a facility, most of the restoration work the Conservancy is recommending in central Washington won't get

Dave Ehrmantrout and his son, Mackey, with one of their highly modified thinning machines. These machines are specially designed to remove very small trees from forests that have grown too dense.

done because there won't be a market for the trees or biomass that restoration forestry generates.

The links below lead to four *Evergreen* reports detailing forest collaborative work underway in Washington, Idaho and Montana. You'll find some fascinating interviews with some of the West's leading conservationists. I learned a great deal from these men and women and so can you.

The Washington Report -Evergreen State No More? [56]

The Ticking Time Bomb in Idaho's Natioal Forests [57]

Montana's National Forests - Burning an Empire [58]

The common threads in these interviews are:

- Thinning and Good Fire are very useful forestry tools.
- If we don't have a sawmill nearby we don't have a market for the products that thinning and Good Fire yield.
- If we don't have a mill and a market, we won't have a forest. Bad Fire wins. We lose.

The "politics" are even simpler. Minus a federal guarantee of a small log supply sufficient to justify investing $100 million-plus in a new, state-of-the-art sawmill, private investors will move on. The environmental renaissance we seek will have been lost and the increasing presence of fire and smoke will be our constant reminder that we missed the brass ring.

Serial litigants know this. They appeal and litigate Forest Service projects in hopes of running out the clock – meaning the trees slated for removal will have rotted or burned before the court rules on the merits of our project.

Public anger has reached the boiling point in many rural timber towns, but Congress has thus far refused to modify the Equal Access to Justice Act. It forces taxpayers to pick up the tab for thoughtless lawyers who represent several groups including the Alliance for the Wild Rockies, the Center for Biological Diversity and the Sierra Club.

56 

57 

58 

I have a copy of a 1995 report written by Michael McCloskey, who was then chairman of the Sierra Club Board of Directors, in which he recommends that the organization do everything in its power to derail a Clinton Administration plan to test the collaborative waters.

McCloskey was clearly alarmed by the Administration's fascination with collaboration as a tool for encouraging wider public engagement, particularly with the EPA's Project XL, which envisioned pilot projects as vehicles the private sector could use to build broader community support for their work.

What he feared most was erosion of the Sierra Club's death grip on the forest policy process. He also complained about the fact that collaboration consumed "huge amounts of time, wore people down and left little time for regular environmental activism."

I'm not sure what constitutes "regular environmental activism" but by 1995 some 50,000 loggers and sawmill workers in western Oregon and Washington had lost their jobs in the wake of the federal government's 1990 decision to list the northern spotted owl as a threatened species.

Seven years earlier, Andy Stahl, who was then a resource analyst with the Sierra Club Legal Defense Fund, had famously declared, "Thank goodness the spotted owl evolved in the Northwest, for it hadn't, we'd have to genetically engineer it. It's the perfect species for use as a surrogate."

McCloskey told Sierra Club board members that what he found "most troubling" about the Clinton Administration's interest in publicly-based collaboration was that it tended "to de-legitimate conflict as a way of dealing with issues and of mobilizing support."

"It is psychologically difficult to simultaneously negotiate and publicly attack bad proposals from the other size," he wrote. "This tends to be seen as acting in bad faith. Too much time is spent in stakeholder processes may produce the result of demobilizing and disarming our side."

McCloskey thus saw collaboration as a "transfer of power to a local venue" well beyond the reach of the Sierra Club's national office and its urban membership base. Although the Forest Service had not weighed in on the possibility that it might have to engage with local forest stakeholders,

McCloskey was concerned about the outcome.

"We should worry about agencies abdicating responsibility for the overall interests of the public," he warned. "Local interests do not necessarily constitute national interests."

What probably worried him most was the fact that several Sierra Club members were actively engaged in two early collaborations – southern Oregon's Applegate Partnership and northern California's Quincy Library Group. As trust relationships formed, the Sierra Club's national office shut them down, despite the quite vocal support of U.S. Senator, Diane Feinstein, who took it upon herself to learn all she could about the work the Quincy Library Group was trying to do.

McCloskey is certainly correct about the enormous amount of time collaborators invest in sorting through thorny environmental problems, but his disdain for local engagement with the Forest Service was alarming. He clearly had no interest in sharing power with anyone who threatened the Sierra Club's grip on a forest policy making process that undermined early attempts to reduce the risk of wildfire in western national forests.

Fearmongering has been a Sierra Club staple for decades. It has repeatedly railed against clearcutting, most egregiously in *Clearcutting: The Tragedy of Industrial Forestry*, a 291-page large format picture book edited by the Club's Bill Devall. The real tragedy in this book is its inaccuracies. Many alleged clearcuts are actually photographs of the aftermath of wildfires. I know this because I revisited and photographed two photo points overlooking the aftermath of the Houghton Creek Fire, a conflagration so hot that it melted the asphalt where it jumped Highway 2 about 20 miles west of Libby, Montana.

Devall's book prompted a quick response – another book – funded by the landowners whose forest practices had been misrepresented in the Sierra Club book. I have no idea whether Book No. 2 repaired the damage done by Book No. 1, but I doubt that No. 2 did much to drown out the Sierra Club's never-ending drumbeat. Industrial landowners are too cheap to fund the kind of offensive the Sierra Club mounts daily. No wonder most Americans don't trust "timber industry" motives. Why should they?

I'll readily concede that clearcuts are ugly. But I love the smell of freshly cut timber and watching newly replanted trees grow. A five-year-old Douglas-fir sapling can grow an additional five or six feet tall annually, so it doesn't take long for an old clearcut to be obliterated by new growth. If you are a careful observer, you can watch a stunning array of sun-loving plants emerge from the bare soil logging exposes. You'll also see lots of small mammals scurrying about and you'll hear songbirds you'll never hear in the solitude of an old growth forest. I love both settings.

I also love a story told by my late father-in-law, Wes Rickard, who is widely credited with having invented "industrial" forestry. Wes was the first forest economist hired by the old Weyerhaeuser Timber Company. Not long after his 1957 hiring, George Weyerhaeuser, Jr., who was then the company's executive vice president, called him into his office and said, "Wes, I want you to pretend that everything we've ever done on our timberland was wrong. Now tell us how to do it right."

Wes and the small team he assembled spent nearly three years writing code and feeding IBM punch cards into a mainframe computer in Tacoma, Washington, but they eventually found the answer Weyerhaeuser sought – and the news was not well received by the company's board of directors. Wes picks up the story.

"What we determined was that the board-approved 140 year-rotation age was twice as long as it needed to be," Wes explained. "This meant that to maximize the internal rate of return, the company needed to harvest its timber every 70 years, not every 140 years."

The 140-year number had been based on a long-ago board decision to match timber growth to milling capacity, the goal being to make certain the company's sawmills never ran out of harvestable trees.

"Carrying all that timber for so long was costing Weyerhaeuser a lot of money in lost growth," Wes told me. "From our extensive analysis of soil productivity, we knew the company could grow far more timber if it cut the rotation age."

My father-in-law was a very perceptive man, so it didn't take him long to conclude that there was no way Weyerhaeuser's board could be per-

Dave Ehrmantrout beside a western white pine he found in a thinning project near Bonners Ferry, Idaho. Because white pine conservation is so important, he carefully removed other small tress and brush from the area so this tree can grow larger and naturally reseed the area.

suaded to cut its time-honored rotation age in half. What to do?

"We picked 90 years out of a hat and went upstairs to talk to George," he replied.

It took some doing, but Wes and his team were finally able to convince the board of directors to try 90 years. The new program needed a name, so Wes decided on "target forestry" because 90 years was only a target in his mind. Soil productivity and circumstances – including market prices – would certainly influence when, where and how company lands were harvested.

When Weyerhaeuser's advertising agency got wind of what Wes and his colleagues had done they immediately renamed the program "high yield forestry." Wes hated the name because it ignored the whole target forestry concept, which was to match rotation ages to soil fertility so that the growth capacity of a particular forest was never exceeded or abused.

The agency – I think it was Cole and Weber in Seattle – eventually sent a camera crew to the woods with Bill Lawrence, a PhD wildlife biologist who was then Weyerhaeuser's Director of Environmental Science.

Bill was right out of central casting: a big guy with a big beard and a marvelous gift for gab, all decked out in his trademark red plaid woods shirt. He was a walking encyclopedia who oozed enthusiasm as he explained how Weyerhaeuser was creating more elk habitat by opening stands of timber on its western Washington lands. The camera loved Bill. Maybe you saw him in the television commercial the company aired on Monday Night Football during its early years. Maybe 1974.

I have vivid memories of watching Bill while standing on the sawdust-covered floor at Moose's Saloon in Kalispell, Montana, ice cold beer mug in one hand and a slice of pizza in the other. God it was fun!

I love Wes's story because it speaks to the art and science of good forestry. It adds context to the much larger story of our country's quest to sustainably grow as much wood as possible on as much land as possible.

I could ask Wes any question about forestry that came to mind and his answer always began with a question in return: "What do you want from your forest?"

If I could tell Wes what I wanted – be it wildlife habitat, a secluded homesite, more birds and wildflowers or a perpetual revenue stream – he could tell me how to get it. The fact that he had invented what we today call "industrial forestry" never deterred him from his belief that soil productivity was central to every forestry equation.

"We can't save the trees," he told me over and over again. "But we must save the soil because without good soil we can't grow anything."

Every forested state in our nation has a set of rules and regulations – usually called Best Management Practices – that are designed to protect soil and water quality in forests. Soil because if you don't have good soil you can't grow a forest; water because most municipal water supplies in our nation come from forests.

Oregon, Washington and California, have more stringent Forest Practices Acts dating from the 1940s. These laws require landowners to replant their forests within two years of harvest. If they don't replant, state crews will do it and send the bill to the landowner, and if the bill isn't promptly paid, the states will slap a lien on the property, and if the lien isn't satisfied, the land is sold at auction.

Most states now have logger training programs. Montana's Accredited Logging Professional program is fairly typical. Workshops – some taught by college professors – cover an extensive list of topics: forest stewardship, third party forest certification, streamside management zone logging practices, first aid, CPR and emergency evacuation. There are 140 ALP-certified loggers in Montana. All are required to complete 32 hours of continuing education annually.

I got an up close and personal look at forests and forestry in the United States about 20 years ago. Sold my home in southern Oregon, bought a 42-foot Teton fifth-wheel and spent three years roaming the backwoods of our beautiful land.

Forestry certainly differs from region to region, mainly as a reflection of forest types and landowner management goals and objectives, but I never saw a forest I thought was being abused by its owner. Not one. Not in the North, South, East or West did I see anything that looked remotely like the doomsaying we hear daily from the likes of Bill Devall and Michael McCloskey.

What I *did* see was a bountiful and productive land cared for by private landowners who have invested much more than money in their life's work. What I heard, again and again, was a story about "place," a word my grandmother used countless times when describing the ranch she shared with my grandfather for 65 years. "Place" was home and home is where hearts live.

There are more than 10 million family forest landowners in the United States and just as many stories about "place." Amazingly, they provide more of the nation's lumber supply than the so-called "industrial landowners." More amazing though are the reasons why these 10 million-plus landowners manage their forests.

Yes, some are in it for the money, but a re-occurring woodland owners survey conducted annually by the Forest Service's Northern Research Station at St. Paul, Minnesota reveals a multitude of reasons why families hang on to their forests for generations.

- Most cite their interest in creating or maintaining wildlife habitat.
- Some simply enjoy nature's great beauty.
- Others relish hunting and fishing on their property.
- Many stick with it to honor their family's "place" in the American story.

I talked to many of them during my road trip. Their stories never varied much, save for the story of the late Jack Rajala, a Big Fork, Minnesota lumberman I met at the insistence of Jerry Rose, who was then Minnesota's state forester. Jack was an amazing man – quiet, a little too intense for his own good but deeply devoted to bringing back the eastern white pine forests that once dominated Minnesota.

"I know of no other tree growing in Minnesota forests that can fulfill so many economic and environmental needs," Jack told me while taking me through his family's Tree Farm between Deer River and Big Fork. "It grows beautiful wood, provides a wide range of wildlife habitat, can be grown under a wide variety of conditions, doesn't need to be clearcut to ensure adequate regeneration and is a sentimental favorite among Minnesotans who love forests."

And Jack certainly loved his white pine, so much so that he had planted more than one million seedlings on his Tree Farm by hand. Armed only with hand clippers, he had also carefully pruned thousands of saplings and bagged thousands of more in tiny white paper tents intended to keep browsing deer from eating their buds.

Although not a trained forester, Jack knew more about eastern white pine silviculture than anyone I had ever met, and he happily shared his vast knowledge with anyone who asked him for help. He even wrote a book, *Bringing Back the White Pine*, which was both a forester's manifesto and a how-to guide for anyone interested in taking up his cause.

Jack garnered so much press coverage that he soon found himself in the crosshairs of environmentalists who had for years insisted that the only way to return eastern white pine forests was to stockpile more public forestland in no management reserves.

"It's a romantic notion with no scientific basis," he told me. "Self-regeneration hasn't worked in a hundred years and it won't work now. The key to successful white pine restoration is regeneration, not preservation. The only places where white pine is reseeding itself is in areas that have been subjected to nature or human disturbance – wildfire or timber harvesting that creates openings and exposes mineral soil where natural regeneration can occur."

Most people lack the discipline and fervor that Jack brought to his labor of love.

"The future of white pine of any abundance in Minnesota has to do with methodically and religiously carrying out well-thought plans and rigorous silviculture," he wrote in his book. "It requires up-front commitment, disciplined execution and a willingness to stick with it."

How Jack's devotion to eastern white pine squares with the wild-ass claim that lumbermen are "greedy" and only want to "chop down all the trees" is beyond me, but you can read this crap daily in the rantings and ravings of social misfits and malcontents who call themselves "environmentalists."

When Jack died in 2016, he left behind a marvelous legacy that included not just his beloved white pine Tree Farm, but also five white pine sawmills, some 250 employees, a $7 million-a-year payroll and a slew of volunteer assignments on school and church boards and state and national forestry associations. For his tireless work, he was named Minnesota Small Businessman of the Year in 1988.

"We will continue to do well even if Minnesotans don't embrace white pine restoration in a meaningful way," Jack told me the last time I saw him. "But I hope they do because the scale of restoration I envision will support many small family-owned businesses in rural Minnesota. But equally important is the fact that it will significantly increase productivity and biological diversity on many thousands of acres of Minnesota forests. Everybody wins."

I told Jack's story in the Spring 2000 edition of Evergreen Magazine. You'll find the PDF on our website https://www.evergreenmagazine.com. I took the photo on the cover from the front porch of a lovely little cabin on a lake on his Tree Farm. At his invitation, I stayed there several nights. It was heavenly.

I heard bits and pieces of Jack's hope-filled story in every "place" I visited during my three years on the road: Bethel, New Hampshire; Cherokee, Tennessee; Sylva, North Carolina; St. Croix, Indiana; Laclede, Idaho; Shreveport, Louisiana; Columbia Falls, Montana; Colville, Washington; Cave Junction, Oregon; Yreka, California; Summerville, South Carolina; Chillicothe, Ohio; Wetumpka, Alabama; Kilgore, Texas; Hulett, Wyoming; Benton, Arkansas; Grand Junction, Tennessee; South Royalton, Vermont; Moose River, Maine; Old Forge, New York; Prentice, Wisconsin and, of course, Jack's place in Big Fork, Minnesota.

My late friend, Hal Salwasser, was Dean of the Oregon State University College of Forestry for 12 years before he died in 2012. I had been one of his biggest fans for years. We met when he was still Northern Region Regional Forester, stationed in Missoula, Montana. He followed my cross-country odyssey and later told me he thought I'd earned the equivalent in a PhD in forestry.

Maybe Hal was right. The Jack Rajala's and Dave Ehrmantrout's of the world teach powerful lessons by their actions and words. For sheer entertainment though, you can't beat an afternoon spent watching Turtle and Bob at work in the back of beyond. But then I remind myself that Unit 7, where Dave and Mackie were hard at it was a biomass unit – meaning the trees they were removing were too small to be sawn into lumber. Not that there is anything wrong with burning woody debris in power plants. It beats storing all that carbon in our lungs.

My friend, Barry Wynsma, who introduced me to Dave and Mackie, was the principal author of the Forest Service's *Biomass Utilization Desk Guide*, a how-to manual designed to help entrepreneurs assess costs and market opportunities for all the dead crap that fuels our godawful wildfires.

The *Desk Guide* [59] is easier to wrap your brain around than the Billion Ton Report, a series of long but very interesting Department of Energy studies that estimate the amount of biomass available from domestic forest, farm and municipal sources.

The link for the 2016 Billion Ton Report is three feet long. Google Billion Ton Report 2016 and the PDF will pop up.

Lord only knows how many billion tons of biomass are laying around in our forests waiting for the next lightning strike or carelessly tossed cigarette, but unlike wind and solar power, it's there even when the sun doesn't shine and the wind doesn't blow. And converting all that woody biomass to energy would reduce greenhouse gas emissions by millions of tons annually. Yet the West's wildfire pandemic isn't even mentioned in the apocalyptic Green New Deal proposal. What am I missing?

Unit 7 was the smallest chunk of a 1,000-acre thinning project within the Bonners Ferry Wildland Urban Interface. My back-of-the-envelope estimate suggests that our western national forests still hold about 89,999,000 acres that look about the same or worse than Unit 7. And the serial litigators are still blocking the road back to sanity. And our federal government lets them do it!

We long ago learned how to make useful products out of biomass that is of such poor quality that it can't be made into lumber: Presto logs, wood pellets, animal bedding, charcoal water filters, mats that minimize soil erosion, groundwood for muddy playgrounds and small powerplants.

59

Lumber and plywood manufacturers have been turning their wood waste into electric energy for decades. Some even sell their excess power into electric grids operated by public and privately-owned utilities.

The product list is long. So are the barriers associated with transforming biomass into liquid fuels, but entrepreneurs will eventually cross this technological barrier, possibly sooner than many people expect.

Cost has always been a limiting factor. If the cost of raw material – in this case biomass – is too high entrepreneurs can't afford to make the investment. It costs north of $100 million to build a new small diameter sawmill, but you can build a new five megawatt wood-fired powerplant for about $20 million. Ten megawatts, $40 million. No matter the capital cost, the investment can only be justified if the raw material supply is of sufficient size and duration to pay off the investment and operating costs from profits.

The Forest Service has known this since 1917. Three years before he was named Chief, Bill Greeley wrote a report titled "Some Public and Economic Aspects of the Lumber Industry," in which he explained that sky-high timber and financing costs were undermining the lumber industry's ability to profit – and thus its interest in replanting cutover timberland.

Greeley resigned from the Forest Service in 1925 to devote his full energy to convincing lumbermen that replanting made sense. He finally succeeded in 1942. The American Tree Farm System transformed a timber industry mired in its own destructive tendencies into a conservation colossus.

The Forest Service knows this, yet it refuses to embrace the clear connection between its wildfire pandemic and private industry's ability to help it solve the problem by developing technologies and markets for the least valuable material in forests – the biomass that is fueling these uncontrollable fires, destroying both our national forests and the Forest Service itself.

Why won't the Forest Service step into the breech? My Forest Service retiree friends tell me that "Don't mess up" is the whispered warning at the highest levels in the agency.

Don't mess up? Are you kidding me? How much bigger can this mess get? We should be rewarding the boat rockers – especially District Rangers and Forest Supervisors who exhibit the courage to think big and act bigger.

If we continue to tip-toe through the halls reminding each other to not "mess up" we will lose our national forests. Show me someone who is willing to "mess up" and I'll show you someone who is going to solve big problems.

Dave Ehrmantrout and his forwarder, "Turtle," wind their way through a thing in northern Idaho. Turtle puts fewer pounds per square inch on the ground than a horse, so there is little soil disturbance.

CHAPTER 27

No mill, no market, no forest

By the time Congress got around to establishing the U.S. Forest Service in February of 1905, its mission had already been clearly spelled out by many times by both President Roosevelt and his occasional boxing partner, Gifford Pinchot, who he named the agency's first Chief.

Both men were ardent conservationists, but the word "conservation" connoted something very different then than it does today. Their primary goal was to make damned sure the nation never experienced a "timber famine."

Timber theft from federal forest reserves was commonplace, much of it associated with mining and railroad construction. Sensing great financial gain, "robber baron" industrialists and grubstake miners were laying waste to public domain timberlands. It was easy. There was no one to stop them.

Amid rising public concern that their lawlessness might trigger a nation-wide timber famine, Congress passed the 1891 Forest Reserve Act, which was supposed to cure land fraud defects in earlier homesteading laws, but the 18 forest reserves subsequently designated by Presidents Grover Cleveland and Benjamin Harrison sparked such an outcry from western House and Senate members that Congress was forced to revisit the matter in its 1897 Sundry Civil Appropriations Act.

In a mere 83 words, the Pettigrew Amendment, which we know today as the Organic Act, set the future Forest Service on a management course that remained contextually unchanged until the 1970s:

> *"No national forest shall be established, except to improve and protect the forest within the boundaries, or for the purpose of securing favorable conditions of water flows, and to furnish a continuous supply of timber for the use and necessities of the citizens of the United States; but it is not the purpose or intent of these provisions, or of the Act, to authorize the inclusion therein of lands more valuable for the mineral therein, or for agricultural purposes than for forest purposes."*

In defining and limiting the reasons for designating forest reserves, the Organic Act also authorized their management by the federal government, specifically the Interior Department's General Land Office. President Roosevelt added clarity in his 1903 instruction to the founding members of the Society of American Forests, noting that "primary object of our forest policy, as of the land policy of the United States, is the making of prosperous homes." Gifford Pinchot echoed Roosevelt's dictum in his 1905 *Use Book*, a set of instructions his first forest rangers were expected to follow to the letter.

Many regard Pinchot as "the father of American conservation." I'm not so sure, but it hardly matters. His contributions to the formation of the Forest Service and the nation's long-lasting forest policy were enormous. So were Bill Greeley's. He had handpicked Greeley to be one of his "boys" in the early Forest Service. But the two men clashed publicly over Pinchot's belief that the Forest Service should have regulatory control over private timberlands in the West. He never forgave Greeley for siding with lumbermen. Strong passions all around.

What passes for forestry in our national forests today bears no resemblance to anything that Roosevelt, Pinchot or Greeley envisioned. Frustration and anger are festering in the same rural communities Pinchot characterized in his Use Book. It is reminiscent of the political range war that erupted in the West after Presidents Cleveland and Harrison created 15 forest reserves without any public discussion of the consequences. That war led Congress to add the Organic Act to its 1897 Sundry Appropriations Act.

Now – 122 years later – what proactive steps might Congress take to build on the Roosevelt-Pinchot-Greeley legacy?

Most recently, the House and Senate have spoken their intentions through the 2014 and 2018 Farm Bills – and it does seem as though Congress understands the dreadful economic and environmental fallout caused by the convergence of our wildfire pandemic and the collapse of the long-gone federal timber sale program set in motion by principles espoused by Pinchot and Roosevelt.

Two diametrically opposing fears are at the heart of the "What to do" question. The first is that our wildfire crisis will destroy the intangible forest assets that form the cornerstone of our New West lifestyle. The second is that Congress breathe new life into the old federal timber sale program, undermining the philosophical underpinnings of the New West.

There isn't a chance on earth that the old federal program will ever return because as a commodity federal timber isn't needed anymore. Private, state and tribal forest landowners are providing all the timber we need.

However – and this is a biggie – logging as a by-product of a forest restoration projects *supports the building blocks of the New West lifestyle:* clean air, clean water and all the other intangible amenities that flow from healthy and naturally resilient forests. The symbiotic relationship between thinning, Good Fire and the New West lifestyle demands precision coordination within and among every federal resource management agency.

Remember, our western national forests hold plus or minus 90 *million* troubled acres that fire ecologists tell us are ready to burn or soon will be. Half the entire federal forest estate. What on earth would Roosevelt, Pinchot or Greeley think? What will our children and grandchildren think when they inherit our mess?

Environmentalism's fearmongering conflict industry – led by the Sierra Club Legal Defense Fund, the Alliance for the Wild Rockies, the Wild West Institute and the Center for Biological Diversity – loves to paint a picture of "greedy lumbermen" salivating at the possibility that the old federal logging program will return.

Not going to happen and the reasons are many, but none more important than the fact that the "timber industry" has moved south into the politically friendlier environs they've found in Carolinas, Georgia, Alabama, Arkansas, Tennessee and Texas. The welcome mat is out and the trees grow much faster there than they do here in West. Yes, we still have state-of-the-art sawmills in western Oregon and Washington, but they prosper on private timber.

The *only* mills left in the West that are interested in working with the federal government are the smaller, family-owned mills that have been here since the end of World War II. These are the mills that serial litigators are trying to drive out of business because , once they are gone, no one in his or her right mind will invest the capital necessary to start anew. How much money, you ask? About $100 million – with no guarantee that the federal government will sell the timber needed to operate the mill long enough to amortize the investment.

I can't name one lumberman who is looking for a government handout. There is no need for public subsidy to make forest restoration projects work profitably. Simply include a few commercially valuable trees within each project – it doesn't take many – to turn a money loser into a collaborative enterprise that can pay its own way without taxpayer subsidy.

Carl Fiedler, the University of Montana PhD forest ecologist I mentioned a few pages ago, did some research in this realm in New Mexico and Montana in the 1990s. His initial goal was to figure out what trees and how many trees had to be removed from a forest that was too dense to give it the opportunity to recover on its own. He asked Chuck Keegan, a PhD forest economist at the university to put a pencil to his idea to see if it could pay its own way.

It turned out that about 70 percent of the thinning projects Carl studied could pay their own way if three or four commercially valuable trees per acre were added to the mix. I don't believe the Forest Service has ever tried to validate Carl's work, which is a shame.

Here's the bottom line on lumbermen. Minus a more favorable political climate and long-term contracts that stipulate an operationally sufficient annual harvest level, private capital will not flow to projects that require costly computer-aided wood processing technologies capable of milling small diameter trees and forest biomass. Our efforts to rescue the New West from a fiery grave will fail.

Why? Because as the late Forest Service Chief, Jack Ward Thomas was fond of saying, "There isn't enough gold in Fort Knox to pay for all the work that needs doing." Jack's pragmatism never allowed him to think that taxpayers would be willing to pay the bill. Private investments and private markets were the only realistic solution. Serial litigators know this, too.

No mill, no market, no forest. What to do? What if I told you there is an easy-to-run software program you can install in your computer than lets you see what a logging job will look like before a single tree is cut, and what if I told you the same program will let you watch your replanted forest grow anew?

It's called BioSum and it's the latest in a sensational array of harvest simulation tools that foresters are using to compare the downstream tradeoffs associated with different forest management alternatives and techniques.

My old friend, Chad Oliver, a PhD forest ecologist, demonstrated an early simulation model for me one morning at a truck stop near Issaquah, Washington. Yup, a truck stop – complete with a gum-chewing waitress looking on at 6:00 o'clock in the morning.

As the simulator first removed trees in various configurations, then grew them back in several patterns, she looked at Chad and said, in a voice that could have broken glass, "What's that?"

In seamless propriety, for which Chad is legendary, he gently explained what she was seeing. Without missing a beat, she loudly exclaimed, "Well, I'll be damned." She then quickly retreated to the kitchen, only to return moments later with the entire cooking crew in tow.

It was a moment in time I will never forget. There we were, huddled around a small table in the wee hours of the morning, our eyes glued to a harvest simulator built by an unassuming forest scientist who is now Pinchot Professor of Forestry and Environmental Studies at Yale University, and Director of the school's Global Institute of Sustainable Forestry.

Last year, I got to see BioSum in action at the Forest Service's Pacific Northwest Research Station in Portland, Oregon. My wife, Julia, and I were there as part of our in-depth investigation of the Forest Service's Forest Inventory and Analysis Program, which is housed in five Forest Service locations around the nation, one being the old Gus Solomon federal courthouse in downtown Portland.

BioSum is an acronym for FIA's "Biomass Summarization System." Its principal architect is Jeremy Fried, a PhD forest economist at the PNW station in the old Gus Solomon Courthouse in downtown Portland. Fried and six of his colleagues explain the system in considerable detail in Chapter 12 of a 321-page report titled *A Comprehensive Guide to Fuel Management Practices in Dry Mixed Conifer Forests in the Northwestern United States.* Wildfire Ground Zero.

The framework Fried and his colleagues built combines forest inventory data representing an analysis region – an FIA staple since 1928 – with "a treatment cost model, a fuel treatment effectiveness model and a raw material hauling cost model to explore alternative landscape-scale treatment scenarios that achieve a variety of management objectives."

The rough translation of Fried's considerable expertise and well-honed vocabulary goes something like this:

"Here's how much crap we need to remove before this sick forest catches fire, here's what it costs to remove it and here's what the forest will look like based on the treatment scenario selected."

Add in fire behavior metrics – including torching and crown fire indexes – allows Fried to compare fire hazard metrics pre and post-treatment. The result is a user-friendly decision support software, complete with spreadsheets, that visualizes hundreds of alternative management sequences, evaluates fire resilience results

Thinning work done by small, family-owned logging companies is key to restoration of natural resiliency in the West's dying national forests. Here, Rick and Deb Smith, Kalispell, Montana.

achieved, accounts for habitat conservation objectives, weighs carbon dynamics, calculates treatment costs and the dollars associated with transporting woody biomass to existing and proposed wood processing facilities.

"Basically, BioSum identifies and evaluates the low hanging fruit," Fried says of what is the latest of many contributions the Portland FIA shop is making to our better understanding of forests and how they function on physical scales we cannot see.

"We grow trees in a computer, then we ask ourselves lots of questions about different treatment impacts through time," he explains. "We look for answers that either affirm or refute what we think we know. Sometimes we get answers that aren't publicly popular."

The unpopular answers being those that have to do with cutting down trees. Our saving grace being the fact that when Fried demonstrated BioSum for us we were sitting in his small office in downtown Portland, easily 40 miles from the nearest chain saw. Redemption in the certainty that not one tree was felled. But as he ran his software program through its paces we could see how different tree selection and management sequences produced strikingly different visuals. And when the software began growing the next forest, we could see how replanted or naturally regenerated trees filled in the open spaces simulated harvesting had created.

What a marvelous tool and what a welcome relief for concerned citizens who worry about the visual impacts of removing trees from forests – even dead ones. Dave and Mackie Ehrmantrout's wonderful work near Bonners Ferry, Idaho came immediately to mind as I watched Fried choose from dozens of treatment options the software program offers its users.

My mind also flashed back to the Forest Service's annual National Woodland Owners Survey, and those millions of Family Tree Farmers who report that their management objectives are less about harvesting timber and more about creating or protecting wildlife habitat. In their forestry world, timber is a byproduct, yet they deliver more wood to market annually than the big industrial outfits. Why can't the Forest Service replicate anything even close to this remarkable feat in our national forests. Where are our big picture thinkers? Where are our leaders? We desperately need an ideas revolution that recognizes the intersection of the human spirit with capital investments in new technologies and system tools.

BioSum is but one of several stunning visualization tools FIA's four research stations are rolling out for public inspection and use. Charles H. "Hobie" Perry, a PhD soils scientist who organizes his day into minutes, was our host when we visited the Northern Research Station at St. Paul, Minnesota earlier this year. By definition, soils scientists toil at the foundation of all forest ecosystems, so he was a good choice to demonstrate a new interactive visualization tool that seems certain to completely change the way the public looks at forests.

The Northern Region lab occupies a fiftyish building on the edge of the University of Minnesota campus. The century old Department of Forest Resources is just up the hill, a five-minute walk away. I know this school well because Wilbur Maki, a legendary forest economist, taught here, as did my friend, Jim Bowyer, another PhD, who headed the Department of Bioproduct and Biosystems in UM's Forest Resources Department. I feel as much at home here as I do walking the halls of the forestry schools at the Universities of Idaho and Montana.

"Hobie" brought his laptop to our meeting in FIA's conference room on Folwell Avenue. Following a brief explanation of what we were about to see, he projected an image from his laptop onto a large screen at the far end of a long table. As he magnified the image our sylvan neighborhood in Dalton Gardens, Idaho came into focus. We were both astonished. What was this? And why?

What we were looking at was one of dozens of layers of data that FIA's rocket jockeys have assembled at the county level for all 3,242 counties, parishes and boroughs in the United States. We were literally a mouse click away from a vast treasure trove of forest data. Hobie could have chosen any neighborhood in the country to demonstrate the system, but he chose ours for maximum effect – and it was effective to the max for sure.

Each layer tells a story about a different forest value. We could see streams, rivers, watersheds, trees of many different species, fish and wildlife habitats, pretty much all the bits and pieces that make up a mix of state, private and national forest within a 30-minute drive of our home. To show us different forest values in our neighborhood –a different map layer – Hobie simply clicked his mouse and, bingo, there it was in stunning color.

It slowly dawned on us that these colorful maps were interactive – meaning that we could sit in our office in the cottage behind our Dalton Gardens home and dial up FIA data sets for any forest value for every county in the United States. You name it: tree species, tree distribution, soil, watersheds and the streams and rivers they form, the presence of insects and diseases, and the risk of fire.

We were both speechless. This was Star Wars stuff. This was Luke Skywalker flying down Beggar's Canyon, around Dead Man's Turn, past the Stone Needle and on through Diablo Cut. This we the stuff that had my then 10-year-old son and me on the edges of their seats in George Lucas's epic 1977 space opera.

This was – and is – the mother lode of user-friendly information all of us have needed for a very long time. It allows Forest Service scientists to confidently and intelligently enter all of the "what to do" conversations by first alerting us to forest conditions and opportunities in our own back yards.

In our case, the interactive maps Hobie pulled up provide the ground-truthing evidence we have needed to document and explain the risks we and our Dalton Gardens neighbors face every summer because the mountains that touch our backyards hold too many trees that are dying. We are one electrical storm away from a fire storm.

My immediate thought was that these easily navigated maps are going to make it increasingly difficult for serial litigators to fill unsuspecting hearts and minds with fantastic tales about how nature will take care of everything in our dying national forests as long as we keep sending them money so they can keep those greedy loggers and lumbermen from killing the planet.

I know the malcontents who live among us won't give up without an enormous fight in congressional hallways, but information is power and these user-friendly FIA maps hold the power to destroy their taxpayer-funded business model.

On the flight home from St. Paul, I began sorting through 30-some years of teachable moments – sound bites more or less – that I've experienced in the course of interviewing giant minds whose careers have veered close to the brass ring FIA has grasped. Three different but all powerful perspectives came immediately to mind.

In the late 1980s, I stumbled across a PhD sociologist who began his professional life as an undergraduate biologist. His name was Bob Lee. He was teaching at the University of Washington when I found him on the pages of the Seattle Times, condemning the conflict industry's almost daily verbal assault on the region's small logging communities. So I called him for a chat. Here's what he told me about the social upheaval he was witnessing in his travels:

> *"Preserving and maintaining this nation's cultural diversity is as important to the survival of America as is preserving and maintaining its biological diversity. What we are preserving in rural farm and timber communities is people, not abstractions or symbols, but real people who embody basic values which are fundamental to our nation's history and its traditions."*

Because I grew up working on my grandfather's cattle ranch here in northern Idaho, I've thought the same thing for a long time, but I had never been able to put it into words as artfully as Bob did.

In *Evergreen* Magazine's early days, I spent a lot of time wandering the halls of the College of Forestry at Oregon State University. The late Carl Stoltenberg, who was then forestry school's dean, had handed me the keys to Peavy Hall and said I was welcome anytime. I readily accepted his invitation.

On one of my early visits I met a living legend in the forestry research world. Dr. Robert Buckman had earned his PhD in forestry at the University of Minnesota in 1959, then worked in research for the Forest Service until he retired in 1986. He had been director of the Pacific Northwest Research Station in Portland before moving on to Washington, D.C. where he headed the Forest Service's research and international programs, a position that led to his being named vice president and then president of the International Union of Forest Research Organizations, representing 15,000 forest scientists in 110 countries.

Robert Buckman was a world-class heavyweight wrapped in a warm personality that oozed

PhD botanist, Mike Newton, talks with a log truck driver, who is hauling freshly harvested timber from his forest plantation west of Corvallis, Oregon. Newton taught silviculture at Oregon State University for nearly 50 years. Tanya runs a planning machine for the Devil's Tower Lumber Company at Hulett, Wyoming.

confidence. He loved Civil War history – as do I – so we found much to talk about. Biological diversity was all the rage in the newspapers then. Someone had suggested to me that defining it was a lot like trying to nail Jell-O to a wall, so I asked Bob if there was any truth to the environmentalist claim that the older a forest grew the more biologically diverse it became. Here is his reply:

> *"Conservationists need to consider a broader range of land management options. There is currently a significant bias favoring old-growth related research. It is undermining our more complete understanding of how the pieces of nature fit together. For every old-growth related research project, there should be companion research involving young and middle-aged forests. Biological diversity is the sum of all ecological processes, not just those we can observe in old-growth forests."*

I asked a similar question of Bill Libby, an outspoken boat rocker and PhD Professor Emeritus of Forest Genetics in the College of Natural Resources Department of Environmental Science, Policy and Management at Cal Berkeley.

Although Bill had retired in 1994, he was still working on three continents so I knew he had stories to tell. At the time we talked, plantation forestry was a hot topic, the supposed scourge of biological diversity in "natural" forests.

Who better to ask about this dreadful malady that was said to be boring its way into old growth forests in the Pacific Northwest than one of the world's foremost forest geneticists, the very same Bill Libby who was also a member of the Board of Directors of the Save the Redwoods League and was also studying the impacts of climate change in California's coast redwood and giant sequoia forests?

Here is Bill's take-no-prisoners answer to my question about the dangers posed by private lands plantation forestry in the Pacific Northwest's Douglas-fir region.

> *"Plantation forestry saves more endangered species in a month than most American conservationists save in their lifetimes. As federal logging in the Pacific Northwest is slowed to a standstill, species extinction in tropical forests has accelerated at a thunderous rate. Is saving the spotted owl and the marbled murrelet worth the loss of eight to ten thousand species in the Philippines, Malaysia, Indonesia and Madagascar? Not in my opinion."*

I met my earlier mentioned friend, Jim Bowyer, at a conference in Vancouver, British Columbia in the fall of 1991. Then, as now, there was great concern for the environmental impacts associated with the alarming increase in consumption of earth's natural resources and a parallel hope that consumption could somehow be shifted from non-renewable building materials, like steel, concrete, aluminum and plastic to renewables we can grow again and again, like trees.

Jim was one of the conference's keynote speakers. I was mesmerized by his thoughtful presentation, specially his rundown of annual global consumption of raw materials measured in millions or billions of metric tons.

Consumption rates in China and India are stupefying, but why wouldn't they be? Infrastructure buildout in both countries is at least a hundred years behind the more industrialized world. There are places in China that are largely inaccessible from the outside world. India still struggles to supply clean drinking water.

I introduced myself to Jim at a coffee break and asked if he had time for an interview. He didn't but he asked if I was the same Jim Petersen who published *Evergreen* Magazine. I said I was and he asked if he could use our magazines to test the knowledge of his incoming freshmen forestry students. I said yes, that would be great. He did, and the results weren't great. Our schools are failing students who are interested in all things environmental, but that's a story for another time.

I'm a pretty respectable notetaker, but when I interviewed Jim by phone a week after our Vancouver meeting, it was all I could do to keep up. But here is what he told me that I hope you will take to heart in your own consuming life.

> *"Nations that consume more than they produce are exporting their environmental impacts to other nations that provide what is consumed. It is like shipping your garbage to another town that needs the money and is willing to put up with the stench.*

Most of the raw materials consumed by the industrialized world – including the United States – come from impoverished countries that lack the money, technology and political will needed to regulate their own extractive industries. In the emerging global economy nations should be increasing, not decreasing, their dependence on wood fiber because wood is renewable, recyclable, biodegradable and far more energy efficient it its manufacture and use than are products made from steel, aluminum, plastic and concrete. Furthermore, growing forests and the lumber they provide store large amounts of carbon dioxide that would otherwise escape into the atmosphere, adding to the potential for global warming."

Jim's observations bear directly on the pressing need for us to do a much better job of managing our national forests, not because I see them as great sources of commercial timber for our growing nation – I don't – but because our national forests should be metaphors for everything we should be doing to protect our environment. But in their fiery deaths they have become symbols for everything that has gone wrong. I have many Forest Service friends but I do not understand how the agency can claim to be "caring for the land and serving the people."

Jim has retired from the University of Minnesota's Department of Bio-products and Bio-processing but he is still very much involved in the Responsible Materials Program of Dovetail Partners, a Minneapolis non-profit that advises companies and organizations on the impacts and tradeoffs associated with environmental decision making and job creation. Jim's well-documented book, *The Irresponsible Pursuit of Paradise* is well worth reading. Buy a copy on Amazon.

For sheer theatre, it is impossible to trump the well-choreographed wisdom of my late friend, Leonard Netzorg, a fiery lawyer who began his career as a United Auto Workers Union organizer in Detroit. Ben Cohen, a New Deal wunderkind and close advisor to President Franklin Roosevelt, found Netzorg proselytizing atop of a lunchroom table in a General Motors plant and brought him to Washington, D.C. He spent World War II in front line foxholes in Europe, listening to German radio transmissions and passing troop movement information along to codebreakers at Bletchley Park, 50 miles northwest of London.

Following the war, he took a solicitor's job in the Department of the Interior before the long-gone Western Forest Industries Association hired him in the early 1950s. He was retired by the time we met in in 1991, our interview led to a friendship that endured until he died in 2003.

"Distant Thunder" was the title of my 1991 interview with Leonard. After you've read these wisdoms I think you will understand why:

- Government is the practice of politics. It is the institution through which members of society are able to adjust their competing and often clashing opinions in order to evolve decisions by which we all agree we must abide. If the decision is to be wise, the decision making process needs more than biology. We are not governing wildlife. Our decisions are all in print and animals do not read. We are governing people for the pur pose of affecting wildlife. The direct impact of our decisions is upon people, not animals.
- There is no perfect truth that can guide us forward. The larger issues of our time, including those swirling about our forests, require separating society's material wants from its spiritual needs.
- Society has demonstrated an unwillingness to vest in scientists the final authority to make decisions that affect the rest of us. We insist that our non-scientific views be heard – that we whose lives are affected have the right to participate in the decision-making and policy processes that flow from today's scientific facts.
- The timber industry is going to have to learn how to share these forests with others who have different values and want different things from the forest. Frankly, I welcome it and I rue the day when polarized factions no longer tear away at the fabric of our society.
- There are great invisible leveling forces in society. When society decides this or that group is being too grabby, without regard to

the consequences, it slaps them back into the corner.

- The American Revolution is still going on. We are still changing, still learning. If some of us were not constantly tearing away at what others of us think we know, we would all still think the earth flat. What is science today is witchcraft tomorrow.

These wisdoms from Bob Lee, Robert Buckman, Bill Libby, Jim Bowyer and Leonard Netzorg can be rearranged in countless permutations and combinations, but the take home message is always the same: To answer all of our "What now" questions, we must first break through the fog of war and disillusionment that got us into this mess. A more hopeful route lies just beyond the next rise in the road.

A de-limber measures and cuts small diameter logs to the correct lengths on a roadside thinning project in western Montana.

Our daily wood

Who says scientists can't be funny?

Wink Sutton certainly is – and he has three PhD's: chemistry, botany and forest biometrics – bio meaning biological and metrics meaning measurements.

I met W.R.J "Wink" Sutton in 1991 at the same Vancouver, British Columbia forestry conference where I met Jim Bowyer. He was teaching at the University of British Columbia's forestry school, easily one of finest on earth. He is a New Zealand native and, last I knew, he had gone home to contemplate retirement.

I doubt that he did. In fact, he emailed me a copy of a millennium presentation he made in South Africa. He'd been asked to discuss advancements in forestry in the coming 100 years -2,000 to 2,100. I would have liked to have seen the astonished looks on audience faces when my diminutive friend predicted that before 2100, science would unlock wood's molecular code, meaning we could manufacture anything from trees, including the fuel for your car.

Wink's Vancouver conference presentation remains one of the most animated and amusing I've ever seen. To illustrate daily global raw material consumption he had calculated the exact amounts for all the essentials we can't live without in per person units – one for each of us, all 7.7 billion of us.

You might think that such an undertaking would come with lots of whistles and bells. Wrong. Wink's only prop was a picnic basket. No PowerPoint, no charts or graphs. Nothing but a wicker picnic basket filled with nails, wheat flower, corn kernels, a potato and some Ziploc plastic bags brimming with bauxite, iron ore and wood chips. Naturally, I was most interested in the three baggies that held the carefully measured equivalent of the amount of wood each of us consumes every 24 hours.

But let me set the stage for you. Here is this diminutive guy dressed in a grey suit who looks like Happy from the Seven Dwarfs strolling back and forth in front of a spell-bound audience, hauling baggies out of his basket and talking about all the goodies manufactured from the basics of life: bauxite becomes aluminum which equals beer cans; iron ore becomes steel which equals rivets used to assemble skyscrapers assembled from steel beams; wood chips from trees used to make lumber and, ahem, toilet paper. Wheat and corn for thousands of everyday items; potatoes for French fries!

Wink got a well-deserved standing ovation. I rushed the stage in hopes of scoring an interview. My first question landed us in an hour-long conversation. I wanted to know if he could come up with a prop that represented the exact amount of wood consumed every 24 hours by every man, woman and child on earth.

"What do you have in mind," he asked.

"I don't know for sure," I replied. "How about the shape of a slice of pie."

"Ah, my daily piece of pie," he said through his broad grin.

"That's it," I exclaimed. "Our daily wood. Can you do it?"

"I think I can," he said. "I'll send it to you in week or so."

What I got in the mail was a drawing of a slice of pie that replicated daily wood consumption in the United States, which leads the industrialized world in wood consumed every 24 hours. Wink's calculation came with an explanation of wood's numerous environmental advantages of competing structural building materials, specifically steel, aluminum and concrete.

He wrote that he was "delighted" to inform me that wood consumption in the U.S. is 3.5 times the global average. "That's wonderful," he said. "We should be using more of it. No other material offers so many environmental benefits."

In short order, I found a carpenter in Medford, Oregon who said he could make as many pie slices as I wanted in Wink's exact dimensions. While he was busy cutting and fine-sanding my first 100-block order, I wrote a brief explanation that a T-shirt shop in Grants Pass silkscreened on each block. Here's the block:

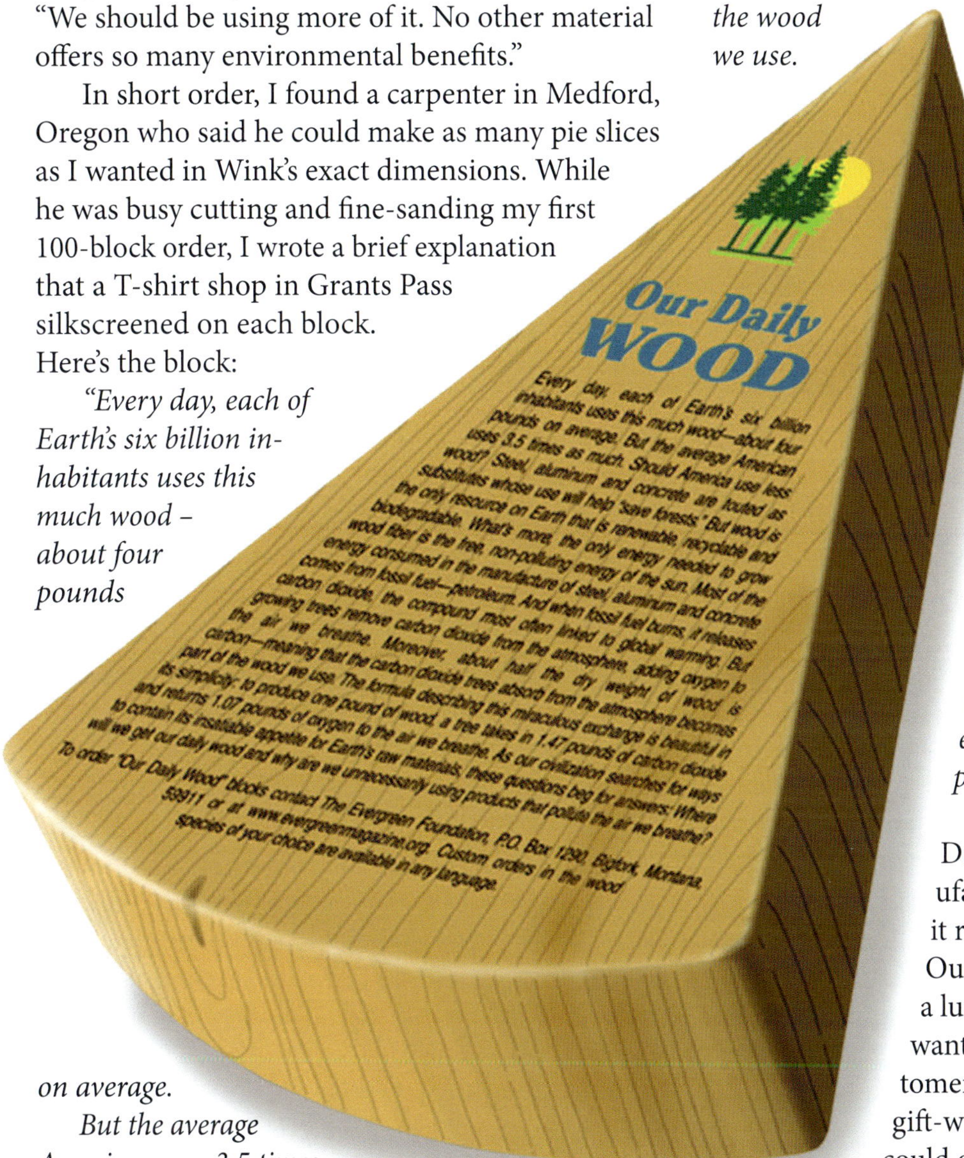

"Every day, each of Earth's six billion inhabitants uses this much wood – about four pounds on average.

But the average American uses 3.5 times this much. Should America use less wood? Steel, aluminum and concrete are touted as substitutes whose use will help 'save forests.' But wood is the only natural resource on earth that is renewable, recyclable and biodegradable. What's more, the only energy needed to grow wood fiber is the free, non-polluting energy of the sun.

Most of the energy consumed in the manufacture of steel, aluminum and concrete comes from fossil fuel – petroleum. And when fossil fuel burns, it releases carbon dioxide, the compound most often linked to global warming. But growing trees remove carbon dioxide from the atmosphere, adding oxygen to the air we breathe.

Furthermore, more than half the dry weight of wood is carbon, meaning that the carbon dioxide trees absorb from the atmosphere becomes part of the wood we use.

The formula describing this miraculous exchange is beautiful in its simplicity: to produce one pound of wood, a tree takes in 1.47 pounds of carbon dioxide and returns 1.07 pounds of oxygen to the air we breathe.

As our civilization searches for ways to contain its insatiable appetite for Earth's raw materials, these questions beg for answers: Where will we get our daily wood and why are we unnecessarily using products that pollute the air we breathe?"

I have no idea how many Daily Wood blocks we manufactured over the years but it runs into the thousands. Our biggest order came from a lumber broker in Rome. He wanted 1,000 for his best customers – individually boxed and gift-wrapped for Christmas. And could our message be translated into Italian? It took some doing but we got it done. The boxes were shrink-wrapped on pallets, trucked to Seattle and shipped to Rome via the Panama Canal.

It would be fun for Julia and me to go to Europe someday to see if we could find any of those blocks. Rome would be a good place to start. Thousands more hang on the walls in lumber company offices all over the U.S. and Canada. We haven't made any blocks for years. Each was handmade and cost us $27 boxed. No one wants to pay that much, so the educational opportunity has been lost.

In recent years, our Daily Wood narrative has morphed into something very different – a graphic explanation of the amount of national forest timber killed annually by diseases and fire – lousy forest policy, neglect and mismanagement.

It all started with my asking a number cruncher in the Forest Service's regional office in Albuquerque if he could come up with a visual that represented forest mortality in national forests in Arizona and New Mexico. To my joyful amazement, he chose a football field. Perfect!

We have used the football field visual to illustrate national forest mortality in several western states: Idaho, Montana, California, Washington, Arizona, New Mexico and Colorado. We assembled *Colorado's Forest Crisis* [60] at the request of Lyle Laverty, an old friend and Forest Service retiree who had been asked to address the Colorado State Legislature.

This PDF holds Lyle's testimony and the bar graph comparing growth, mortality and removals. I hope you'll download it on your computer. I think you'll be stunned by what you see.

Lyle later told me he was deluged by questions from state legislators wondering how such a calamity could have occurred. My wonder is where his legislature has been for the last 25 years. How could anyone miss the near-destruction of Denver's entire watershed in the 2002 Hayman Fire?

The story is much the same in every western state. Legislators from rural areas understand the roots of our wildfire pandemic, but understanding is reduced to disbelief in western urban centers, and you don't have to travel too far east of Denver before you discover that no one gives a damn. Floods, tornadoes and hurricanes are the big worries.

The beautiful and compelling story of trees and the daily miracle they perform for us has been swept away by other more worrisome storylines that preoccupy us but numb our appreciation for what may be the greatest of all natural wonders: the formation of wood and its ubiquitous presence in our daily lives. There is a short history lesson here that I hope you will enjoy.

60 

In 1850, an English landscape architect named Joseph Paxton designed what was surely the most impressive building of its era. It was called the Crystal Palace. Built to celebrate Victorian-era technological advancements, the structure was 1,848 feet long, 108 feet tall and 408 feet wide – more than six times the length of a football field and more than two-and-one-half times its width. Its superstructure supported 293,655 panes of glass; hence its name.

More than six million people – roughly one-third of the entire population of the United Kingdom – strolled beneath the Palace's glass ceiling. No doubt British historian Thomas Macaulay spoke for all his countrymen when he called Paxton's Palace "a most gorgeous site; vast, graceful; beyond the dreams of the Arabian romances."

But Macaulay failed to note one important detail about the Palace. Its most awe inspiring feature – a great glass dome that stretched the length of the building – was framed in wood – more than 60,000 cubic feet of it. Perhaps he did not notice because Paxton had wisely ordered the wood superstructure painted to look like steel. Otherwise the public would never have entered the Palace, fearing its collapse. But Paxton knew the truth about wood's enormous strength and was willing to risk his reputation on its structural integrity.

The magazine *Natural History* attributed Paxton's daring to his discovery of "a simple yet elegant design canon, discovered by plants millions of years ago – the principle of minimum weight. Because every material used to stiffen or support a structure also adds to the total load the structure must bear, adding height unavoidably means trading off between a material's strength and its weight."

What Paxton knew was that, pound for pound, wood is stronger than steel because it has a more favorable strength to weight ratio. The secret to its great strength lies in cellulous, the basic ingredient in all plant cell walls. You can't see this cellular structure with the naked eye, but it is stiffer and stronger than nylon, silk, chitin, collagen, tendon or bone – a fact that goes a long way toward explaining why the largest living organisms are trees, and why wood is a near perfect building material. Lorna Gibson, a professor of engineering at Massachusetts Institute of Technology, attributes wood's mechanical efficiency to its unique-in-nature combination of composite and cellular structure.

Wood's exceptional performance in bending reflects the fact that the trunk and branches of a tree are often loaded in bending; the trunk by the wind and the branches by their own weight. It arises from the honeycomb-like structure of the wood cells as well as the great stiffness and strength of the cellulose fibers."

Writer and filmmaker Delta Willis talked about this in an article published in Natural History in February 1996.

"The whole design of a tree limb employs the yin and yang of good engineering – tension and compression, or pull and push," she wrote. "This allows saplings to become vertical again after being buried by snow. [When wind blows on a tree, the windward side of the tree is in tension and the leeward side is in compression.] In broad-leaved trees, the upper side of a limb normally grows faster than the lower side, and the cells on the upper side shrink longitudinally. When a branch bends under a load of snow, the cells of the tree limb's upper side shrink to allow for recovery."

Joseph Paxton was not the first to exploit wood's wondrous powers. In her fine book, "*The Sand Dollar and the Slide Rule*," Ms. Willis writes that Leonardo da Vinci sketched a sleek hull design based on the movements of fish in water. Five hundred years later the Wright Brothers designed a set of stabilizers for their Kitty Hawk after observing that turkey vultures used their primary feathers to reduce turbulence at low speeds. Alexandre Gustave Eiffel used a so-called fish belly design in the fabrication of light weight lattice-work that holds his 984-foot tall, 10,100-ton Eiffel Tower upright 119 years after construction was completed. More recently, German physicist Claus Mattheck redesigned the threads on a spiral screw to mimic the way a tree limb is reinforced by the trunk. Elsewhere, biomimetics [mimicking nature in scientific applications] has been used to improve the designs of artificial joints, electric razors, automobile parts and washing machines. But it was Paxton who first observed that the five to six foot leaves of giant Guyana water lilies were rigid enough to support the weight of his five-year-old daughter. The pattern of their cross-rib veins was the inspiration for the latticework on his Crystal Palace.

Tensile strength – the stretching ability of a particular fiber, measured in pounds per square inch – is a factor architects and engineers apply in the selection of both building designs and building materials. Cellulous in trees has a tensile strength of 15,000 pounds per square inch, slightly more than a muscle tendon's 12,000 psi but far less than the 35,000 psi registered by spider silk, which is five times stronger than steel.

Bruce Hoadley, who has a PhD in wood technology and teaches at the University of Massachusetts, explained wood's great strength to me in a 1993 interview in his Amherst office.

"Think about this for a moment," he said. "Here we have this natural material created by nature out of free solar energy, water and carbon dioxide. Put this stuff under a microscope and you see millions of wood cells joined together in ways that allow them to transfer and share load-bearing stresses. As trees, these cellular structures engineered in nature make perfect columns and beams. And what are the roof, wall and floor systems in houses? They are systems of columns and beams. This is why wood is an ideal building material."

I have a copy of *Identifying Wood*, a beautiful picture book Bruce assembled in 1990. He has been an expert witness in numerous court proceedings, writes for several wood working magazines and is a widely respected appraiser of period wood furniture. When asked to describe him a few years ago, I said I thought he was a living testament to the fact that most of us feel some sort of mysterious attachment to wood.

"Maybe it's the feel or the touch," he suggested when I asked him about it in 1993. "Or its smell or the knowledge that wood comes from trees; or maybe it's just a natural human response to a world crammed full of artificial environments. Whatever it is it is causing people to reach out for wood in the form of decks, hot tubs, wood floors, open beams, wood-frame windows and even outdoor furniture made from wood."

We also know that when people sit for a few minutes in a wood-paneled room their blood pressure goes down. What we don't know is why. Maybe it's just the act of sitting down and resting for a moment. Maybe the muted wood tones have something to do with it or perhaps wood surroundings have the same calming effect as a walk in the forest.

Might it have something to do with wood's warmth? The microscopic air pockets in its honeycomb structure give it 1,400 times the insulating value of aluminum. If you've ever sat on an aluminum park bench you know how cold they can be. Not so with a wood bench.

In the hope of moving beyond the esoteric and on into the world of measurable and reproducible science, the National Academy of Sciences formed a research group in 1976 called CORRIM – The Consortium for Research on Renewable Industrial Materials. It produced a landmark study that, among other things, compared the amounts of energy consumed in the manufacture of building materials made from aluminum, steel, brick, concrete blocks and wood. The results were startling.

From extraction to finished product, the energy consumed in the manufacture of one ton of aluminum was 70 times greater than the amount of energy consumed in the manufacture of one ton of wood. Steel consumed 17 times as much energy; brick and concrete blocks three times as much as wood.

Even more startling: for each one billion board feet of wood replaced by a wood substitute, oil consumption increased by about 720 million gallons and carbon emissions increased by 7.5 million tons.

You can read more about CORRIM's impressive research on their website.[61] It is an absolute treasure trove for anyone wanting to understand the relationship between energy sources and carbon cycling.

CORRIM is only one of several well-respected research groups available to you. Forintek Canada,[62] a public-private sector research alliance, is another powerhouse whose work is at your fingertips.

Following on CORRIM's early lead, Forintek scientists analyzed two, 10-foot by 100-foot wall assemblies – one made of wood and the other

61 

62 

from steel. Among their surprising discoveries: it took four times as much energy to manufacture the steel needed for a steel wall as it took to manufacture the wood needed for the wood wall; carbon dioxide emissions were three times greater and water consumption was 25 times greater.

"There isn't any doubt about it," my friend, Wink Sutton said of wood's many environmental advantages during our 1991 chat in Vancouver, British Columbia. "The world should be using more wood, not less."

Trees begin their lives in the organic soil layer that is being incinerated in the West's wildfire pandemic. The hottest fires transform organic soil into a pasty substance water cannot penetrate. But let's put a happy face on this story for a moment. Seeds sprout in the right mix of water, sunlight and warmth. Sprouting sends the first shoot upward and the first root downward.

How a seed knows that this is what it is supposed to do is its own mystery. Some say it is God's work. Others credit "intelligent design." Some say it's just "nature."

My memories run to Sunnyside School where, as third graders, we planted beans in half-pint milk cartons from the cafeteria. Mrs. Ross set them on window ledges so we could watch them sprout. Then I took mine home and transplanted them in the back yard. I love fresh cut green beans.

Like all green plants, trees make their own food through a process called photosynthesis. It occurs in chlorophyll-heavy leaves as they soak up the sun's rays. It takes about eight minutes for the free, non-polluting energy of the sun to reach earth's surface. Fueled by the sun's energy, water, soil nutrients and carbon dioxide combine to make sugar and oxygen. Trees releases their oxygen into the atmosphere and use the sugar to produce all of their parts – more leaves, wood, bark, roots, flowers and fruit.

The absorption of carbon dioxide is called carbon sequestration. Carbon is the building block of every living organism on earth, but it's been getting a bad rap lately because of climate change worries that are exacerbated by wildfires that release millions and millions of tons of carbon dioxide and other nasty chemical compounds into the air we breathe – and some of it ends up in our lungs.

Privately-owned forests like this Inland Empire Paper Company forest near Spokane, Washington, provide most of the wood fiber we consume daily.

Sun-powered photosynthesis has stored about 11 percent of all U.S. carbon dioxide emissions over the last 25 years. Trees are said to "breathe" as they take in CO_2 and release oxygen into the atmosphere.

Deepak Chopra, the Indian-born author, lecturer and alternative medicine advocate speaks for many Americans in his lyrical claim that, "The trees are our lungs, the rivers our circulation, the air our breath, the earth our body. Protect our natural world the same way you would take care of a loved one."

Viewed through Chopra's metaphorical lens, we aren't doing this in our national forests, not by a long shot, but I digress.

The actual tree growing process is beautifully described in a pamphlet titled *How A Tree Grows*, written by Virginia Master Naturalist, Mike Steele, and distributed by the Virginia Department of Forestry. Here's a summation of what Mike wrote:

Trees *grow up, out and down* as new cells are produced at the tips of twigs, causing the twigs to grow longer.

Trees grow out as their trunks and branches add new cells beneath their bark. These cells – xylem and phloem – perform different functions.

Trees grow *down* by their roots. Microscopic tube-like hairs near the growing tips take in water from the soil. In a large tree, these tiny hairs can absorb hundreds of gallons of water in a day, though only a small portion is used in photosynthesis. The rest is released from the leaves through a process called transpiration.

On hot afternoons, this bluish vapor can look like smoke. Picture the Great Smokey Mountains in Tennessee and the Blue Mountains in eastern Oregon. What you're actually seeing are volatile organic hydrocarbons – mainly terpenes and isoprenes – two molecules that are linked to photochemical smog. Isoprene drives the rate at which the sun's rays break down nitrogen oxides, producing atmospheric ozone.

Pale blue ozone is formed when oxygen comes in contact with ultraviolet light or an electrical charge, giving it three atoms. It is a godsend in the stratosphere eight to 12 miles above the earth because it screens out cancer-causing ultraviolet rays. But closer to home, it is a toxin that causes stinging eyes, prickling nostrils and severe breathing problems for some people.

We're off course. Back to our oxygen-giving tree.

Active xylem, also called sapwood, carries water and nutrients from the roots to the leaves. Old xylem no longer carries water. It forms the heartwood of the tree and is usually a different color than sapwood.

Phloem, the inner bark, carries food from the leaves to the branches, trunk and roots. Outside the phloem is the outer bark that protects the tree from injury.

A tree's cambium layer is located between the phloem and xylem. Although it is only one cell layer thick, it's all important job is to manufacture new xylem and phloem cells so the tree can continue to grow up, down and out.

Trees grow fastest in the spring and early summer, adding a layer of light-colored wood. Growth slows in the late summer and fall, adding a second layer of darker wood. These layers reveal themselves as rings in the wood. One light plus one dark layer of wood equals one year of growth. The rings are wider when the tree has lots of water and sunlight plus sufficient growing space, and the gap between rings narrows when trees are crowded by other trees and there is more competition for sunlight, moisture and soil nutrients.

The rampant tree mortality we see in western national forests is a direct result of overcrowding. I know I sound like a broken record, but we have too damned many trees for the carrying capacity of the land – the sum of soil fertility, moisture, elevation, aspect and growing space.

Our wildfire pandemic is nature's "three strikes and you're out" response to the mess we've created – the strikes being insect infestations, rampant root diseases and stand replacing wildfires.

The run-up to what we are witnessing in western national forests is recorded in the rings of trees, more precisely the gaps between these rings. These gaps reveal moist years, when growing conditions were favorable, and dry years when there was little or no growth.

Fire scars on trees can be closely matched to the year when the fire occurred. This is because when fire scorches a tree, the tree floods its wound with sap that can protect the wound from decay for hundreds of years if subsequent fires burn at low heat. All bets are off in the 1,500 degree heat of today's wildfires. These fires generate 10,000 kilowatts of energy in any given moment, enough to heat and light our home and office for three months in the dead of winter.

In 2002, we published an in-depth *Evergreen* report titled "The New Pioneers." It was a major undertaking partly funded by the U.S. Forest Service, which wanted to highlight its effort to recruit cottage industries to Arizona and New Mexico in hopes that they could utilize the millions of tons of small diameter trees that needed to be removed from dying national forests.

In my travels around the two states, I interviewed dozens of entrepreneurs and innovators – scavengers really – who were trying to turn mostly worthless trees into profit centers in their small businesses:

Phil Archuletta was grinding juniper and plastic milk cartons at his shop in Mountainair, New Mexico to make road signs for the Forest Service. Gordon West was crafting beautiful pine furniture in tiny Santa Clara, New Mexico.

Steve Hall hoped to make a killing burning biomass in a cobbled together powerplant at Eagar, Arizona. The Ribelin brothers office near Flagstaff, Arizona was surrounded by log decks they could not profitably sell because there were no mills within a hundred miles. Loggers Ray and Louis Cordova of Cuba, New Mexico were also struggling to find markets for their small-diameter logs. So were the Walker Brothers, loggers whose claim to fame was that they had done a good deal of thinning for Ted Turner on his New Mexico ranch.

Meanwhile, Turner was financing the Center for Biological Diversity litigation machine at Tucson, Arizona. Turner was fine with thinning work on his ranch but opposed similar work on national forests in the Southwest. They were so effective that a well-respected logger refused a Forest Service grant that would have paid for a new mechanical harvester because he knew litigators would stop every thinning projects they agency developed for him.

Ninety-year-old Ted Wilbert hoped to solve everyone's problems by building a pulp and paper making complex at Belen, a few miles north of Albuquerque, New Mexico, but with all the new homes being built in the Rio Grande Valley, he could not find sufficient water. The locals breathed a sigh of relief.

Ed Collins, a U.S. Forest Service District Ranger, was doing his damnedest to dispose of ground biomass generated by a 17,000-acre thinning project near Lakeside, Arizona but there were no takers. Taxpayers picked up the tab for the project, which was designed to protect both Lakeside and nearby Show Low from wildfires that had threatened both communities.

In the course of my research Wally Covington, the charismatic director of Northern Arizona University's Ecological Restoration Institute, suggested that I check out the University of Arizona Tree Ring Research project. I did – and I was both surprised and very pleased to find a body of science that helped explain the influence of climate cycles on the widespread tree mortality I was seeing in Arizona and New Mexico.

The Laboratory of Tree-Ring Research was founded in 1937 by A.E. Douglass, a Vermont native and founder of the modern science of dendrochronology – the dating and study of annual tree rings. For some weird reason, I am amused by the fact that Douglass wasn't a forester. Not even close. He was a physicist and mathematician whose fascination with astronomy led him to Arizona Territory in 1894, where he helped Percival Lowell build an observatory near Tucson.

The two men eventually had a falling out – Lowell believed the canals on Mars were built by Martians – so Douglass wrangled an astronomy and physics teaching job at the University of Arizona, which gave him the opportunity to study solar variability – the possibility that there was a connection between observable sunspot cycles and weather changes.

There being no long-term weather data, Douglass turned his investigation in a direction few astronomers would have tried. Might the growth rings in northern Arizona's virgin ponderosa pines act as proxies for the climate data he sought? His initial investigation confirmed a common pattern in precise wide and narrow rings that Douglass could substitute for actual weather data.

Archeologists who knew of Douglass' work asked if the same methodology might be used to date ruins that held old wooden beams. At the time, the ring count in live trees only extended back 600 years – hardly sufficient to date ruins that might be thousands of years old. A series of Douglass-led field expeditions funded by the National Geographic Society proved so fruitful that he was able to map the Southwest's climate in reverse for 2,000 years.

Douglass' remarkable achievement brought him so much acclaim in scientific circles that he was able to found both the modern science of den-drochronology and the Tree Ring Research Center [63] in Tucson.

Notice how our warming and cooling cycles look like undulating sine waves. Wet cycles in the Southwest have averaged 225 years and dry cycles 339 years. The last long dry spell – 1399-1790 – caused Indians in six settlements to move. There wasn't sufficient runoff to fill the irrigation system they had built to water their crops. The wettest winter-spring period in recent years – 1919 – spawned a surge in ponderosa pine growth in northern Arizona and New Mexico. And as dry as it currently is in the Southwest, it turns out the region has been in a wet cycle for more than 200 years.

There are also mini-warming and cooling cycles embedded in the longer cycles. I made good money shoveling snow in our neighborhood in the 1950s, thanks to a cooling cycle that dumped tons of snow in Kellogg winter after winter. Four feet on the level wasn't unusual. The big money was in shoveling roofs.

That same cooling period triggered a change in tree species distribution in Intermountain mixed conifer dry-site forests that we are still battling. Shade-tolerant white fir quickly colonized sites where fire had been excluded or too many ponderosa and western larch trees have been logged. White fir's thin bark and need for more moisture makes them susceptible to insects, root rot diseases and killing wildfires.

Although Douglass died in 1962, his dendrochronology research goes on, blending tree ring research with archaeology, climatology, geology and ecology. If you're traveling in the Southwest, the Tucson, Arizona lab hosts a great tour.

By now, you should be wondering what on earth connects tree ring research to dendrochronology to photosynthesis, tree growth, carbon uptake and storage, the environmental advantages of wood,

63

increasing global consumption of raw materials, climate change and our wildfire crisis. The connect-the-dots answers can be found in several lengthy reports that function as my desk references.

Of these sources, the one I hold in highest regard is "Global Climate Change," the April/May 2008 edition of the *Journal of Forestry*. I know of no other single source that is as comprehensive or even-handed in its treatment of an issue fraught with controversy. I want to walk you through its 173 pages as painlessly as possible so you'll keep turning the pages of this book!

Here are the main points in the *Journal of Forestry* report:

- Forests are shaped by climate and climate is shaped by forests.
- Climate change and increasing atmospheric carbon will affect forests in many ways, not least the increasing presence of insects and disease.
- Climate change is considered to be the primary driver of the increasing frequency and intensity of wildfires in the western United States.
- Increasing tree mortality will feed the wildfire cycle.
- Our recent years have been the warmest since 1850.
- The warming trend is associated with in creasing concentrations of atmospheric carbon dioxide [CO_2] and other greenhouse gases. [GHG]
- The "greenhouse effect" begins when GHG's in the atmosphere allow the sun's short-wavelength radiation to pass through the earth's surface, where it is absorbed. But when this radiation re-enters the atmosphere as longer wavelength radiation, GHG's trap the heat close to earth. Hence, the warming cycle we are experiencing.
- Carbon dioxide is the most common GHG but there are many more.
- Human activity and natural processes produce GHGs.
- Carbon dioxide is the most common GHG produced by human activity.
- Photosynthesis is the natural process by which trees and other plants convert atmospheric carbon dioxide into carbohydrates that yield more trees and plants. This process is driven by the sun, water and soil nutrients.
- Forests are unique among all possible remedies because they can both prevent and reduce GHG emissions while simultaneously providing essential environmental and social benefits.
- To prevent GHG emissions, use more wood and less steel, aluminum, concrete and plastic.
- Life cycle analysis reveals that wood products used in construction store more carbon and use less fossil energy than steel, concrete, brick or vinyl.
- A concrete floor produces more than four times the GHG emissions of a dimensional lumber or wood I-joist floor, and a steel design increases the global warming potential [GWP] by 731. Likewise, steel stud walls increase GWP by 44 percent.
- To further prevent GHG emissions, convert wood waste to biofuels and bioenergy, reducing our reliance of fossil fuels, like oil and coal.
- Wildland fires are a major source of GHGs.
- We can reduce GHGs by modifying fire behavior.
- Combustion and decay from just four wildfires that burned in California in the early 2000s dumped 38 million tons of GHG into Golden State skies, an amount equal to the annual emissions of seven million cars.
- Reducing forestland conversion to other uses – urban sprawl – can reduce GHGs. Globally, forestland conversions between 1850 and 1998 released 149 billion tons of carbon into earth's atmosphere – about one-third of the total for the time period.
- Forests store carbon in trees and soil. They blanket one-third of our nation's 2.95 million square mile land mass. As such, they represent a significant carbon "sink."
- The ability of a forest to store carbon is influenced by soil productivity, tree species mix, the ratio of live to dead trees and the presence of insects and root diseases.
- Forest carbon storage capacity can be in-

creased by prompt reforestation following harvest or a wildfire, controlling tree density which increases natural resistance to insect and disease infestations.
- Although fire can be an effective forest management tool, extinguishing big wildfires as quickly as possible reduces associated environmental impacts and minimizes GHG emissions.
- Thinning trees from overstocked and fire-prone forests reduces both the risk of large-scale wildfire and resulting GHG emissions.
- Forest management and the increasing use of wood products adds substantially to a forest's capacity to store carbon, thereby mitigating the impacts of climate change.
- Substantial net reductions in carbon dioxide emissions can be made by substituting wood for other construction materials – steel, aluminum, concrete and plastic. Carbon can also be stored in wood for long periods.
- Regional "cap and trade" programs that focus on afforestation – planting trees on land not previously forested – increase forest carbon storage. "Cap and trade" thus allows GHG polluters to "offset" their emissions.

Just for the fun of it, think about this for a moment. Fluctuations in the composition of our atmosphere – more or less carbon dioxide, nitrous oxide, methane and what have you – have ushered in profoundly different climate regimes over many millions of years. One hundred million years ago, alligators roamed the Russian north, redwoods grew in Alberta and the carbon dioxide level in earth's atmosphere was four to eight times what it is today – an estimate that has prompted agricultural scientists to note that a warmer planet would yield more croplands for earth's 7.5 billion inhabitants.

There is much more to be learned from reading the entire 173-page *Journal of Forestry* report, but for me the big takeaways are:

- Trees are nature's carbon storage box.
- The two best places to store carbon are [1] forests and [2] environmentally friendly wood products.
- No matter where we live, forests are the apex of our lives. We should not allow wildfires to destroy them without putting up one hell of a fight.

Without mentioning carbon or sequestration, Craig Thomas, a genius of a logger I've known for years put the *Journal* report into a boots-on-ground perspective in a quite memorable note he wrote me in November of 2008.

There being no logging jobs in Montana and needing to feed his family and keep his bills paid, he had loaded some of his logging equipment on a trailer and hauled it to the Midwest where he wrangled a job digging trenches across mile after mile of farmland for a gas line installer. He kept me in progress photos while he was there, then wrote me shortly after he got home from his six-month odyssey.

"Many of my forest restoration projects in western Montana yield 20 to 60 tons of biomass while leaving the best trees properly spaced and ready to grow again," he wrote. "If we figure 30 tons per acre it equals 1,740 gallons of diesel energy, enough value to complete the projects. If carbon credits are added, the economics become very favorable."

Craig is good with numbers. They are the entry point in most of his "communications" with me, a word he uses that reminds me that he is a University of Montana forestry school graduate and most foresters become foresters because they aren't wordsmiths and they prefer the company of trees to the often less pleasant company of people.

"Each pound of green wood fiber contains about 4,000 BTUs of energy and dry much more," he wrote in his November 7 letter. "A gallon of diesel contains about 138,000 BTUs. A ton of woody biomass contains more than eight million BTUs of energy, about the same as 58 gallons of diesel. The problem with rating biomass energy the same way we rate fossil fuels is that we are comparing apples and oranges. Instead of rating wood residual values, we need to compare energy value to energy value in BTUs."

This is Craig's habit of starting a conversation midstream. But we soon enter the introspective world of windshield time and its antecedent, long nights spent living alone in a cramped travel trailer in the godforsaken and windy middle of nowhere of central Iowa. Lots of time to think big

New Mexico entrepreneur, Phil Archuletta, developed a way to press ground wood and ground up milk jugs to manufacture roadside signs and placards.

thoughts because there is nothing else to do except eat, sleep, grease machinery and work.

"When I re-entered my small office here at home this week I was greeted by a note I'd pasted on the wall months earlier," he wrote. In bold letters it read, **DO WHAT IS RIGHT FOR THE FOREST**. "I meant it when I wrote it, and I practice it, but I now believe it ever more. The mills here will come and go and so will guys like me, but if we treat the forest right it will be here forever."

He then went on to tell me that he'd driven to Ovando, a whistle stop about an hour northeast of Missoula made famous by the cold beer and fabulous burgers they serve at Trixi's, a roadside oasis named for a former trick rider and showgirl who owned the place in the 1950s. One of Craig's old thinning jobs is near there, just off Highway 200. He wanted to see how the residual trees were growing.

"We jumped a large blond grizzly bear on a turn in the road," he reported. "What an absolutely beautiful animal. I wish I had another eye that was a great camera because he was gone before I could get my camera from behind the pickup seat."

To Craig's great surprise, his thinning demo had attracted a good deal of mostly favorable public reaction. One man complained – but then he invited Craig to join him for dinner so they could talk about it. The pair parted friends but Craig later reminded me that whenever he shut down his equipment to explain what he was doing to a passerby, it cost him $5 a minute. Trust me, my friend isn't capable of talking for a minute or even five. Figure 20 to 30 minutes on the short side.

"These demos are not logging for logs as those days are history," Craig wrote. "These are treatments that place the forest first, empathizing what is left and removing what is necessary to establish a starting point in the forest's future. They are more expensive to do than industrial logging jobs but are easily accomplished when the cost savings is available in the energy industry."

Now Craig is homing in on the real reason he has written me so soon after his return from the Midwest.

"Pulling together here, we can have a really neat place to live as we collect biomass for fuel. It is as valuable as oil, yet green and renewable, and we leave the larger majestic trees and other plants of choice for other forest residents. Just do what is right for the forest and let the chips fall where they may!"

"Environmentalists have won the war against the logging industry," he wrote without hesitation. "But now that they have won we need leadership for a new direction which can make an important investment in upgrading our forests while contributing much to society's fuel situation. I see great opportunities here and I am completely astounded that the energy industry and mainstream politicians have overlooked these HUGE opportunities."

The next three pages of his letter are filled with BTU calculations that would bore you to tears, but his concluding paragraph will not.

"Leave the best trees well-spaced and remove the brush, dead and sick trees and other biomass. Process the biomass, probably as wood chips, for 50 percent the value of an equivalent energy source and divide the other 50 percent between the landowner, logger and processor. We will have the most economical and environmentally positive energy systems in the history of mankind."

I don't doubt it. How else to explain the millions of dollars oil industry lobbyists and their environmentalist cohorts have spent trying to sabotage the whole idea of converting woody biomass to energy.

"Liquidating old growth to make toilet paper," they claim. Nonsense. We don't cut old growth timber in our federally-owned forests and haven't for nearly 30 years. Most of our country's paper mills moved offshore 20 years ago in search of cheaper labor and raw material. Chances are your toilet paper came from Brazil where it grew in a never-ending seven-year cycle in a meticulously maintained plantation within eyesight of a paper milling complex the size of small town.

Craig Thomas is right. A biomass-to-energy industry would suck up millions of tons of crap that is currently fueling the West's wildfire pandemic.

Wink Sutton is right too. Someday, someone is going to unlock the cellulose molecule at its molecular level and we will be able to replace fossil fuels forever with Real Green Jobs. More on this later.

Meantime, we need to hunt up someone here in northern Idaho with a good table saw and some free time who can cut up a hundred new wood blocks for us. Then someone to silkscreen a new message and seal coat the blocks so the words can't be smeared or easily rubbed away.

I think "Our Daily Tankful" ought to turn some heads.

The small tree revolution

When I started Evergreen Magazine in 1986, Oregon led the nation in lumber production and bustling Roseburg in Douglas County on Interstate 5 three hours south of Portland billed itself as "The timber capital of the World." The armada of sawmills based in Douglas County manufactured more lumber and plywood than any other county in the United States. Neighboring Lane County was close and adjoining Josephine, Jackson, Curry and Coos counties weren't far behind.

The late Kenneth Ford, the mega-force behind the Roseburg Lumber Company, was probably a billionaire by then. At least Forbes magazine thought so, but he refused to be interviewed, so no one knew for sure.

All I know is that when I asked him how he did it, he stared at me for what seemed like an eternity, then said, "Some people learn how to play. I learned how to work." Then he sidestepped me and was gone down a long hallway. It was the only time we ever spoke and I felt fortunate that he hadn't ordered me out of the company's office for daring to speak to him. He was an intensely private man.

Ford's biggest sawmill at Dillard, nine miles south of Roseburg was the largest in the nation. It ran 24/7 and consumed 600 truckloads of logs every day. Local lore had it that Ford knew how many logs were in every deck. I doubt it but he was almost always in the log yard by daylight because he preferred the company of men who got their hands dirty every day.

God only knows how many log trucks there were in southern Oregon. I'd hazard a guess there were at least 1,500 in the five-county area. Ireland Trucking at Myrtle Creek had about 300 log trucks and Stalcup Trucking at Coos Bay had maybe 100 chip trucks. Trucks belonging to R.B. Browns, R.B. Slagle and Floyd Martin seemed to be everywhere.

You could not drive more than three or four minutes on Interstate 5 or any of its state or county arterials without seeing a loaded log or chip truck, a reminder that you lived in the midst of the largest lumber and plywood manufacturing complex on earth. Paraphrasing Stephen Ambrose from his transcontinental railroad epic, "There was nothing like it in the world."

Back then, some 30 years ago, most of the loaded log trucks rolling up and down I-5 held three to five good-sized logs, occasionally only one log – a giant eight feet in diameter and 32 feet long. You could not miss them. They were huge.

As impossible as it seems, the Forest Service of that era was focused on harvesting all of the old growth timber standing in the region's national forests, and they were doing it with congressional blessing!

It was assumed that everyone understood that old trees took up a lot of space on productive land better suited to growing "the next crop." The goal was to "get the land back into production" as quickly as possible – every acre fully stocked with Douglas-fir seedlings that grew like crazy in sun-filled clearcuts. "Site 1" ground bore seedlings that shot up four and five feet annually, a growth rate unmatched anywhere else in the world. If ever there was a place where the good Lord intended to grow timber, this was it.

I no longer recall the first time I heard about the northern spotted owl, but it was soon after we started publishing *Evergreen*. At the time, I was so focused on the Forest Service's first decadal forest plans – mandated by the 1976 National Forest Management Act – that I paid scant attention to the owl drumbeat that could be heard from Portland and Seattle, light years removed from the security blanket that was southern Oregon's mammoth timber industry.

It took a long time for the seriousness of the owl situation to settle in where I lived and worked, and by the time it did, it was too late. The federal government listed the owl as a threatened species in June of 1990 and the comfortable world we had known became a trauma ward filled with loggers and sawmill workers who had lost everything. Those in the bottom of the barrel existed in rest areas along Interstate 5 between Eugene and Medford.

Job loss estimates varied widely. Some said maybe 25,000 in western Oregon and Washington and northern California. Others pegged it as closer to 80,000. I think the direct losses – millworkers and loggers – were probably around 40,000, but if you added indirect and induced losses – those whose jobs were dependent on lumber and plywood manufacturing – possibly 70,000 lost their jobs.

It hardly mattered in the big scheme. Life did not change in Portland or Seattle but the bloodletting went on for years in places like Grants Pass, and Roseburg. None of these communities has ever fully recovered from the loss of so many high paying jobs, but they've done better than smaller, more remote places. One-mill towns like Cave Junction, Oregon and Yreka, California host tourists who are too tired to drive any further. The influx of Californians fed up with California has probably saved the southern Oregon economy from total collapse.

I was luckier than most. I found a buyer for my Colonial Valley home and used the proceeds to buy a 42-foot Teton fifth-wheel. I drove away in July 1995 and never looked back. Most of the friends I made during my 10 years there are dead now and all of the family-owned lumber companies that helped fund *Evergreen's* startup are gone too.

The only dire prediction that didn't come true is that the timber industry did not collapse. Measured in terms of annual production, it's bigger than it was before the spotted owl was listed and the federal timber sale program collapsed. You can be forgiven for wondering how this could happen. It happened because the companies that survived the owl listing invested billions in wood processing technologies that enabled them to manufacture lumber and panel products from progressively smaller-diameter trees. I watched this hope-filled story unfold on the bunks of log trucks traveling north and south on Interstate 5 beginning in the mid-1990s.

Two overlooked factors made this transition possible. First, these new logs were sourced from private lands replanted following World War II. They were uniformly sized and of far higher quality that the old growth logs that were harvested from national forests in the years following the war.

These new logs were products of genetically-superior seedlings that grew faster and straighter and resisted disease. They were grown from seeds collected from trees that displayed genetically superior growth characteristics. Ever in the hunt for a memorable six-second sound bite, environmental doomsayers were soon calling them "Franken-trees" in hopes of turning public opinion against their use. Former Forest Service Chief Jack Ward Thomas had been right. Some people are so hateful that they enjoy strolling the battlefield bayonetting the wounded.

The second factor that spawned the small tree revolution was unexpected. Many lumbermen feared the collapse of the federal timber sale program would trigger a costly bidding war for private logs. Never happened. So many mills had gone out of business that supply and demand soon stabilized for the first time in anyone's memory. One long time federal timber purchaser told me he'd be fine if only 10 percent of his logs came from national forests.

Throughout the long spotted owl war, environmentalists argued that job losses in mills were a direct result of "automation" by "rich" lumbermen who "didn't care" about their employees. Lumbermen claimed the losses were the result of a steep decline in federal timber sales and a corresponding increase in log prices. There was a kernel of truth in both arguments, but the marvelous story the owl-fixated press missed completely was the story of the new jobs and products that technological

Part of the Freres Lumber Company's mass panel plywood plant at Lyons, Oregon

advancements were creating before our very eyes.

But technological advancements in wood product manufacturing began long before computers, high speed band mills which replaced clunky circle saws or any of the laser-guided sawing systems that hit the market emerged in the 1980s .

The first "engineered wood product" made its debut at the Lewis and Clark Centennial Exposition in Portland, Oregon in 1905. It's presumed inventor was Gustav Carlson, manager of Portland Manufacturing, a maker of wooden fruit boxes. Carlson's "three-ply veneer work" drew the attention of several door, cabinet and trunk makers who eagerly placed orders.

The veneer panels were assembled from hand-peeled sections of Douglas-fir glued together with a paste made from animal residues that apparently smelled awful, then pressed using modified house jacks. From start to finish, the process took several hours. Even so, there were 17 plywood mills in the Portland-Seattle area by 1929 and the final product soon caught the eye of car builders who were soon using veneer to make running boards and car floors. But the market fizzled because the glue dissolved in water.

James Nevin, a PhD chemist at Harbor Plywood in Aberdeen, Washington, solved the problem in 1934 with a waterproof glue that opened the door to plywood's use in home construction, but its real fame came during the Second World War. The Navy chose it over steel for its fearsome Packard supercharged PT boats and its seeming indestructible Higgins landing craft because wood was more quickly and easily repaired in remote locations.

Plywood was soon on every war front. The Army crossed the Rhine River in plywood boats, the Seabees in the South Pacific lived in plywood huts, the Army Air Corps flew gliders made from plywood, the Merchant Marines packed nearly everything they shipped in plywood containers, and the Quartermaster Corps and Army Corps of Engineers built thousands of Series 700 barracks from exacting plans drawn by military architects.

None of this was good enough for my father.

Nor did it matter to him that Egyptian Pharaohs had used wood laminates to construct ornate tombs that survive to present day. When we doubled the size of our home in 1950, Dad chose one-by-six tongue and groove larch for the subfloor and floor.

I was six when he handed me a hammer and a carpenter's apron filled with 16 penny nails and showed me how to nail on the blue chalk line he had struck in perfect alignment with the floor's two-by-12-inch joists. The subfloor and floor both ran diagonally – the subfloor one way and the floor the opposite direction. The finished two-inch-thick floor could have carried a loaded freight train, which was exactly what Dad wanted.

By 1954, there were 101 plywood mills in the United States producing some four billion square feet of the stuff annually. Enough to cover 69,444 football fields. It was everywhere – except beneath the fortress my father built at 106 West Mission in Kellogg, Idaho.

I wonder if it ever occurred to him that all we'd done was fashion our own engineered product by cross-layering lumber in the same way veneer layers are laid. We were simply taking advantage of the added strength that comes with layering wood diagonally.

In that era, veneer was peeled mainly from old-growth Douglas-fir harvested from the West's national forests. God only knows how many homes were made from it but it must run into the millions. Old-growth veneer was expensive so the search for a less expensive substitute was soon underway. Oriented strand board [OSB] hit the homebuilding market in the late 1970s. Made from small wood strands, not solid sheets of veneer, it is glued together in cross-laminated layers. Same principle as plywood, but lower quality wood.

OSB spawned an even wider array of engineered wood products: I-beams and joists, laminated veneer lumber [LVL] and oriented strand lumber. The first piece of LVL I ever saw would have put an old growth log to shame. It was 40 feet long, eight feet wide and four feet tall. It was laying on a set of glistening steel rollers in an LVL plant in White City, Oregon. The spotless concrete floor was painted grey and the cavernous building was so quiet my tour guide and I could talk in normal tones of voice.

When I asked the plant manager what he could make from such a large piece of wood, his memorable reply was, "Anything you can afford. Big beams, the top and bottom pieces for I-joists, anything. Want some nice wooden salad bowls? We can make those too."

Building code writers and inspectors love these products because they are stronger, more stable and more predictable than dimension lumber. They don't expand or contract or twist or turn. Homebuilders love the stuff too because they can assemble a house with a small crane. Not many carpenters are needed so labor costs are a fraction of what they once were.

I saw my first glulam plant in 1972. I had been hired away from my cozy newspaper job with the Grants Pass Daily Courier by a hardscrabble Riddle, Oregon sawmill owner who admired my writing and needed a public relations guy for his company. I threw in the towel about eight months later because I was sure I was wasting his money learning his business, but I learned a great deal from Donald Ray Johnson, and we remained good friends until he died in 2010.

D.R. had a glulam plant next to his cogeneration plant which ran on wood waste that powered two General Electric generators he bought in upstate New York for $7.5 million. His peers thought he was crazy, but they often did and they were usually wrong. The cogen plant and the glulam plant made DR a bloody fortune, the former because he had secured very favorable rates from the Bonneville Power Administration and the latter because he had wrangled a sweetheart of a deal with the California Highway Department to make pre-cut glulam beams for roadside rest stops along Interstate 5 between Redding and San Diego. Glulam gave D.R. a lucrative market for his lesser quality Douglas-fir logs.

Five years after D.R. died, the company he founded in 1951 became the first U.S. company certified to manufacture cross-laminated timber panels [CLT], a product already in wide use in commercial high rise construction in Europe and Canada. The product draws on architectural elements present in both plywood and D.R. original glulam process.

Like LVL, CLT panels are assembled in billets eight to 10 feet wide, up to 20 inches thick and

64 feet long. The panels are made by gluing layers of dimension lumber of varying sizes and, like other I-joist and LVL assemblies, CLT products are quickly assembled by cranes. D.R. would be very pleased by what his daughters, Valerie and Jodi have done. Both girls were in grade school the first time D.R. took me home for dinner. I had such admiration for his fearless determination. Still do.

Not surprisingly, CLT already has a competing product – a wonderous collaboration of German-Austrian manufacturing prowess and youthful American genius. Twin brothers Kyle and Tyler Freres, grandsons of T.G. Freres, a legend among Oregon lumbermen are the driving forces behind North America's first Mass Panel Plywood [MPP] manufacturing facility.

I know this wonderful story well because I just finished assembling the 97-year history of the Freres Lumber Company. *Santiam Song* is so named because the company is based at Lyons, Oregon in the heart of the beautiful Santiam River Canyon east of Salem. In 1922, T.G. bought a steam powered circle saw overlooking the canyon.

Today the company that bears T.G.'s name is the largest family-owned veneer and plywood manufacturer in the nation. Its $23 million investment in mass panel technology the twins first saw in Austria took the engineered-wood world by storm. Every wood industry trade journal photographed the story of the plant's construction. So did my wife, Julia. She's a marvelous photographer with a keen eye for the innerworkings of machinery.

Santiam Song would not have been complete without us telling the behind-the-scenes story of the Freres family's decision to embrace MPP, a decision disrupted by the tragic death of Kyle and Tyler's father, Ted, T.G.'s youngest son. Ted was the heart and soul of the company's byzantine manufacturing complex and one of the nicest guys I've ever known. He was 68. His nephew, Rob, a friend of more than 30 years, is now the company's president.

Like LVL before it, veneer-based mass panel plywood is laid up in billets. Freres billets are 48 feet long, 12 feet wide and two feet thick. They are manufactured from suppressed Douglas-fir – suppressed meaning the trees grew slowly in tight quarters in forests that should have been thinned years ago but weren't. Once the billets are pressed, a CNC [computer numerical control] machine cuts them to exact customer specifications. Want a wooden sign, a wall assembly, stairs, an entire building? Done to a standard you can measure with a micrometer.

For reasons that defy rational thought, the nation's architects began to shy from wood use during the spotted owl wars. Such was the mind-numbing effectiveness of the environmentalist-led effort to publicly brand wood manufacturers as planet killers. At *Evergreen*, our well-received wood block became our main prop in our effort to call attention to wood's well-researched environmental advantages, but it took a tremendous amount of work by some very prestigious research outfits to encourage architects to reconsider wood use.

CORRIM – the Consortium for Research on Renewable Industrial Materials – led the way. Its ephemeral roots date from President Truman's 1952 Materials Policy Commission, which was charged with assessing post-war industrial raw material needs, but no real progress was made on the environmental assessment front until 1970, the year Congress fortuitously ratified the National Environmental Policy Act and the National Materials Policy Act.

NEPA's provisions would subsequently be used to nullify the use of domestic raw materials at the same time the lesser known National Materials Policy Act was attempting to encourage domestically-sourced raw materials because NEPA regulations favored domestic sources over imports from impoverished third-world nations where few, if any, environmental regulations existed.

Oddly, the National Commission on Materials Policy made no mention of wood in its 1973 report to Congress, despite the fact that retired Forest Service Chief, Ed Cliff, had written an entire section focused on renewable building materials. The oversight led several wood scientists, including Peter Koch, who was then chief scientist at the Southern Forest Experiment Station at Knoxville, Tennessee, to engage the National Science Foundation and the National Research Council. The two groups subsequently

Markets for small to medium size logs are robust in northern Idaho and northeast Washington. The Forest Service and private landowners can always profit from log sales, though some environmentalists think it is immoral for the Forest Service to sell its logs at a profit.

formed CORRIM, which was initially chaired by Jim Bethel, Dean of the College of Forestry at the University of Washington.

I knew both Koch and Bethel but in different venues. Koch for his magnificent post-retirement work with lodgepole pine at his laboratory in Corvallis, Montana and Bethel during the Iraqi oil panic of the late 1980s. Jim had retired by then but he was still up to his eyeballs in projects and he was horrified by Congress' failure to craft policies that favored domestic energy production from woody biomass.

We were seated at his kitchen table on Mercer Island when he said something so unforgettable that I turned it into a red, white and blue bumper sticker. It read, "If you like Iraqi oil, you'll love Russian timber!" It got a lot of laughs.

More important was CORRIM's progress against NIMBY-led public resistance to the use of domestic production of raw materials. NIMBY being "Not in my back yard," the battle cry of all who prefer an "out of sight, out of mind" approach to saving the planet. I don't so I was pleased to be invited to the 1991 Vancouver, British Columbia conference where I met both Jim Bowyer and Wink Sutton.

The conference, titled "Wood Product Demand and the Environment" drew scientists and policy analysts from a dozen countries. World population growth and skyrocketing demand for wood products were the focal points. It was a refreshing departure from the "stop doing that" hobgoblin peddled daily by environmentalists who hadn't had a new idea in decades.

Informal discussions at the conference led to the subsequent formation of CORRIM II, a nonprofit entity housed at the University of Washington and led by Bruce Lippke, Professor Emeritus at UW's School of Environmental and Forest Science. CORRIM II's primary focus has been on development of a consistent database for measuring environmental performance standards associated with the production, use, maintenance, reuse and disposal of alternative wood and non-wood materials used in light construction.

It is CORRIM II's work and its linkage to life cycle or "cradle to grave" assessments of various building material that persuaded the architectural profession to rethink its earlier decision to dismiss wood. More recently – and most likely at the behest of architects – CORRIM has taken on carbon mitigation. It is a far more complex task than anything described in the much ballyhooed Green New Deal. Tracking carbon inflows and outflows from structural building materials – including solar panels and wind turbines – will be no small chore. Likewise, the most common structural building materials: steel, aluminum, concrete, plastic and wood.

But here is what we currently know about cross laminated timbers and mass panel plywood that is playing to great applause in the architectural world. Both products can be made from small diameter trees – the very trees that we need to be removing from overcrowded national forests before they die and burn, before we instead store the carbon in our lungs.

This is a big, big deal in the forest restoration world because there now exists a viable and unsubsidized market for trees that had no commercial value a decade ago. It's also a big, big deal in the building design world. Skyscrapers are giving way to "plyscrapers" in the lexicon of architects who see exciting new possibilities for wooden buildings. Freres already has the fire certifications to construct MPP buildings up to 18 stories tall in the U.S. and Canada, but I have seen architectural renderings for buildings 50 and 60 stories tall – plyscrapers that integrate many structural materials including mass panel plywood and cross laminated timber.

Like the "farm to fork" movement, with its emphasis on sustainable, locally sourced farming – especially organic – the "forest to frame" movement has captured the fancy of a multitude of rainmakers: prestigious architectural firms, global engineering giants, national and international building code writers, major construction companies, forest policy analysts, conservative and progressive think tanks and the social media mavens at Twitter, YouTube, Daily Motion and Vimeo. This story – the story of what technology has wrought at the intersection of environmental passion and public need is big. Very big. But how do we become part of it with the U.S. Forest Service barely crawling through our national forests at a time when it should be sprinting flat out toward the finish line? That's next

CHAPTER 30

Solving forestry's Rubik's Cube

"I'm just an old Alabama farm boy. Around here, the squeaky wheel gets replaced. We don't carry grease and I'm not good at blowin' sunshine." Welcome to the take no-prisoners-world of Robert E. Lee, former District Ranger on the Chickasawhay Ranger District on southern Mississippi's Desoto National Forest and driving force behind the U.S. Forest Service's 2005 Hurricane Katrina Environmental Assessment – a *15-page* EA that his collaborative team completed in a mere *53 days* after Katrina tore through some 484,000 acres of the Desoto on August 29, 2005.

I have italicized 15-page and 53 days because, in the normal course, Forest Service Environmental Assessments take at least a year to complete and run hundreds of pages. Environmental Impact Statements can take from three to five years and run more than 1,000 pages.

More astonishing, the Katrina Assessment announced the agency's intent to salvage log and/or burn or otherwise treat 329,000 acres on the Chickasawhay Ranger District and another 249,000 acres on the adjoining Desoto Ranger District. Out west serial litigators would have had a field day.

"How did you do it," I ask Lee? And in the same breath, "Why aren't you still in federal court? "We're the Forest Service," he says. "We serve the American people, not special interests. The whole country. Right?"

Well, yes, I reply, you are the Forest Service, but out West where we live Environmental Assessments seem to go on forever and Environmental Impact Statements take forever times two. The Forest Service is very timid in its approach to anything having to do with EAs or EISs and salvage logging following a natural disaster is taboo. Getting sued can end careers.

"You have to know your business and you have to know what the National Environmental Policy Act allows and disallows," Lee replies. "As for the touchy-feely stuff, you have to get to the issues, get to the bottom line and take the risk necessary to do the job right."

The last Forest Service guy I knew who was this tough was the late Joe Pomajevich, who was Flathead National Forest Supervisor when I was hired by the *Daily Inter Lake* in Kalispell, Montana in 1968. He commanded great respect and he gave it in return. You asked a direct question. You got a direct answer. Sing-songy was not in Pomajevich's DNA, nor is it in Lee's.

Sensing disbelief that is surely written all over my face, the cheerful and non plussed Lee explains his role in completing the Desoto National Forest's Katrina EA in an unheard of 53 days.

"Here's my secret," he begins. "It's all about process and content, process and content. You have to train your environmentalists. Down here they know I'm a straight shooter. We're all trying to do the best we can for the land and that meant we were going to cut some timber that had been flattened by Katrina."

"That's it," I replied in a disbelieving voice that said I expected the other shoe to drop at any moment.

"We live in a show and tell world," Lee explained. "We either create the narrative we want the public to hear or someone else will create one we might not like. My narrative was simple: "We have a lot of damage on the Desoto. We are going to manage a recovery as best we know how for the American people. Not special interest groups. The whole country."

I asked Lee if he had a check list of things he

Following 2005's Hurricane Katrina, the Forest Service's Robert E. Lee led a Desoto National Forest team that produced a 15-page Environmental Assessment in an unheard-of 53 days. EA's generally take at least a year to complete and are hundreds of pages long.

felt were necessary to stay on track and on schedule following Hurricane Katrina. He did but only in his head. It reads more like a manifesto than a check list:

- Take charge
- Train your environmentalists
- Educate your collaborators
- Challenge the experts to do better
- Everyone is trying to do the best job possible but we have to find the middle ground and that means we can't all be right all of the time
- Dumb it down and keep it simple
- Lots of visuals and lots of field trips
- Know the law and the law is NEPA
- Use the tools in the 2003 Healthy Forest Restoration Act tool box
- There is always a way to mitigate the impacts of your project
- Know your business
- My line officers don't make decisions. I do.
- In a perfect world, Forest Plan comments would be limited to peer reviewed science
- The world is not perfect

Lee comes by his clarity naturally. He grew up in a family of 11 on a farm in the South. His 87-year-old father logged and farmed. There were never enough hours in the day and there was certainly no time for the circular debates that promote management indecision in western national forests. There was work to do and it had to get done promptly. The same mindset has characterized Lee's 31 year Forest Service career and it is written all over the Katrina EA.

In a September 27 "Dear Shareholders" letter Desoto National Forest Supervisor, Tony Dixon, announced [1] that the Forest Service would be relying on the 2003 Healthy Forest Restoration Act in its Katrina planning work and [2] that there would be a four-hour collaborator meeting on October 4 in Laurel, Mississippi.

"I know this is short notice, but action is needed now," Dixon wrote. "Delays will cause a further decline in the value of the timber, affecting the ability of the Forest Service to effectively remove the timber through salvage sales. Also, it is important to remove or otherwise treat the heavy fuels to safely reintroduce the use of prescribed burning as soon as possible in the longleaf pine ecosystem."

"We found a lot to talk about and many areas of agreement," Lee recalls. "We all knew time was short and we got right to it."

Indeed they did but it was shear genius on someone's part to convince eight Indian tribes and 15 others representing academia, timber, private landowners, historic preservation and archeology to pick Ray Vaughn to lead the collaboration. Vaughn, the founder and executive director of WildLaw, a public interest litigator, brought vital standing and credibility to the group's work.

"Was it you who recommended Vaughn?" I ask. Lee smiles broadly. "Never argue with an ol' southern boy. He'll beat you to the punch every time."

Both Vaughn and Lee make friends easily, so for many it was lamentable when WildLaw closed up shop in 2011. The same recession that pushed *Evergreen* to the brink pushed Vaughn's organization over a cliff. In a widely published letter announcing his decision, Vaughn thanked both his friends and his opponents for their courtesy, even when common ground could not be found.

"Finally, at the risk of sounding corny, but so what, thanks be to God," Vaughn wrote. "Everything in life is a gift and WildLaw and this work have been gifts beyond measure."

Public references to God are far more common in the South than anywhere else in the country. Why I don't know, but in his heartfelt letter Vaughn conceded that he had been privileged to live the life he dreamt for himself, doing work that, for him, truly mattered.

"If I have made a difference in this world, it is because God has made a difference in me and with me."

Lee has moved on, too. He is Assistant Director of the Forest Service's Forest Inventory and Analysis Program within the Southern Research Station in Knoxville, Tennessee. He tells me he likes working in the supporting cast for Station Director Bill Burkman. I have no doubt Burkman thanks his lucky stars at least once a day. I certainly would, but what I really think is that Lee has all the right stuff to be a spectacular Forest Service Chief.

"I'm just an ol' country boy from Alabama," the self-effacing Lee reminds me as he gently deflects my question about his Chief's credentials.

Robert E. Lee isn't the first person in Forest Service history to figure out how to make the trains run on time, but he is unquestionably the first to orchestrate a legally sufficient 15-page Environmental Assessment in just 45 days – counting weekends and holidays: Dear Stakeholder Letter dated September 27. Signed Record of Decision dated December 5. Amazing.

It's a shame Lee never met my friend, John Marker. John was a Pennsylvania native and guiding light in the formation of the National Association of Forest Service Retirees [NAFSR], a stellar group of men and women who have worked tirelessly to put some spine the Forest Service's current leadership. I don't know how well their advice is received but I do know they have the ear of Agriculture Secretary, Sonny Perdue, and it is Perdue to whom the Forest Service answers.

Ever a gentleman, John would have been greatly amused – but not fooled – by Lee's good ol' southern boy routine. He admired courage and decisive thinking and went to great lengths to nurture it in Forest Service employees who crossed his remarkable career path.

I no longer recall when I met John but it was during the worst of the spotted owl wars. He was Forest Service legislative and public relations liaison for Region 6, stationed in Portland, Oregon, Ground Zero in dozens of nasty skirmishes that pitted the city's tree huggers against rural Oregonians who made their living logging old growth timber in the region's national forests.

The late Ben Stout, PhD silviculturist and well-traveled forestry school dean, assembled an anthology of the writings of Harvard's Hugh Miller Raup, one history's most controversial field biologists. Stout later compiled *The Northern Spotted Owl: An Oregon View,* a running account of the events and political forces that led to the owl's 1990 listing.

What I remember most about our first meeting is that John was the consummate professional and a skilled listener who clearly understood the fears of loggers and millworkers whose lives had been turned upside down by a war they were losing.

Portland was John's last stop in a Forest Service career that spanned some 40 years and included assignments in fire management in northern California, public relations in southern Oregon, public relations and fire in Region 4 headquarters in Ogden, Utah, and the Washington office, where he helped design the Forest Service's wildland-urban interface program.

John joined our Evergreen Foundation Board of Directors after he "retired" to a cherry and pear orchard he purchased near Hood River, about an hour east of Portland. NAFSR was still in its early years and, much to John's frustration, still struggling to find its footing.

We agreed that we could help one another so he joined our board and we began to pound the table for NAFSR's work on our website. A decade hence we're still at it and my list of Forest Service retiree friends has grown considerably. I am privileged to be included in many of their email networks.

I admire these men – and most are men – for what they stand for and for what they accomplished during their working years. They get a bad rap for presiding over an era when the congressionally-blessed federal timber program provided about 15% of the nation's lumber supply and at least twice that amount in western states that grew rapidly following World War II.

NAFSR's 700-plus members constitute the largest repository of on-the-ground experience available to the modern-day Forest Service – more than 21,000 years of problem solving experience in our country's 154 national forests, including 87 in the 11 western states.

Former Forest Service Chief, Jack Ward Thomas, lamented what he called "the crazy quilt" of overlapping and conflicting mission statements and environmental regulations that made it increasingly difficult for the agency to do the thinning and stand tending work necessary to protect western national forests from insects, diseases and wildfire.

You would think Forest Service leadership would have the organization on speed dial, but NAFSR has had to work hard to get the Forest Service to pay attention. In fact, my late friend, Jack Ward Thomas, the agency's thirteenth Chief, refused to join NAFSR. Jack could be aloof at times and I suspect he concluded that joining the organization might further sully his already well-worn reputation. Whatever the reason, my friend Marker, who considered NAFSR membership a sacred duty, soon began calling Jack "God." Had he known, Jack would have been amused.

When Donald Trump was elected President, NAFSR's current leadership seized the opportunity to open a dialogue with former Georgia Governor, Sonny Perdue, Trump's pick to be Secretary of Agriculture and the son of a Georgia farmer and a Democrat-turned-Republican in 1998.

Perdue is a deeply religious man. In the midst of the worst drought in Georgia in decades, he led a prayer rally on the steps of the Georgia capital. He invited some 200 faithful to "reverently and respectfully pray up a storm."

"God we need you, we need rain," he prayed aloud. Two years later, the state was awash in the worst flooding in its history. Who knows.

NAFSR hopes they've found a willing listener in Secretary Perdue. Though he knows little about the West's wildfire pandemic, he has pressed the Forest Service – and Congress – to increase the pace and scale of forest restoration work in overcrowded and dying western national forests. I will hazard a guess that most of what he has learned over the last two years has come from a series of letters and briefing papers written by Michael Rains, a Forest Service retiree whose brilliance is matched only by his shyness.

Although we've never met, Michael and I have become comrades in arms. We share a rock solid belief that it is possible to manage the West's national forests in ways that reduce the outsized risk of wildfire without jumpstarting the dreaded federal timber sale program that has been the focal point of so much public angst since the Clinton Administration granted threatened species status to the northern spotted owl in 1980.

Michael is the only guy I've ever known with five degrees from five different universities. He spent most of his Forest Service years in the agency's State and Private Forestry division, one of three agency branches that seem to function without controversy or disarray.

The other two are the Forest Inventory and Analysis Program and the Forest Products Lab, a highly regarded wood and paper research laboratory at Madison, Wisconsin. We featured the lab's long and admirable history in "Giant Minds, Giant Ideas," a 2003 *Evergreen* report you can download from the "Magazine Archive" [64] in our website,

These are the folks who invented the postage stamp you don't have to lick and an array of wood preservatives you should not lick. If you share my love of science, you could spend days in Madison. There are machines for testing the strength of various wood species and products and there is a three-bedroom house filled with sensors that monitor moisture in walls and the durability of different building materials. Fascinating stuff.

I no longer remember when my email correspondence with Michael Rains began, but I soon learned that after he retired from the Forest Service he got his school teaching ticket punched in Pennsylvania. Now he tutors kids with limited physical and emotional strengths. Such is his compassion for young people for whom life itself is a struggle.

Once I realized the depth and breadth of Michael's 48-year Forest Service career I began peppering him with questions about the agency's seeming inability to get out of its own way amid a wildfire crisis that threatens life as we know it here in the 11 western states.

Why was this so hard, I asked. Where was the courage to say we are headed in the wrong direction in our national forests and here is our course correction? Isn't the Forest Service the tipping point? Where are the big picture thinkers? Where is the grenade and who will pull the pin?

I was not prepared for what followed – a 30-page draft report titled "Restoring Fire as a Landscape Conservation Tool; Non-traditional Thoughts for a Traditional Organization." If the Forest Service can be thought of as a Rubik's Cube, Michael solves it in a thoughtful disassembly of the linkage between our wildfire crisis and an organizational structure that has outlived its usefulness.

Michael advises that what I have before me is an early draft of an essay destined for publication in a Society of American Foresters desk reference titled "193 Million Acres: Toward a Healthier and More Resilient U.S. Forest Service." It features 32 essays by some of the leading forest conservation thinkers or our time – a must read for anyone searching for pathways forward in western national forests.

Among the essayists: Michael, of course; former Forest Service chiefs, Dale Bosworth, Jack Ward Thomas and Tom Tidwell; Sharon Friedman, a retired PhD forest geneticist and host of The Smokey Wire, an utterly fascinating blog that accepts the opinions all comers who behave themselves; Dennis Becker, interim Dean of the University of Idaho's College of Natural Resources and director of its Policy Analysis Group; Keith Argow, the ever-candid founder and president of the National Woodland Owners Association; Rich Stem, who like Robert E. Lee, knows how to make the trains run on time; Char Miller, a Senior Fellow at the Pinchot Institute for Conservation and a spectacular writer in his own right; and wildfire guru, Tom Harbour, whom Michael had picked to be his Director of Fire and Aviation Management when he was Deputy Chief of the Forest Service.

64

Tom was the perfect choice to help Michael weave the wildfire story into his unraveling of an organizational structure that is broken beyond repair. The result is partly a fix-it kit and partly a post-mortem for someone who hasn't died yet but soon will.

Here is my summation of their main points:

- To fix the wildfire mess, first fix the forest management mess.
- The Forest Service – world's premier conservation organization - is devolving into a Fire Service.
- Aggressive fire suppression has left us with a Wildfire Paradox: the more aggressively we fight wildfires the more aggressive they become.
- To fix the management mess, Congress must repopulate the Forest Service with the nearly 14,000 men and women with management skills who were dismissed as annual firefighting costs sucked up an increasing share of the agency's forest management budget.
- This repopulating will cost about $2.2 billion annually over the next five to seven years – in addition to the Forest Service's current $5.14 billion annual appropriation – but eventually gains on the management side will translate into fewer fires, less destructive fires and lower firefighting costs.
- Measurable success will turn on the repopulated Forest Service's ability to use fire to fight fire without succumbing to the temptation to simply allow wildfires to burn themselves out without regard to the environmental and economic consequences.
- Effective fire management rests on finding innovative and profitable markets for the billions of tons of woody biomass and small diameter trees that are fueling our Wildfire Paradox. Here, the Forest Service needs help from impacted communities, private capital markets, scientists exploring wood-based nanotechnology, architects engaged in constructing "green" buildings and conservation groups that hope to return natural

fire to our western national forests without first burning them to the ground.

- The Forest Service's organizational structure is outdated and riddled with inefficiencies and redundancies. Combining some research programs and merging some of the agency's 10 regional administrative offices will yield an immediate $200-$300 million in annual savings that should quickly be redirected to high priority restoration projects.

Although Michael and Tom's essay makes scant mention of thinning in overstocked forests, their approach reminds of a caution shared with me by Peter Kolb, during one of our many conversations.

"Most western forests are fire adapted, not fire dependent," he said. "There is a big difference. Too much fire can dumb down a fire adapted forest in the same way that too much old growth logging did decades ago. We want to return fire in a way that encourages natural resiliency while balancing our human dependence on what forests offer. It's complicated but doable if we avoid value judgements that have us tilting at political windmills."

The prologue to Michael and Tom's essay suggests that they clearly understand that returning fire depends totally on a clear-eyed assessment of forests in what my late friend, Ben Stout, called "the here and now," uncluttered by romantic notions about ecosystems perpetuating themselves in perfect harmony.

Ben was a well-traveled PhD silviculturist, a former dean of the University of Montana's forestry school and colleague of the late Hugh Miller Raup, Bullard Professor of Forestry at Harvard University and possibly the botany world's most legendary boat rocker. And he surely enjoyed challenging the comfort zones of his colleagues. Before Harvard University would publish his 1938 "Botanical studies in the Black Forest," the director of the Harvard Forest, who was clearly offended by Raup's heretical conclusions demanded that someone write a disclaimer that would distance the University from Raup's opinions. Never one to shy from controversy, Raup wrote his own disclaimer.

In 1981, Ben assembled an anthology of Raup's writings. He had spent his entire academic career as a Harvard field biologist, searching for evidence to support the widely held belief that nature existed in some sort of steady state, with every action eliciting an equal and opposite reaction, and always coming back to some invisible mid-balance point. But all he ever found was chaos – evidence of upheavals he attributed to insects, diseases, floods, wildfires, tornadoes and hurricane-force winds in his native New England.

There was no orderly system of interdependent communities in which every living thing l found a pre-existing niche and the whole community moved through a stately succession toward what foresters call "climax," the evolution of old growth forests representing stability in the long run.

Ben's anthology, which he autographed for me, bears a title befitting Raup's conclusions and his own concerning the role of disturbance in natural ecosystems: *Forests in the Here and Now*. It was Ben's way of affirming his belief that Raup was correct about the role natural disturbances played in the life, death and rebirth of forests. The quest to find an invisible balance point was fruitless. There was no balance point and there were no indicator species, so-called "canaries in coal mines," that could warn us of impending natural doom. There was only what you could see. What we do with what we see in the here and now is up to us.

Ben's colleague, Calvin Stillman, wrote the forward to his Raup anthology. In it, Stillman took a remarkably circumspect view of chaos, recalling the observations of Robert Jay Lifton, a former Air Force psychiatrist who has written widely about the impacts of war on human behavior.

"Lifton tells us that identification with on-going Nature is one of the devices we use to deal with really major stresses," Stillman wrote. "This is clear in the United States in the last century, at every period of particularly rapid social change with distortions of human status."

Stillman thought the most recent example of distortion could be found in the 1970s rise of the environmental movement. "It was preceded by a general rise in affluence and opportunity, sparked by civil-rights agitation, and then by the unrest occasioned by military operations in Vietnam."

I have veered close to this same line of thinking in my own research concerning the social undercurrents that drive contemporary thinking and policy formation that swirls around the widely held human desire to "save forests." I think it is this desire that continues to fuel unrest and debate about our West's wildfire crisis. Some demand that we "fix it now." Others say, "leave it to nature."

I suspect this same debate is going on inside the

Forest Service. Many – especially Forest Service retirees – want an immediate fix because the West's wildfire crisis is quite literally consuming everything they stood for and believed about forests and forestry.But many of the agency's newer employees seem more inclined to pursue a more minimalist approach that at least acknowledges the history role fire has played in the West's forests.

I can see good points in both longings, but with so much at risk in the West, it is vital that we understand the difference between Good Fire and Bad Fire. Unless we are prepared to fully accept the long-lasting environmental consequences that accompany Bad Fire, we cannot allow Congress or the Forest Service to substitute "nature" for "management" by allowing Bad Fire to do the cleanup work the agency seems unwilling to do. Thinning is the perfect catalyst for encouraging Good Fire to snuff out Bad Fire.

Current Forest Service Chief, Vicki Christiansen, oversees a convoluted regulatory process that has the agency spending more than half its annual $5.14 billion budget extinguishing wildfires, leaving less money for restoration work necessary to reduce wildfire risk.

We recently completed a series of unscripted street interviews with randomly selected people living in urban and rural communities in the Pacific Northwest. As you might imagine, rural folks who have more hands on experience with nature fall mainly in the "fix it now" category.

What surprised us was that their urban neighbors aren't parroting the radical environmentalist claim that our forests should be "left to nature." Not one was willing to say that we should stand by while "nature" destroys forests we love.

It is this maelstrom of debate that led the Society of American Foresters to ask some of its leading lights – including Michael Rains – to offer solutions based on their own careers. *193 Million Acres: Toward a Healthier and More Resilient U.S. Forest Service* offers a quite remarkable compendium of opinion.

What Michael may not fully understand about forest ecosystem function is generously compensated by his intimate understanding of what ails the Forest Service's ecosystem – its ethos and its failure to define its corporate structure. We know all about the McDonald's brand and those of Apple, Amazon and Walmart, but does anyone know what the Forest Service brand means? I don't. Neither does Michael, nor do any Forest Service retirees I know.

Michael's well-informed assessment of the Forest Service's death spiral was all the encouragement I needed to ask him a question I'd been contemplating for a long time. If NASA can put men on the moon and six rovers on Mars – the most recent last November – what the hell was wrong with the Forest Service? What happened to the organization that was compared to the United States Marine Corps in an early 1950s opinion survey? Michael's answer is almost six pages long. It traces the history of a U.S. Department of Agriculture belief that the Forest Service was frequently "off the reservation," meaning that Forest Service leadership tended to sail its own ship as it had since its formation in 1905. If things looked a little messy from the outside, it was only because you did not understand what was going on inside the agency.

"Our 'farm system' grew weak as time passed," Michael wrote of his latter days. Apart from Max Peterson, who was Forest Service Chief from 1979 to 1987, few worried about leadership succession.

"The notion of reaching outside the agency for top leaders to join us was foreign," Michael said. "So, existing leaders trained new leaders to be 'just like them.' We talked about diversity, but that was always about gender and then race. We did not apply diversity to creativity, being visionary, the ability to lead from the front and behind, talking calculated risks or constantly trying to stay up with the demands and needs of a new constituency."

Plainly stated, the Forest Service's gene pool was a mile wide and an inch deep. Faced with mounting public and congressional criticism, agency leadership grew increasingly cautious. Risk-taking soon gave way to a "do not mess up" mindset, what Michael called "leadership deterioration," the absence of well-schooled skill sets that we sometimes see in private industry today. Here I think of Lee Iacocca at Ford and later Chrysler. Or Marine Corps Major General, Charlie Bolden Jr., who led NASA for eight years and flew on four space shuttle missions, twice as pilot and twice as commander.

Where are the Iacocca's and Boldens in the Forest Service? And where, for heaven's sake, are the Ross Perot's when we really need them? Perot defined an activist as "not th them – should do the cleanup work.

The ever-practical Perot hated bureaucratic inefficiency in government and private industry. He thus famously said, "If you see a snake, just kill it. Don't appoint a committee on snakes."

Translation: First, put out the fire.

Where are the Forest Service's Pinchot's and Greeley's today? The closest we've come in recent years was during Chief Dale Bosworth's tenure, 2002-2007. Dale and I both attended the University of Idaho in the same years – he in forestry and me in whatever moved my spirit for longer than 15 minutes.

I didn't know Dale during our UI years, but I've interviewed him twice in recent years and think highly of his insights. His 193 Million Acres essay "A Failure of Imagination: Why we need a Commission to Take Action on Wildfire," is a great read. He co-wrote it with Jerry Williams, whose 39-year career spanned the agency's effort to come to grips with its macho wildfire mentality.

Dale's tenure as Chief followed the inglorious term of Mike Dombeck, a fisheries biologist known to be on good terms with Vice President, Al Gore, whose principle environmental mission seems to have been the destruction of the Forest Service, or at least what it had stood for since its founding.

Suffice it to say, many in the Forest Service never trusted Dombeck. Nor did many rural western congressmen who believed the Chief of the Forest Service should be a forester. They got their wish in Dale Bosworth, a quiet and cerebral professional who continues to travel the world offering advice to nations looking for better ways to manage land.

Despite what Michael described as "the very calming influence" of two Agricultural Secretaries – Marty Glickman and Ann Veneman – the Forest Service continued to lose its edge. "We were becoming soft," he told me in his six-page answer to my NASA question. "There was still no talk of succession to the chief's position and the notion of a corporate and contemporary Forest Service was still foreign to us."

When Dale retired in 2007, Gail Kimball replaced him. She was the first woman to be named Forest Service Chief. Her resume suggested big things to come – BS in forestry, University of Vermont; MS in forest engineering, Oregon State University [did we hear an "oorah"]; pre-sale forester in Alaska, logging engineer and district planner in Oregon, district forester in Kettle Falls, Washington and La Grande, Oregon, and forest supervisor in Alaska and Wyoming. The right stuff.

"But ultra conservative," Michael advised. No out-of-the-box thinking. The do not mess up mentality had overtaken Forest Service leadership before she arrived and she did nothing to challenge it.

"I was the author of the American Recovery and Reinvestment Act of 2009," he reminded me. "We were ready to submit a $4 billion package to Congress and she was afraid it was too much. We submitted half that amount and got it, all the while congressional staffers questioning why we had asked for so little."

Tom Tidwell followed Gale Kimball. The third Chief to ascend from Northern Region headquarters in Missoula. And like his Missoula forebearers, he knew the West's forest health/wildfire story inside and out. I know this because Tom and I shared the podium at least twice during his Missoula years. Michael told me he was even more cautious than Gail. That was my read, too, but I was always willing to give Tom the benefit of the doubt because I liked him personally.

Tom announced his retirement eight months after Donald Trump entered the White House. He had presided over the worst wildfire years in modern history and he had explained the wildfire crisis to Congress many times, but I don't think Congress saw anything new or bold in Tom's easy-going manner. What they heard from him was a story they'd heard many times before from earlier Chiefs.

Agriculture Secretary, Sonny Perdue, thanked Tom for his "dedicated leadership and service" on his Twitter account and Tom slipped out the back door. Last I knew he planned to return to Boise, Idaho, his hometown. Good for him.

Early on, Tom had asked Michael's permission to recommend him for consideration as Deputy Chief of the National Forest System – a huge and influential post ideally suited to big thinkers like Michael. He thought about it overnight and told Tom he wasn't interested. What a shame. But I understood his thinking. He was nearing retirement and he believed the job demanded a more forceful personality than his own, someone able to break the Forest Service free of its stodgy culture. Rearranging the deck chairs on the Titanic would not be enough to steer clear of looming disaster.

Sonny Perdue being a southerner – think Robert E. Lee – saw to it that the skids were greased for Tony Tooke, a hard charger who began his Forest Service career in Mississippi when he was 18 years old, eventually becoming Regional Forester in Region 8, headquartered in Atlanta, less than five miles from the Georgia Capital building, Perdue's old stomping ground.

Perdue swore Tooke into office on September 2, 2017 but his tenure was cut short by widely publicized allegations of sexual misconduct. He resigned on March 7, 2018. Might he have been the big picture thinker the Forest Service needs?

I doubt it. His core values swirled around loyalty – a widely admired southern attribute – but not one that inspires the kind of out-of-the-box thinking the agency so desperately needs.

Vicki Christiansen replaced Tooke, first as Interim Chief, then as Chief. Like her western predecessors, she knows the wildfire story well, perhaps better than they because of her storied career: Arizona State Forester, Washington State Forester, Deputy Director of Fire and Aviation Management for the Forest Service and Deputy Chief of State and Private Forestry.

But if Christiansen's recently issued "Letter of Intent for Wildland Fire for 2019" is an indicator of things to come, the news isn't encouraging, even in its chosen title. We don't need intent. We need action.

Aggressive fire management won't solve our wildfire problem any faster or better than aggressive forest management. They are not mutually exclusive. What is still missing is the NASA-like courage and vision that put us on the Moon and Mars; the corporate will to change – and a budget that matches the daring.

Meantime, we are left to consider one of Jack Ward Thomas' many wisdoms. This from one of his four books. I no longer remember which one and it doesn't matter because I heard him say something similar many times:

> *"We don't just manage land—we're supposed to be leaders. Conservation leaders. Leaders in protecting and improving the land...with a broad view of natural resource leadership, and that includes people, because people are part of ecosystems.... The Forest Service is going to be a leader in ecosystem management...right now it's more a concept than a practice.... What does ecosystem management mean? It means thinking on a larger scale than we're used to. It means sustaining the forest resources over very long periods of time. And from that will flow many goods and services, not just timber. Ecosystem management is not just a timber sale; it's putting the timber sale into a bigger picture, including the watersheds, wildlife, roads, and people's needs and values... Wood production will continue to be a significant part of our program, but we will look more at multiple variables, not just production. We will be more pro-active on wildlife programs, fish programs, and recreation programs...we have to involve the citizens of this country... We are going to have to improve our technical skills across the board... We need to be prepared to move into the 21st century or we'll be left in the dust."*

And so the question...

Is the Forest Service being left in its own dust?

Before you answer, read the articles [65] Michael Rains has written for *Evergreen* and the letters and reports [66] he and his NAFSR colleagues prepared for President Trump and Agricultural Secretary, Sonny Perdue. But be forewarned. What you will see when you click on this link is going to look a lot like homework to some of you, but I urge you to hunker down and learn. You aren't going to find this stuff on any of the "news" by algorithm social media platforms.

One of Michael's letters includes an eight-page Executive Order ready for the President's signature. "A Comprehensive Strategy to Ensure Healthy, Sustainable and More Resilient Forests" sets in motion the organizational and cultural changes that Michael and Tom outlined in their *193 Million Acre* essay.

Now that's leadership. That's how you solve forestry's Rubik's Cube.

65 

66 

CHAPTER 31

A real green new deal

Dad turned 13 the day his father was buried, August 3, 1928.

Paul Randolph Petersen had emigrated from Trondheim, Norway in 1902. He married my grandmother in Spokane in June of 1908. They had three children. Dad; his younger sister, my Aunt Myrtle; and an older brother, my Uncle Howard. My grandfather died on Uncle Howard's fifteenth birthday.

My grandfather's death so devastated Dad that he quit school midway through his eighth grade year and never went back. Aunt Myrtle told me years later that he ate in his bedroom for an entire year. In the 42 years I knew my father, he never talked to me about his father. Not once. Not one word.

Wall Street cratered the following October, leaving my grandmother to run my grandfather's sawmills until she was able to sell them in 1939. Dad worked in the log yards and cut dead timber in Vergobbi Gulch north of Kellogg. He bucked the logs into stove wood lengths, split them into firewood and sold the firewood for 25 cents a cord – a cord being a stack of wood eight feet long, four feet tall and four feet wide. I have done it and it is backbreaking work.

My grandfather built three sawmills on the North Fork of the Coeur d'Alene River. The "honeymoon house" – so labeled by my grandmother on the back of a black and white photo she took – was on the Eagle mill site near Murray, a still bustling gold camp. She took the picture with a camera she had built. Years later, she built her own darkroom in an apartment house she owned in Spokane. She was a fine photographer who, in later years, counted on me to drive her all over eastern Washington so she could take more pictures with her home-built cameras.

Between his sawmills and a thriving home-building business in Kellogg, Paul Petersen employed more than 100 men. Being Norwegian, he felt obliged to buy a round for the house in three uptown bars every day at quitting time. The bar owners loved him, but I don't think my teetotaling grandmother thought much of the idea. There were other perks, though. My grandparents owned the first touring car in Kellogg, a magnificent Oakland ragtop. Life was good.

Alexander Fleming discovered life-saving penicillin in September of 1928, two months after pneumonia killed my grandfather. In her resolve to treat her dying husband at home, my grandmother forced their family doctor to show her how to drain fluid from his lungs. It worked until it didn't. He was buried in a bronze casket that came with a 100-year guarantee. Friday, August 3, 1928.

Dad reopened his father's gravesite overlooking Kellogg in June of 1967 so we could lay my grandmother beside him . We buried her cancer-ravaged body on Friday, June 16. I remember standing next to her open grave and wondering how my grandfather's body was holding up after 39 years in the ground. How strange.

When the Civilian Conservation Corps was formed in 1933 my totally lost father joined immediately. He soon found himself in familiar surroundings in a CCC camp on Crooked Ridge, high above the Little North Fork of the Coeur d'Alene River, about a day's walk from his late father's Eagle mill.

True to form, Dad never talked much about his time in what became known as "Roosevelt's

President Franklin Delano Roosevelt arrived for dedication of the spillway at Bonneville Dam on the Columbia River on September 28, 1937. (Courtesy Library of Congress)

Tree Army," but I know he battled blister rust, a parasite that was killing western white pines by the millions. He also built trails and fought forest fires, one being a ferocious reburn of the Great 1910 Fire.

Dad also made friends with a towering Indian he called "Choo-Choo." I have no idea why. Choo-Choo called Dad "Pee Wee," no doubt because Dad stood all of five-foot-six and couldn't have weighed more than 100 pounds dripping wet. If Dad needed protection, he had it in spades. No one messed with Choo-Choo.

When I was going through some of Dad's things after he died in 1986, I found the official eight-by-ten black and white photograph of the Crooked Ridge crew. Dad is seated in the second row behind the cooks. Choo-Choo is standing in the back row. Counting the three cooks, there are 31 mostly young men looking back at a government photographer. Three are smiling. The rest – including Dad – are not. I am guessing many of them were a long way from home.

The pay was $30 a month – $1.00 a day – and Dad had arranged for his checks to be sent directly to his mother. Times were tough and there were three sawmill payrolls to make every Friday. How my grandmother managed to keep the mills running in the depths of the Great Depression is beyond me, but she did.

When the camp closed for the winter, Dad walked the 60-some miles back to Kellogg, down Leiberg Creek, then down the Little North Fork, across the main river, up the Graham Creek Trail and down the other side to Kellogg. It took him two days. When he walked in the back door, his mother had to look twice to be sure it was him. He had grown five inches and gained about 50 pounds. Camp cooking and a change of scene had agreed with him.

During its nine-year run – 1933 to 1942 – three million young men worked for the Civilian

In their nine-year history, Civilian Conservation Corps workers planted three billion trees, built 97,000 miles of trails in national forests, erected 3,470 fire lookouts and recorded 4.2 million man-days on fire lines. The CCC had been Franklin Roosevelt's idea. It was part of his Depression-era New Deal. Workers were paid $30 per month.

Conservation Corps. Most went on to fight in the Second World War. Dad did not. He was beyond draft age, so he was "frozen" on his ditch digger's job at the Bunker Hill and Sullivan Mining and Concentrating Company in Kellogg. Lead, silver and zinc were essential war materials, so Dad dug ditches until he was transferred to a plumbing crew that laid pipe in the same ditches.

Two days after Franklin Roosevelt's March 4, 1933 inauguration he had declared a bank holiday – closing every bank in the nation – to give the Treasury Department a chance to check the banking industry's pulse. The goal was to prevent a "run" on banks by panicky depositors like the run portrayed in "It's a Wonderful Life," Frank Capra's marvelous 1946 Christmas film about life turned upside down in mythical Bedford Falls.

In his July 2, 1932 acceptance speech at the Democratic National Convention in Chicago, Roosevelt had epochally declared, "I pledge you, I pledge myself, to a new deal for the American people."

The "new deal" phrase had come from Stuart Chase, one of Roosevelt's closest advisors. Chase had borrowed it from humorist, Mark Twain and novelist, Henry James. No one in the campaign operation expected it to be remembered, but it quickly entered the nation's political lexicon where it is still thrives today.

Roosevelt called Congress into special session on March 5 to begin work on his New Deal agenda for America's vanquished labor force. Dozens of federal aid programs were created in a matter of days, none more important to millions of young men standing in bread lines than the Civilian Conservation Corps.

In a March 21 communique, Roosevelt asked Congress to approve his plan for putting at least 250,000 young men to work in the coming weeks.

"I propose to create a Civilian Conservation Corps to be used in simple work, not interfering with normal employment and confining itself to forestry, the prevention of soil erosion, flood control and similar projects.

"More important, however, than the material gains, will be the moral and spiritual value of such work. The overwhelming majority of jobless Americans who are now walking the streets and receiving private or public relief would infinitely prefer to work. We can take a vast army of these unemployed out into healthful surrounds. We can eliminate, to some extent at least, the threat that enforced idleness brings to spiritual and moral stability."

It was as though the President himself had been channeling my young father's broken heart. But the spiritual and moral connections to forestry that Roosevelt referenced in his March 21 letter to Congress had a far more direct link to the soil than destitute Americans ever realized.

"I am a forester," their newly-minted President would later declare in several letters. He wasn't in an academic sense, but in his own privileged youth he had planted thousands of trees at Springwood, his family's lavish 600-acre Hyde Park estate, 90 miles north of New York City. He took over land management duties on the estate following his father's death in 1900, so he understood the basics. By his own estimate, an 11-man CCC crew could plant 5,000 to 6,000 trees daily, depending on weather.

Congress approved his Emergency Conservation Work Act on March 31 and he gleefully signed it. The fine print stipulated that $22 to $25 of each CCC worker's $30 per month government check had to be sent home to help with family expenses. They could spent the rest themselves. Grateful enrollees joked, "Another day, another dollar; a million days, I'll be a millionaire!"

"Forests, like people, must be constantly productive," Roosevelt prophetically told a writer from the *Forestry News Digest*. "The problems of the future of both are interlocked. American forestry efforts must be consolidated and advanced."

Roosevelt took a personal interest in the CCC's and their work, pouring over maps of rivers, streams, deserts and forestland. "I want to personally check the location and scope of the camps."

Roosevelt envisioned three kinds of camps: forestry camps in national forests, like the Crooked Ridge camp I see in Dad's picture; soil camps dedicated to combating Midwest flooding and erosion and recreational camps where the work would be focused on developing parks and scenic areas.

He sketched his CCC vision for cabinet members on a scrap of paper. Frances Perkins, his Labor Secretary and the first woman in U.S. history to hold a cabinet post, later recalled that the President had "put the dynamite" under his cabinet and let them "fumble for their own methods."

Roosevelt's hard-charging Interior Secretary, Harold Ickes, became so obsessed with implementing the President's CCC vision and his other New Deal initiatives that he ordered the doors to Interior's headquarters locked promptly at 9:01 in the morning. If you were late, you were fired.

At its peak in 1935, the CCC program was housing a half-million young men in 2,650 camps around the nation. Dad was among the initial 250,000 unemployed young men hired – unmarried "boys" 18 to 25 years old.

The hiring pool was soon expanded to include 25,000 World War I veterans who had fallen on hard times. Because the Forest Service was shorthanded, they were assigned to National Forest camps, most in need of their wartime organizational and leadership skills.

To bolster job-training another 24,000 "Local Experienced Men" were hired: biologists, physicians, architects, climatologists, naturalists and teachers who helped 40,000 illiterates learn how to read.

Then 10,000 Indians were added and assigned to projects on reservations, which meant that Dad's friend, Choo-Choo, who was an early hire, had somehow slipped by recruiters. To get hired, jobless young men frequently lied about their age.

The Civilian Conservation Corps' stunning nine-year record of accomplishment has never been surpassed:

- Three billion trees planted
- 3,470 fire lookouts built
- 97,000 miles of trails constructed
- 4,235,000 man-days on fire lines
- 1,240,000 man-days on floods in the Ohio and Mississippi valleys
- 84,400,000 acres of flooded farmland drained and ditched

Congress abolished the CCC's on July 1, 1942, seven months after Japan bombed Pearl Harbor. Thousands of young men had already left their CCC camps to enlist in our armed forces. But not my too old ditch-digger father, though so many of his mining buddies had enlisted that it crippled mine output in the Silver Valley. The military was obliged to find several hundred of them and send them back to the mines where they were needed most.

Franklin Roosevelt was a President like no other in American history. Dad's mother thought Roosevelt was a gift from God. I know this because she told me so many times. Such was her irrational hatred for President Hoover, who had been unable to stave off the runup to the Great Depression.

Having lost his father before his thirteenth birthday, I doubt my father thought much about God for a long time. My parents were regular churchgoers but God and politics were never discussed around our kitchen table, the single exception being local school bond elections. My college-educated schoolteacher mother and my solitary father, who always regretted dropping out in the eighth grade, were avid supporters of education, mine especially.

I'd like to ask FDR where he got his CCC vision. Was it really rooted in his Hyde Park boyhood? He had been born in the second floor tower bedroom at the south end of his father's sprawling mansion and he had taken over landscaping duties after James Roosevelt died in 1900. Did FDR learn that much so soon in life?

Or had one of Roosevelt's New Deal advisors whispered the idea in his ear? I'm going with the Hyde Park story because his CCC vision, sketched on Oval Office scrap paper, is said to have caught his newly-formed cabinet totally by surprise. Had they not remembered his famous "Portland speech," delivered September 21, 1932 on the Broadway Street steps of the old Benson Hotel in downtown Portland, Oregon – a speech in which he laid out his vision for hydroelectric development of the Columbia River.

"We have, as all of you in this section of the country know, the vast possibilities of power development on the Columbia River," he told supporters and journalists gathered on Broadway. "And I state in definite and certain terms, that the next great hydroelectric development to be undertaken by the federal government must be that on the Columbia River."

As governor of New York State, Roosevelt had supported joint U.S. and Canadian hydroelectric development along the boundary waters of the St. Lawrence River. To the depths of his soul he believed that energy development and distribution was a national problem that could only be resolved by federal investment and ownership of utilities that charged rates low enough to encourage public use.

Roosevelt did not believe privately-owned utilities in the Pacific Northwest had made sufficient investments to encourage greater public use of electricity but had instead funded and waged what he called "a systematic, subtle, deliberate and unprincipled campaign of misinformation, propaganda and if I may use the words, lies and falsehoods."

It was vintage Roosevelt and no one who had watched him orchestrate hydroelectric developments on the St. Lawrence River could have missed it. He railed against President Herbert Hoover's opposition to federally-owned power developments. FDR told his Portland throng that federally-funded hydro was "as radical as American liberty" and "the Constitution of the United States."

Of the Columbia he declared, "This vast waterpower can be of incalculable value to this whole section of the country. It means cheap manufacturing production, economy and comfort on the farm and in the household."

Roosevelt had voiced a similar vision 12 years earlier. He had boated through the Columbia Gorge during his 1920 campaign for the vice presidency and the Gorge had made a lasting impression on him. He shared his vision for developing the river during a stopover in Portland.

"When you cross the Mountain States and that portion of the Coast States that lies well back from the ocean, you are impressed by those great stretches of physical territory now practically unused but destined someday to contain the homes of thousands and hundreds of thousands of citizens like us, a territory to be developed by the nation for the nation. As we were coming down the river today, I could not help thinking, as everyone does, of all the water running unchecked down to the sea."

That same year – 1920 – Congress passed the Federal Water Power Act authorizing a series of studies that, when completed in 1926, proposed the construction of eight dams on the Columbia. On September 28, 1937, near the end of the first year of his second term, President Roosevelt spoke at dedication ceremonies for Bonneville Dam. Grand Coulee would be completed in 1941 and by 1942, every school kid in the Pacific Northwest could sing the lyrics to "Roll On Columbia," the most famous of 23 ballads folksinger Woody Guthrie wrote and sang under contract to the Bonneville Power Administration.

Eleven dams were eventually built on the Columbia and its major tributaries. Most were multi-purpose facilities that generated power, limited springtime flooding and directed reservoir water through a vast system of canals that irrigated millions of arid acres in eastern Oregon and Washington.

Millions of families, including my own, benefitted mightily from Roosevelt's hydroelectric vision. Dad's brother, my Uncle Howard, was a cement finisher at Grand Coulee Dam. The wartime aluminum industry, so vital in the construction of heavy bombers, flourished in the Pacific Northwest. Likewise, our Bunker Hill, which mined and smelted most of the lead we threw at Germany and Japan.

Roosevelt's vision was perfect, but it took years to build out our region's electric grid. Until 1951,

That's Jim Petersen's father, Darrell, in the second row in a CCC camp on Crooked Ridge in the old Coeur d'Alene National Forest. Like thousands of other young men, he lied about his age and joined the CCC when he was 17 years old. Three million joined Franklin Roosevelt's "Tree Army" to escape the crushing poverty of the Great Depression.

my cattle-ranching grandparents lit their log home with beautiful kerosene lamps. The last one sits atop our antique player piano, a wedding gift from my Norwegian grandfather to my grandmother in 1908. We still light it occasionally and the piano still plays. The glow of memory is powerful.

Where are the Roosevelt visionaries today? Those who can look down on our nation from 30,000 feet and say, "This is what we need."

Where are the big, big thinkers. Where is the someone who can lead the U.S. Forest Service and its stakeholders out of the wilderness? Who can pull us out of the hellish fires that are consuming our national forest heritage?

Scads of ideas have been floated. We need a commission, we need this, we need that, we need money, we need more people. Alright, but where is the Roosevelt visionary who can sketch out a solution on scrap paper and confidently sell it to Congress and the American people?

Progressive Democrats are offering their "Green New Deal" as the solution to all our planet's ills, but it bears no resemblance to its namesake New Deal. Solar and wind power replacing all fossil fuels? Zero carbon emissions in 10 years? And a $7 trillion price tag? Is this what we've come to? Are we really this intellectually lazy? Our best idea is to keep throwing Jell-O on the wall until some of it sticks?

President Roosevelt worked very hard to unify Americans behind his uplifting vision for our country. I don't find anything unifying or uplifting about a plan that threatens the livelihoods of millions of Americans and their families.

What vision is there in a plan that deputizes the banking industry so that it can keep a watchful eye on its customers in oil and gas drilling, mining and forestry. *Forestry?* Yup, forestry – the only industry on earth that grows trees that absorb atmospheric and terrestrial carbon and the only industry that manufactures and sells structural building materials that are products of the free, non-polluting energy of the sun. This looks like an extortion racket to me.

I don't have a problem with solar power. We heated our swimming pool in southern Oregon with solar blankets on the backside of the pool house and they worked great. Saved us some money too, but so did the four energy-saving hot water tanks that Pacific Power and Light installed in our house. They were free, and as Tom Peterson used to say when he was hawking appliances on Portland television stations, "Free is a very good price!"

Wind? Not so much, I agree with the lovely folks who hang out at Martha's Vineyard all summer. Unlike clearcuts, these wind turbines are permanent eyesores. They're everywhere now in the Columbia River Gorge with their semi-truck-size blades turning slowly and chewing up birds in flight with their every revolution.

What about all that steel and concrete it takes to make a turbine? And all that copper and steel wire. Mining, you know. Bad for the planet. And what about the carbon emissions released into the atmosphere by turbine manufacturers? And why aren't environmentalists up in arms about the reports that the big offshore turbines set up vibrations that disturb whales and disrupt spawning.

Not good people. We look like hypocrites.

The basic problem with wind and solar is that they don't work when the wind isn't blowing and the sun is shining. This is why the federal power regulations classify them as interruptible sources. Power companies that market interruptible power are required to maintain sources that are always there, day and night, rain or shine, no matter what: nuclear, hydro and fossil-fueled power. Oh, dear.

And then there is the disquieting fact that if the U.S. were able to go carbonless by 2100, global atmospheric carbon dioxide levels would be reduced by a mere 29 parts per million, an amount the Intergovernmental Panel on Climate Change says would make no difference in the mean global temperature. What to do?

How about we take a few steps back and consider the low hanging fruit. What if our Green New Deal included a manifesto that pledged all of us to do something BIG to pull our western national forests back from the brink of fiery ruin? What if we implemented a "to do" list that looks a lot like the proposal that Michael Rains and Tom Harbour assembled for the Society of American Foresters?

And what if the first item on our "to do" list was the resurrection of Roosevelt's Tree Army? I suspect millions of Generation Y kids would jump at the chance to live in a tent in the back of beyond and work from sunup to sundown the same way my father did more than 80 years ago. I'm not kidding! If I were 25 and not 75, I'd sign up in a heartbeat.

Ours is a blended family. My son will be 52 next month. My step-daughter will be 20. She went to Thailand last summer to plant trees, teach English to Thai kids who live in remote villages and commune with elephants. It's Sophie's dream come true. I get it and she has my 110 percent support in her efforts to save elephants while also saving kids and our planet.

Souvenir pillow case on display at the CCC museum in Michigan.

So why not bring back Roosevelt's Tree Army? Why not give kids like Sophie the opportunity to do something meaningful for their country and our environment? Why not give us a fighting chance to save our national forest legacy? Look at the legacy of the Civilian Conservation Corps. Look at all the good those young men did. You think we can't do this again? I beg to differ. We can.

Thankfully, the Trump Administration has retreated from its proposal to close nine of 26 Job Corps Civilian Conservation Centers and transfer the rest to the Department of Labor. Ag Secretary Perdue unveiled the plan on May 24, 2019, only to reverse course less than a month later amid strong public resistance. I can't imagine President Roosevelt approving of such a decision.

The Job Corps CCC program focuses on youngsters who come from tough circumstances and are having a hard time figuring out what life holds for them. It also teaches some of the same skill sets Dad learned in the CCC 80-some years ago: tree planting, brush clearing, trail construction and wildland firefighting.

You can also learn how to weld, carpenter or cook, three very successful programs I saw in action when I was Community Services Director for Rogue Community College in Grants Pass Oregon in 1972. RCC took over an old Job Corps Center, so I know this drill well. Many who came went on to earn undergraduate and graduate college degrees.

A Forest Service retiree friend sent me the "Inside the Forest Service" announcement concerning the agency's decision to wash its hands of the Job Corps CCC program. In a matter of hours, I also had 23 pages of angry reaction from people I don't even know. No, that's not true. The first comment came from Michael Rains who wrote, "I can only hope that common sense will ultimately prevail. To do what is being proposed is an incredibly stupid [yes, stupid] decision. This program is one of the true success stories of our time. I am at a loss for words for this extremely short-sighted proposal."

The proposal was as stupid and short-sighted as Michael suggested. It sent the *absolute wrong message* to young people who are looking for pathways out of their own wildernesses. What was missing from the proposal was a realization that there isn't an immediate payoff in any social program designed to rescue wayward kids. The payoff comes years later when they become productive citizens and we don't have to feed them in jail cells.

Remember Roosevelt's still true analogy. "Forests, like people, must be constantly productive. The problems of the future of both are interlocked. American forestry efforts must be consolidated and advanced."

We have youngsters who want to be productive and forests that need to be productive again. We can travel a good distance down both roads if we first bring back the old Civilian Conservation Corps. This is a Green New Deal that a new Roosevelt can easily explain to Congress and the American people.

As for all the handwringing about greenhouse gases in our atmosphere, how about we *first* get most of the damned wildfire smoke out of western skies and see how things look. No country on earth is going to choose poverty, disease, hunger and illiteracy over cheap electricity and hope. That's how Roosevelt sold publicly-owned hydroelectric power to our Depression-wracked nation. It's also how he sold the Civilian Conservation Corps to a nation of heartsick men and women, including my father and my grandmother.

The pathway ahead

Michael Rains, a friend and colleague for many years wrote the Foreword for this book. He also contributed the essay you are about to read. Some of you will like it because he writes about aggressively thinning trees from national forests that have grown too dense. Some of you will hate it for the same reason. My hope is that those who hate it will at least consider the pragmatic science it represents.

Michael wrote this essay for *SMOKEJUMPER*, a quarterly publication of the National Smoke-jumpers Association. These are the young men and women who bravely ride parachutes into small wildfires in hopes of putting them out before they become big fires. They have been the stars in several fine books including *Young Men and Fire*, Norman Maclean's second and last book. If you have not read it, please do so. It is the finest book I own, which explains why I reference it in Chapters 12, 14, 30 and 31.

Michael's essay is titled *"Aggressive Forest Management: We Can't Avoid It any Longer."* It is one of the best of many he's written over the years I've known him. He's also written several letters to President Trump describing the root causes of the wildfire tragedy that is unfolding in the West.

I have no idea if Michael's letters reach the President but I want to believe that someone with close ties to him is reading them because there is much that Mr. Trump could do to untie the Gordian Knot that prevents more aggressive forest management that doesn't require Congressional action. Michael has also given the President a laundry list of things he could do to speed forest restoration in western national forests.

Michael takes a more direct – you might say more aggressive – approach in this essay than in his earlier work. He does so because he's frustrated by the inaction that continues to plague the U.S. Forest Service. The 48 years he worked for the agency give him tons of credibility and plenty of room to criticize the Forest Service's unexplainable reluctance to use the tools Congress has provided.

Contrary to the baseless claim made by some environmental groups, greedy lumbermen and loggers are not "chopping down all the trees" in western National Forests. Michael proves this – not by challenging the hucksters – but by pointing out that about five percent of what grows annually in our national forests is harvested. This means that 95 percent continues to grow year after year.

Some will say, "What's wrong with that?"

What's wrong is that our cumulative 95 percent growth rate isn't sustainable. If we continue down this pathway our national forests are going to start dying faster than they grow because we have exceeded the carrying capacity of the land – the number of trees per acre that nature can accommodate. Sadly, several western national forests are now dying faster than they are growing.

Think of our national forests as the reservoir behind a big dam. What if we only release five percent of the water that flows into the reservoir ever year? We will soon have an uncontrollable flood on our hands. That's what's happening in our national forests. We are witnessing an uncontrollable "tree flood." There are only two ways this flood can be quelled. We can harvest some trees, or we can let Nature do the harvesting for us.

Nature's toolbox includes insects, diseases and

like until the embers die out. Our toolbox yields more predictable results because we get to pick the methods based on what science tells us is the best one. We can hand-pick the trees and tree species we want to remove. We might want to deliberately set fires to clear out unwanted brush or focus on clearing out the diseased and dead trees, and then burn the debris before we replant. Our options are many, diverse and well regulated.

Nature isn't this careful or discriminating. We get whatever nature serves up. Currently, we are annually losing millions of acres of fish and wildlife habitat to insects, diseases and wildfires along with just as many acres of outdoor recreation opportunity. So, while reading Michael's essay ask yourself, "What do I want from my forest? What do I want it to look like? Who best delivers the result I want? Nature or people? Or maybe some of both."

Aggressive Forest Management: We can't avoid it any longer

by Michael Rains

I am a Forester by training, so I have a bias toward forest management. That is, through aggressive actions, keeping America's forests healthy, sustainable and more resilient to disturbances like insect and disease outbreaks and wildfires. Currently, with some exceptions, there is a lack of active forest management across our country – especially the public lands. Our forests are in decline. From the rural to urban land gradient, this decline is not in harmful to us all. It does not have to be this way.

Recently, I was reading "Print and Paper Myths and Facts" [version 4, 2018] from Two Sides North America, Inc. A quote caught my eye: "…Avoiding the use of wood is not the way to protect forests for the long term. It is precisely the areas of the world that consume the least wood that continue to experience the greatest forest loss."

During the past few years I have written extensively about the lack of forest management in our country, specifically as it influences the terribly destructive wildfire situation we have been confronted with during the last two decades. My notion is "…aggressive forest management will help ensure effective fire management" and eventually the large, high intensity wildfires we are experiencing now will subside and become again, a tool for landscape scale conservation.

Unfortunately to date, most of my words have had little effect at influencing change. I am not sure exactly why. People seem to be entrenched in a specific ideology or simply do not care. Have we become so divisive that removing any vegetation from our forests and woodlands causes what former Forest Chief Jack Ward Thomas described as "gladiators form and fights ensue?" Well-managed forests that provide goods and services and slow the ravages of wildfires is the conservation issue of our time, let there be no doubt. Surely there must be some common ground and a desire to change the status quo.

Thus, I have started to look at the issue differently, perhaps more pragmatically: the use of wood. American's like to use wood and enjoy its benefits housing; furniture; paper products; carbon positive; low energy production; and it's renewable and can be easily recycled. And, most of it comes from America's forests. We each use about 636 board feet of wood and wood products each year. That's about 2 times more than the global individual average! So, if we like wood so much, why do we seem to avoid ensuring a sustainable supply through aggressive forest management? It does seem like a paradox. Maybe most people do not know where their wood comes from. And as long as it does not come from "my forest," then that's okay. But it does come from "your forest."

Across our country, there is a total inventory of about 12 trillion board feet of wood. According to a recent publication on Forest Resources of the United States by Oswalt, et. al., that's enough wood to "…fill the Great Pyramid of Giza 12 thousand times." That's huge from a standpoint of helping mitigate the impacts of a changing climate through carbon sequestration. For additional reference, the total wood inventory is enough to build about 732 million homes!

And, each year, about 317 billion board feet of new wood is produced from forests and woodlands in the United States. Offsetting amounts for exports and imports, we essentially use each year about one-half of the wood

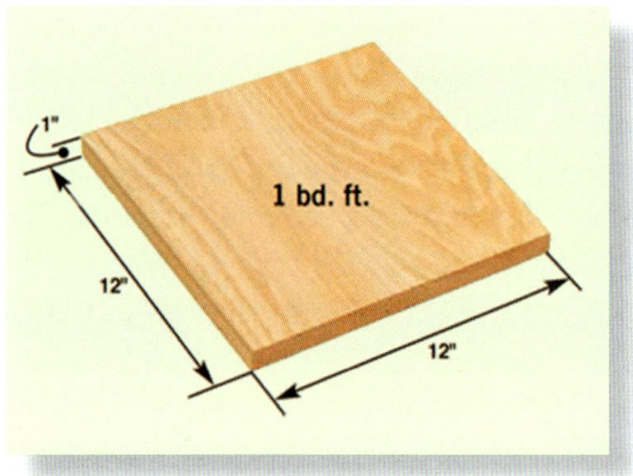

that is produced from our forested lands. That in itself has created a problem: our forests are getting clogged up. For example, there are more trees now than 100 years ago. Forests, which include more than just trees [i.e., the chaparral forests of Southern California], are getting stressed, they are dying, and are becoming a tinderbox for fire. And, once a fire gets a foothold, they become destructive behemoths that destroy everything in their paths.

Nationally, America consumes about 204 billion board feet of wood each year [including the offset of exports and imports]; about 144 billion board feet from just America's forests and woodlands. According to reliable sources, projections indicate yearly demand for wood and wood products [for example, lumber, plywood, pulpwood and advanced composites] in our country will be about 292 billion board feet in 2030; 330 billion board feet by 2050. That's close to the current annual growth [about 317 billion board feet] to ensure a sustainable proposition. Simply put, more wood can and should be removed from our forestlands.

Approximately one-quarter of the lumber used in the United States last year was imported. About 80 percent came from Canada. While I am all for free-trade, if more of America's forests were aggressively managed, there would be a much better balance in domestic production, use and imports -- especially for the more conventional wood products such as lumber for building construction. For reference, an average-size residential house uses about 16,380 board feet of wood. And, commercial construction using wood is on the rise.

Who controls the management of our forests? About eight percent of the world's forests are in the United States and this is split into three ownership categories: federal [30 percent]; state and local [10 percent]; and private [60 percent]. About 67 percent of all the forestlands have an objective to produce wood. According to a Forest Resources Report of the United States, "...about 55 percent of the volume of growing stock and half the volume of sawtimber is in private ownership. In the eastern states, about 90 percent of the timber volume is on private land; in western states, by contrast, only 40 percent of the timber volume is in private ownership. More than 90 percent of the growing stock on western public lands is on the National Forests or other areas managed by the federal government."

This last statement is telling. There was a time when I was with the United States Forest Service when the annual timber harvest level from the National Forests [NFS] was about 12 billion board feet. Now, it is about 3 billion board feet each year. That's about 1 percent of the today's total wood production level [or, about 5 percent of the total NFS growth] – from a high of about 12 percent from the production level of the late 1970s. About 19 percent of America's forests are designated National Forests.

Clearly, from a resource sustainability and processing capability point of view, the National Forests could easily increase their contribution of wood and wood products for our country. And, as a result, the forests in the west – which are especially vulnerable to large, intense wildfires – could become less "clogged" and much more resilient. Simply put, we could begin to reverse the current trend of "lack of management" to "aggressive management" to help protect lives, property and communities. And, produce more wood and wood products for a growing America. To me, "aggressive forest management" can easily be translated, for example, into an annual wood removal program on the National Forests to a very minimum of 9 billion board feet per year; three times the current level. The economic benefits to local communities will be significant. Yes, this will take additional resources and some infrastructure expansion, but it's well within the range of science-based, sustainable vegetative management and will help increase the flow of wood and wood products to meet projected demand increases.

Let me go back to that opening quote: "…Avoiding the use of wood is not the way to protect forests for the long term…" Healthy, sustainable, resilient forests make our lives better. They protect us. They nourish us and provide comfort. They improve our health. The current decline of our forests does not have to be. We owe it to ourselves and future generations to band together and do all we can to enable our lands to be more fulfilling to everyone and everything that depends on them. With the dynamics we impose to be a vibrant and growing country, the notion of "let nature takes its course" is not a good plan. Now is the time to stop avoiding aggressive forest management in America. Support and funding from the current and future Administrations will be fundamental to success. To this end, readers are encouraged to sign on to a Petition. [67] We can no longer avoid being aggressive about the management of our forests. We have waited far too long. Now is the time.

Primary Sources:

1. United States Forest Products Annual Market Review and Prospects, 2015-2019. James L. Howard, Economist Shaobo Liang, PostDoc Scientist. Forest Products Laboratory, Madison, Wisconsin USA.
2. An Analysis of the Timber Situation in the United States: 1952 to 2050. Richard W. Haynes Technical Coordinator. U.S. Depart ment of Agriculture, Forest Service Pacific Northwest Research Station Portland, Oregon General Technical Report PNW-GTR-560 February 2003.
3. James Howard and Kwameka Jones, U.S. Timber Production, Trade, Consumption, and Price Statistics, 1965-2013, USDA, FPL-RP-679, 2016.
4. Forest Resources of the United States, 2017 A Technical Document Supporting the Forest Service 2020 RPA Assessment Sonja N. Oswalt, W. Brad Smith, Patrick D. Miles, and Scott A. Pugh. https://www.fs.fed.us/research/publications/gtr/gtr_wo97.pdf
5. Print and Paper Myths and Facts. Version 4, 2018. Two Sides North America, Inc. 330 N. Wabash Avenue Suite 2000 Chicago, IL 60611. T: 855-896-7433 E: info@twosidesna.org
6. https://twosidesna.org/wp-content/uploads/sites/16/2018/07/Two-Sides-Myths-Facts-Version-4-NA.pdf
7. https://www.everycrsreport.com/reports/R45688.html
8. Woodworks. 2011.
9. U.S. Forest Resource Facts and Historical Trends. USDA Forest Service, FS-1035. 2014: https://www.fia.fs.fed.us/library/bro chures/docs/2012/ForestFacts_1952-2012_English.pdf

a. Conversions: 766 million acres of forestland; 145 million = NFS or 19 percent. 317 billion board feet of total wood growth x 19 percent = 60.2 billion board feet from the NFS. 3 [current harvest level]/60.2 = about 5 percent of NFS growth or 1 percent to total wood growth in America.

10. Planting for the Future. How Demand for Wood Products Could Be Friendly to Tropical Forests. October 1, 2014
11. R. C. Wilson, Chief, Forest Survey Branch, and George Vitas, Forestry Information Specialist, Forest Service, United States Department of Agriculture.
12. Conversions: 1 cubic foot = 12 board feet. 6.3 board feet per square foot for home construction.
13. U.S. Census Bureau. 2013. Average size house = 2,600 square feet, or 16,380 board feet.
14. Federal Lands in the West: A few facts and figures. https://www.westernplanner.org/201604issue/2017/8/9/federal-lands-in-the-west-a-few-facts-and-figures

67 

CHAPTER 33

Turn out the lights. The party's over.

You'd have to be living on a different planet not to have heard or read about the PG&E wildfire fiasco/bankruptcy/keelhauling underway in California. Some of the public scorn is richly deserved, but not all of it.

More on this in a moment, but first read the letter I wrote last September to PG&E CEO and President, Bill Johnson. Frankly, I didn't expect a reply. Only the rarest of corporations is willing to confront controversy head-on. Mr. Johnson did not disappoint me. I'm still waiting for a reply. Hell will freeze over first.

My letter to Mr. Johnson included a copy of the bar graph imbedded in Lyle Laverty's 2017 testimony before the House Subcommittee on Federal Lands. Lyle and I have been friends for many years. Even interviewed him a couple of years ago when he was thinking about tossing his name in the nomination pot for Chief of the Forest Service. He would have been a good one: Former Assistant Secretary of the Interior for Fish, Wildlife and Parks, former Director of Colorado State Parks, former Associate Deputy Chief of the Forest Service and former Rocky Mountain Region Regional Forests. That's a lot of formers.

I did not include Lyle's testimony in my letter to Mr. Johnson, though I probably should have. Just the bar graph, which I thought was gruesome enough to get his attention. I was wrong. Anyway, what Lyle told subcommittee members about the roots of the West's wildfire pandemic and my letter to Bill Johnson are on the following pages. His statement is long but well worth reading.

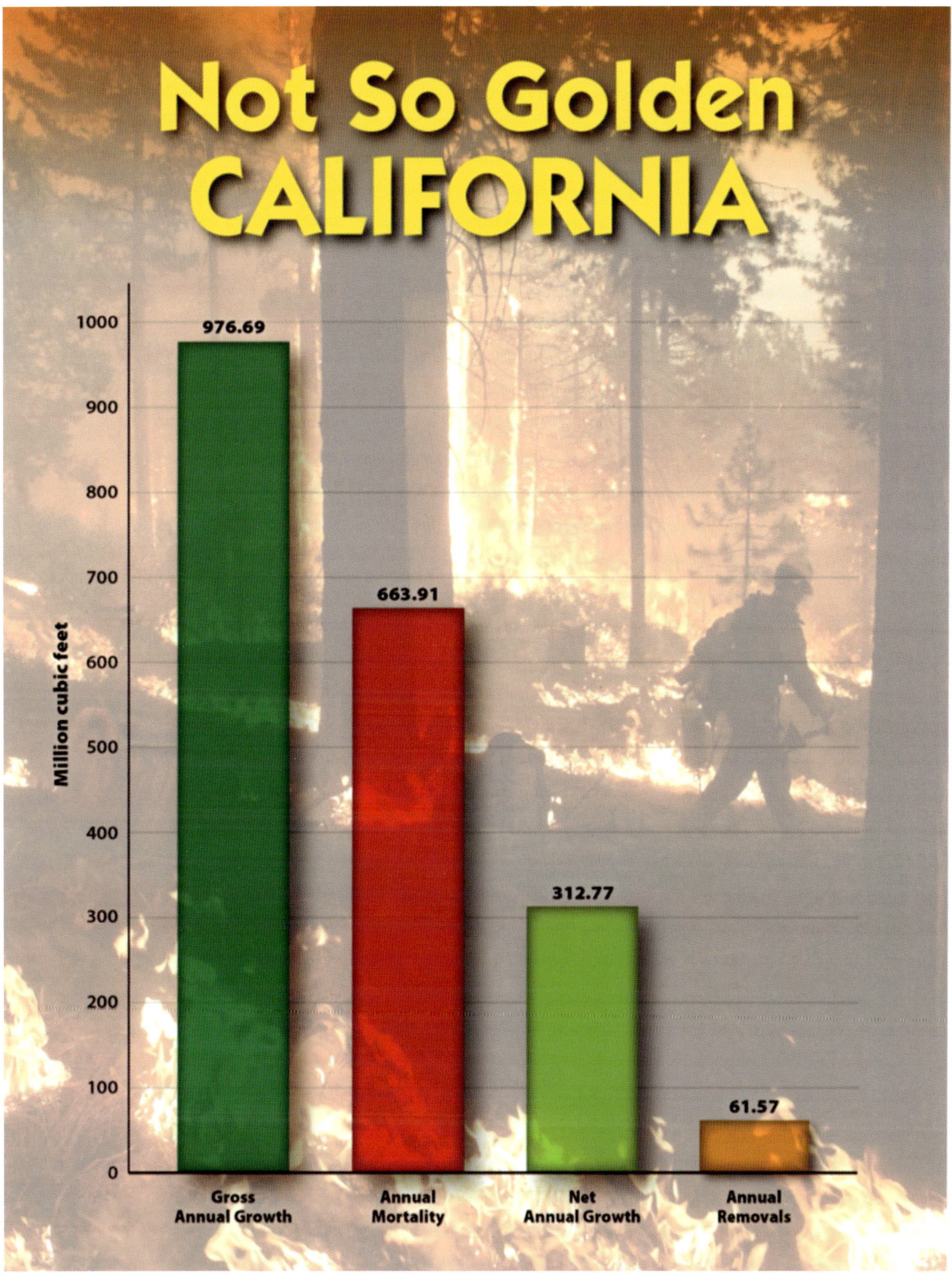
Not So Golden
CALIFORNIA
Million cubic feet
1000
900
800
700
600
500
400
300
200
100
0
976.69
663.91
312.77
61.57
Gross
Annual Growth
Annual
Mortality
Net
Annual Growth
Annual
Removals

What do you want from your forest?

September 23, 2019

Bill Johnson, CEO and President
Pacific Gas & Electric, Inc.
245 Market Street
San Francisco, CA., 94105

Dear Mr. Johnson:

We have been following your efforts to contain the public relations and financial nightmares that have developed in the aftermath of the Camp Fire. No doubt you are anxious to put this tragedy behind PG&E and its shareholders. Your $11 billion settlement with insurers is certainly a step in the right direction.

Unfortunately, you can't end this tragedy because PG&E isn't the root cause. To be sure, better maintenance along transmission lines will help, but the federal government is not doing its part. Specifically, the United States Forest Service is years behind in its maintenance responsibilities in California's national forests.

The larger problem isn't associated with rights-of-way or equipment maintenance. It is the disgraceful state of federally-owned forest lands adjacent to transmission routes. No matter how well you do your job, one spark, regardless of its source, can trigger a firestorm as soon as it reaches your power lines.

Of the 976.69 million feet of timber that grow annually in California's forests, 663.9 million cubic feet die. Imagine a 68 percent failure rate at PG&E. Imagine a solid block of wood the dimensions of the Rose Bowl stretching 2.18 miles skyward. That's how much timber dies annually in California forests. Until this problem is resolved, PG&E faces enormous and continuing financial risks. Likewise, every public and private electric utility in the West.

The crisis you face is quantified on the enclosed bar graph, which we assembled from field survey data collected by the U.S. Forest Service's Forest Inventory and Analysis Program. FIA has been collecting and analyzing this data from designated research plots since the 1930s.

We use FIA field, aerial and remote sensing data in all of our forestry education work. I am enclosing recent reports from Montana, Idaho and Washington to give you a sense of what we could do to assist you in exposing the underlying forest management challenges facing every California community you serve. These reports underscore the wealth of vetted and publicly sourced information at our fingertips. There are many options open to you.

The Evergreen Foundation has been on the front lines in the West's "forest health" debate since 1986. With the able assistance of our partners at the Society of American Foresters and the National Association of Forest Service Retirees, we can help you craft a collaborative public dialogue focusing on the underlying causes of this costly and unending tragedy.

Please contact me if you wish to discuss this invitation more fully.

Sincerely,

James D. Petersen
Founder and President
The non-profit Evergreen Foundation

Roseville firefighters put out hotspots in Paradise, California. (Mason Trinca for The Washington Post)

Statement of Lyle Laverty
Former Assistant Secretary of the Interior, Fish, Wildlife and Parks
Before the House Subcommittee on Federal Lands - June 8, 2017

Chairman McClintock and distinguished members of this Subcommittee. Thank you for the opportunity to share some perspectives on the challenges facing active management of America's National Forests and Grasslands.

Today our forests are in crisis. Wildfires are burning with unprecedented ferocity due to prolonged drought; insect and disease infestations in over stressed stands; too many trees for the carrying capacity of the land, and I believe the lack of active management to name just a few. There are many other reasons. My friend and colleague Jim Petersen, publisher of Evergreen Magazine shared there is no cause, "more damaging than a suite of well-intended but conflicting environmental laws administered by federal agencies whose missions and regulations make it impossible for the Forest Service to attack the forest health crisis on meaningful ecological scales."

The National Forest System offers unsurpassed opportunities to fulfill the goal of Making America Great Again and restoring vibrancy to rural America. Actively managing these forests and grasslands will enhance our Nation's watersheds, forest health and resilience, benefit wildlife, protect and produce tens of thousands of direct and indirect jobs that will benefit communities, gateway communities dependent on healthy forests. Sustainable management of these lands will create investment and employment opportunities within natural resource based communities and return wealth and health to rural America.

The forest health crisis is evident across the country, but I share the situation on the National Forests in California and Colorado as examples. Today, there are more than one billion dead trees just on the National Forests in these two states. I recently shared with the Colorado Joint Agriculture/Natural Resources Committee highlights of the condition of Colorado's National Forests. It is not a favorable picture. Due to the widespread bark beetle epidemic, we have over 5 million acres of dead trees. In 2015 annual tree mortality exceeded annual growth. The following information is based on the Forest Service Timber sale information and Forest Inventory and Analysis data.

Colorado's National Forest Crisis	
2015 Gross Annual Growth	119,857,000 cubic feet
2015 Mortality	266,113,000 cubic feet
2015 Annual Net Growth	146,256,000 cubic feet
Standing Dead Volume	6,700,000,000 cubic feet
Timber offered for sale	29,122,000 cubic feet

California's National Forest Crisis	
2015 Gross Annual Growth	976,690,487 cubic feet
2015 Mortality	663,917,476 cubic feet
2015 Net Annual Growth	312,773,011 cubic feet
Standing Dead Volume	7,672,698,704 cubic feet
Timber offered for sale	64,881,700 cubic feet
Timber cut	61,566,800 cubic feet

Putting these large figures in perspective, the standing dead volume in California and Colorado would supply building material to construct nearly 6 million 2400 square foot homes. The Idaho Forest Product Commission estimates roughly 35 jobs are created for each one million board feet of raw logs. The 2015 mortality volume in just California and Colorado would support approximately 11,500 jobs.

We are bankrupting the future. Lack of active management on America's National Forests threatens our watersheds and communities. It also increases future environmental impacts such as lost economic opportunity resulting from blackened landscapes and subsequent flooding. America's green infrastructure is on life support, perhaps even on the brink of ecological collapse.

I believe there are three general areas of impediments constraining the necessary pace and scale of management to sustain healthy resilient forest ecosystems; (1) wildfire funding must be permanently resolved immediately, (2) the Equal Access to Justice Act and other conflicting laws must be amended to unencumber active management of America's National Forests without the chilling effect of litigation, (3) regulations and agency policies which restrict active managements of our National Forests must be reviewed, identified and eliminated.

Chris and Nancy Brown among the remains of their home in Paradise, California. (Noah Berger/AP)

Continued underfunding of wildfire suppression has forced the agency to engage in "borrowing" or transferring funds from non-fire accounts to pay for wildfire suppression costs. The impacts of this broken fire funding system are severe. Over the past three or four years, funding for non-fire programs of the Forest Service has been slashed by hundreds of millions of dollars. Redirecting these funds, intended for programs that improve forest resiliency – such as mitigation and active forest management activities – exacerbates poor forest health conditions and actually increases future fire risks and suppression costs.

Programs for watershed, wildlife, timber, recreation, range, road and trail maintenance, research and cooperative programs have been decimated as a result of the current leveraging of funds to pay for wildfire suppression activities. Consider trying to manage a large proactive resource organization like the Forest Service when you have to hold in reserve, funds appropriated for resource management activities, to make sure adequate firefighting funds are available for the last 3 months of the fiscal year – July, August, and September. These are the critical months for major, expensive fires in the west. Catastrophic wildfires, just like hurricane season for FEMA, put the Forest Service in an almost unmanageable situation.

The consequence of the agency's inability to actively manage forest landscapes is amplified in the Forest Service's inventory data for the national forests in California showing an average of 266 trees per acre on a landscape that generally can only support 40 to 100 trees per acre. The increasing tree density creates a tinderbox of fuel creating huge, intense wildfires on California's National Forests.

Extreme deteriorating conditions of our forests have led to unprecedented cost of wildfire suppression and control across our country. Each year we see unacceptable impacts to watersheds and communities from wildfire in regions of our great Nation. Wildfire is not just a western issue, but rather an issue to which all forests are vulnerable, as evidenced by last year's devastating Gatlinburg wildfire. We must recognize that wildfire suppression funding is as critical to our national infrastructure as funding for hurricanes, floods and earthquakes. Under the current budgeting process, funding for wildfire preparedness and suppression is consuming an ever-increasing amount of the Forest Service budget line items not intended for suppression. Each year the result is a decrease in available funds for work that could be done to reduce the risk, size and cost of wildfires. Secretary Perdue testified just two weeks ago, that of the 2018 Budget for the Forest Service, 53 percent is for Wildland Fire Management, up from just 16 percent in 1995. The most important action Congress can do to advance the pace and scale of active management on America's National Forests is to aggressively fix the wildfire funding problem.

The Equal Access to Justice Act (EAJA) as adopted by Congress in 1980 focused on removing a barrier to justice by helping individuals, small businesses and nonprofit organizations recover money and other resources they spent suing the federal government. Unfortunately, this well-intentioned law has been hijacked by groups intent on stopping active forest management activities and projects, using taxpayer's money to fund their litigation and further their own narrow political agenda. Wyoming rancher/lawyer Karen Budd-Falen found in 2009 that non-profit environmental groups filed more than 1500 lawsuits and the federal government paid out more than $4.7 billion of taxpayers' dollars in settlement and legal fees in cases against the United States, specifically from the Judgement Fund.

The Government Accountability Office (GAO) recently indicated we do not know the totality of EAJA costs as most agencies do not compile this information. In addition to these settlement costs, the Forest Service incurs the added burden and cost in planning management projects, attempting to defend them from nuisance appeals and litigation. This new legal industry is a large burden on the federal decision-making process, America's taxpayers and America's communities and must be reformed.

Recently passed House Resolution 1033 begins to capture information relating to the amount of fees and expenses awarded by federal courts when the United States loses or settles a case. The inclusion of a standing requirement for a "direct and personal interest" will greatly reduce the extent to which 501(c) (3) organizations can intervene

A vintage car rests among debris in Paradise, California. (Noah Berger/AP)

and assert their right to compensation along with individual citizens. Others have suggested excluding forest management activities from the EAJA suggesting that differences of opinions should be settled through binding arbitration. The National Association of Forest Service Retirees suggests courts give deference to resource professionals on the ground, making it harder for courts to halt forest restoration projects with injunctions.

One of the most important reforms to increase the pace and scale of active management of America's National Forests would be efforts to reduce the regulatory burdens of ESA on restoration and active management activities. For over 40 years, the ESA has been one of our nation's strongest and respected environmental laws. While the original intent of the ESA was to conserve and protect American species of plants and wildlife threatened with extinction, the law has been increasingly used to block projects and deter the legal use of privately owned land. Healthy and productive private and public forests support essential habitat for listed species and species at risk. The challenge today is to develop effective and balanced legislative and administrative improvements to the ESA that support the protection of fish, wildlife and plant populations as well as responsible land, water and resource management.

Steve Mealy, Vice President of Conservation for the Boone and Crockett Club in 2013 provided testimony before the Subcommittee on National Park, Forests and Public Lands. His remark echoes the growing concern regarding healthy function ecosystems. *"Recent assessments of uncharacteristic wildfire risks indicate the absence of active management to mitigate fire risks in such areas may be the greater risk to vulnerable species. Ironically, continuation of highly restrictive precautionary principle driven, short term risk averse protection measures will likely lead to the continued deterioration of the very resources the environmental laws were intended to protect."*

Twenty two years after the listing of the northern spotted owl in 1990, the Fish and Wildlife Service issued a Revised Recovery Plan. The plan recognized that "many populations of spotted owls continue to decline … even with extensive maintenance and restoration of spotted owl habitat… it is becoming more evident that securing habitat alone will not recover the spotted owl… competition from the barred owl poses a significant and complex threat…" Mr. Mealy continues *"Overall northern spotted owl numbers have been declining nearly 3 percent per year, leading to an estimated 40 percent decline over the last 25 years."*

There are significant and burdensome costs associated with listing decisions. Mr. Mealy's testimony articulates the listing impact. "Since 1989, the year before the northern spotted owl listing to 2012, timber harvest on federal forestland in western Oregon has dropped from about 3.5 billion board feet per year to under .5 billion board feet per year, an 86 percent decline owing to the effects of environmental litigation and an emphasis on mature and old forest retention. Final harvest acres declined from nearly 100,000 per year to less than 10,000 per year."

Management action and inaction or things we do and don't do, have the potential to cause serious environmental harm as well as good. On fire prone forests of the West, the focus of regulatory environmental laws has been mostly prevention of harm from action. The potential for harm from inaction has largely been ignored. This has contributed to the decline of the very resources the laws are intended to protect. Unnatural fuel accumulations lead to the uncharacteristic wildfires that can and will ultimately harm listed species and water quality.

The scope of the Endangered Species Act should be updated and expanded to include consideration of the short-term effects of management inaction, and then compare and balance them with short and long-term effects of action. These comparative assessments would allow managers to consider the full ecological contexts over space and time in decision making and offer improved prospects for restoring and sustaining resources.

To accelerate active National Forest management, streamlining the interagency consultation process is essential. Forest Service biologists are trained and capable of determining whether a project or activity complies with ESA and should only be required to consult with US Fish and Wildlife Service should there be questions of ESA compliance.

The Council of Environmental Quality (CEQ) regulations implementing the National Environmental Policy Act (NEPA) have slowed the federal land management agency decision making process to a crawl, adding little value to the process but swelling the cost of projects. The Act requires an environmental analysis on "major Federal actions significantly affecting the quality of the human environment". The Act simply requires agencies to fully consider environmental values along with social and economic values in making major decisions affecting the human environment. Over the decades, agencies have transformed the environmental *assessment* process into a political decision making process. By adopting the current application of the NEPA process as its decision making process, agencies have placed an environmental bias into federal decisions by forcing agencies to justify why they are willing to disturb the environment in order to provide some economic and social benefits or even longer term environmental values.

Logic would support using an economic or social decision model to drive decisions but consider the environmental effects as required by NEPA. For an agency such as the Forest Service, it makes a significant difference in the management, implementation and impact on affected communities. Starting with economic or social objectives to create jobs, create recreational opportunities, provide timber to a local mill, thin the forest to reduce fire hazards, improve fish and wildlife habitats, or improve the health of our Nation's watersheds, then identify the environmental effects of the project and determine if they need to be mitigated. Within this decision framework, environmental values are considered in the decision process as required by NEPA, however the outcome would most likely be different with a focus on economic or social goals and objectives, rather than environmental side effects.

GAO has found that the Forest Service conducts more NEPA analysis, produces more Environmental Impact Statements (EIS), and takes longer to do so than most other agencies whose projects have more lasting impact on the landscape.

NEPA requires an environmental analysis for significant projects with potential adverse impacts on the environment. Perhaps the major trigger for passing NEPA was Tellico Dam in Tennessee which became controversial when significant environmental effects were overlooked in the decision making process. Through regulations and agency policies issued over the years, significant projects have been liberally expanded to include individual timber sales, construction of roads, trails and other minor projects. The Forest Service routinely repeats the same type of projects, projects that have well recognized but minimal environmental impacts and should not have to repeat the environmental analysis each time that type of project is conducted.

Congress should streamline and clarify NEPA, that for the Forest Service:

- Application of NEPA should be restricted to truly "major" actions, not routine land management activities such as thinning of forests in general forests or lands "suited for timber production" under existing National Forest Management Plans. Taking active steps to address forest and watershed health conditions following wildfire and insect infestations should not be considered "major."
- Clarify that (1) environmental impact statements only require an agency to analyze the proposed action and a no-action alternative, and that consideration of additional alternatives is solely at the discretion of the Forest Service line officer; and (2) environmental assessments do not require analysis of a no action alternative.
- Amend the Act to explicitly define "major" and "significant," thereby eliminating pages of regulations implying that NEPA applies to every ground disturbing activity.
- Provide greater authority for the use of categorical exclusions for emergency actions to protect watersheds and communities from impending wildfire.
- Provide clarity of what constitutes "extraordinary circumstances," facilitating greater use of categorical exclusions.

The condition of America's National Forests and Grasslands is in immediate and grave jeopardy. Actively managing these lands by engaging collaboratively with citizens, states, and counties with credible science will return significant benefits. Active management of these lands will:

- Produce sustained employment opportunities,
- Enhance forest health and resilience,
- Improve wildlife habitat,
- Sequester carbon,
- Protect and restore our nation's watersheds, by reforesting millions of recently burned areas, and
- Bring health and wealth to America's rural communities.

Today, conflicting laws, regulations and polices as well as endless litigation and political gridlock threaten the resources that made America great! This gridlock results in catastrophic wildfires, destruction of critical habitat, and the loss of millions of dollars to local gateway economies.

Former Forest Service Chief Jack Ward Thomas once said, "It's over time now to assemble a group of folks to look at the whole body of federal law and determine their function and dysfunction and make recommendation about how they should operate."

It is time for Congress and Federal agencies to act and chart a renewed course for conservation leadership in America. Thank you for the opportunity to share these perspectives with you today.
I am happy to take your questions.

I suppose I should feel vindicated by the fact that an increasing number of respected publications including the Wall Street Journal have belatedly weighed in. The Journal – for which I have written several times – has published a series of informative essays that explain the underlying causes of our wildfire calamity. Yet despite my 33 years in a front line trench in the wildfire debate, I'm still not feeling any of the "I told you so" satisfaction I expected.

What I see in my mind's eye that frustrates the hell out of me are maybe 30 million Californian's with their hands cupped over their ears yelling, "La, la, la, la, la, la." They refuse to hear or consider the truth about the underlying causes of our wildfire crisis. They have wrapped themselves in shrouds of naturalness and nothing is going to disturb their séance.

- Not millions of dead trees.
- Not thousands of homes reduced to ash and ruin.
- Not hundreds of people killed fleeing flames.
- Not skyrocketing home insurance premiums.
- Not homeowner policy cancellations.
- Not carcinogenic wildfire smoke.
- Not the hundreds of millions of tons of carbon wildfires release annually into California's otherwise sunny skies.

PG&E's high-voltage lines typically carry 345,000 volts of electricity. These lines pass through more than 5,000 miles of drought-stricken forest – mostly publicly owned national forests that beg for better vegetation management – including some fairly aggressive thinning. At last count, there were an estimated 147 million dead trees in the Sierra Nevada's. When flames touch these trees, they explode like Roman candles. Boom. Gone.

Unfortunately, many Californians no longer see science-based forestry and rangeland management as solutions to our wildfire pandemic. They love nature and they're deeply suspicious of any private sector action that disrupts what they perceive to be nature's fragile web of life. Especially if it involves "greedy" loggers "profiting" from clearing away dead and dying trees in California forests.

PG&E has done a lousy job of maintaining their vast California transmission system, but it pales when compared to the horrible job Congress and the federal government are doing to protect and restore insect and disease infested across the West – forests that belong to every American. Protecting our nation's forest heritage demands bipartisan support – not the partisan bickering that the fear-mongering conflict industry continues to feed.

This is an excellent time to remember that allowing the West to burn to the ground just because some screwball says "it's natural" is a terrible idea. We have all the tools, manpower and time-tested science we need – including thinning and Good Fire – to restore natural resiliency in publicly- owned forests that are being incinerated by Bad Fire.

Remember Chief Oshkosh's wisdom from Chapter 1:

"Start with the rising sun and work toward the setting sun, take only the mature trees, the sick trees

and the trees that have fallen. When you reach the end of the reservation, turn and cut from the setting sun to the rising sun and the trees will last forever."

Alan Houston nailed it in the same Chapter:

"When we leave forests to nature, as so many people seem to want to do, we get whatever nature serves up, which can be very devastating at times, but with forestry we have options and a degree of predictability not found in nature."

So did Alston Chase – also in Chapter 1: "There is no such thing as leaving nature alone. People are part of nature. We do not have the option of choosing not to be stewards of the land. We must master the art and science of good stewardship. Environmentalists do not understand that the only way to preserve nature is to manage nature."

Given the enormous amount of misinformation, disinformation and plain old propaganda that passes for "news" today, no one should be surprised that many Californians oppose PG&E's efforts to thin vegetation from the routes its aging transmission lines follow.

When asked, most say they understand the need to pick up branches and fallen trees beneath power lines but does anyone understand that big wildfires create their own weather, generating cyclone-like winds that can throw burning embers a mile or more ahead of the conflagration?

A broken hook on a PG&E transmission line at Tower 27/222 started the Camp Fire. High winds broke the hook, dropping the line to the ground. Has everyone forgotten that the ensuing fire storm traveled for miles in a couple of hours before it reached bucolic Paradise Valley, where it killed 85 people and destroyed 18, 804 structures – more than the Great Chicago Fire of 1871.

Does anyone remember that the Camp Fire moved through tall grass at 100 yards per second. And we're going rake leaves and chip broken limbs and call it good?

Spraying fire retardant on every tree within 300 feet of a PG&E transmission line isn't going to stop the firenadoes that are destroying California's forests. It might prevent powerline sparks from starting a fire, but that's not the problem. Less than 10 percent of all fires are caused by powerlines. The problem is a near total lack of forest and vegetation management – actions that would prevent the buildup of flammable woody debris that is fueling our wildfire pandemic.

PG&E has done the only thing I can do given the regulatory noose around its neck. It is shutting down its transmission lines during high winds, prompting Wall Street Journal opinion writer, Holman Jenkins, Jr. to pose a very timely question in "Revolutionary California," his October 30, 2019 column:

- Can 40 million Californians go overnight from First World electric reliability to Third World electric reliability without a voter revolt?

"The wildfire crisis is ultimately the product of a state politics controlled by interest groups whose agenda has drifted out of any cognizable relationship with the daily well-being of the state's average citizen," Jenkins wrote.

"A generation of ill-judged environmental activism had all but ended forest management in favor of letting dead trees and underbrush build up because it's more 'natural.' At the same time, residents resist any natural or planned fires that could consume this tinder before it gives rise to conflagrations like those now menacing Los Angeles and San Francisco."

I have a hard time understanding how or why a state that is so wedded to reducing California's less than one percent contribution to global emissions can summarily ignore its major contributor to atmospheric pollution: wildfire smoke. But then I remind myself of something the late Michael Crichton said during a 2008 lecture at Caltech titled Aliens Cause Global Warming. He said, "Once you abandon strict adherence to what science tells us, once you start arranging the truth in a press conference, then anything is possible."

Over the last 40 years, I have observed a great deal of arranging and rearranging the truth by fearmongering reporters. If you care to take the time, here's a long list of apocalyptic predictions [68] that turned out to be wrong.

But if you're not much for dredging up the past, my colleague Mike Archer, a Los Angeles copywriter, publishes a terrific Monday through Friday global

68 

A deer stands amid the remains of a burned home. (Josh Edelson/AFP/Getty Images)

wildfire news digest you can access for free at Wildfire Today.[69]

If your main interest is in bayonetting the wounded, hire a good personal injury lawyer. PG&E will shell out billions before it goes broke. Then the utility will fall into the hands of the same state regulators who recently declared that carbon released by burning trees was more "natural" than carbon released from fossil fuels. This is like saying that vaping is better for your lungs than cigarettes.

PG&E customers, who already pay among the highest power rates in the nation, are loading up on generators powered by – you guessed it – fossil fuels! Gasoline, propane and diesel! How else to keep their homes and businesses going when the utility shuts down its system because the winds is blowing like crazy and they fear its aging grid might start another forest fire?

You can be forgiven for wondering why PG&E fears its grid might start a fire. Bear with me and I'll explain.

Credit Suisse estimates that PG&E's long-term contracts with green energy developers cost the company $2.2 billion a year more than current market power rates. And because green power – solar and wind – is more expensive than coal or natural gas, the government subsidizes the added cost of green power to make it more palatable to people who otherwise wouldn't even consider it. Here, the word "government" means taxpayers and rate payers.

69

Public utility regulators set power rates in California, not PG&E. Clearly, they're more interested in promoting green energy than grid safety. How else to explain the fact that PG&E's grid continues to crumble?

The company estimates that inspecting its 100,000-mile grid and clearing away hazardous trees will require a 400 percent rate increase. It is the price of 40 years of regulatory mismanagement of publicly-owned forests and rangelands in just one western state. Who's next? Idaho? Eastern Oregon or Washington? Montana? Colorado? Maybe every western state.

Recalibrate your conservation compass. Re-read Lyle Laverty's testimony. It's time for the fearmongers and bullshit artists to turn out their lights. The party's over.

Black ghosts and climate kids

I re-read Norman Maclean's *Young Men and Fire* every winter. It is one of the three or four best books I've ever read. Maclean and my great aunt, Genevieve Alberton, were Shakespearean scholars and teachers of considerable renown. They were also Montanans to the depths of their souls. He taught at the University of Chicago, she at Montana Western in Dillon.

I harbor the certainty that they must have met somewhere at some conference reserved only for those who really understood Shakespeare. I would not have been admitted because I preferred more contemporary greats: Eugene O'Neill, William Faulkner, Tennessee Williams and the lesser known Walker Percy.

Genevieve knew this and kept me supplied with their works, which I still have. I did not attend Montana Western, and thus never took a class from her, but she remains a giant in my life nearly 50 years after her death. What I admire most about her is that she never gave up on wandering souls, including mine.

Maclean outlived Genevieve by 17 years, and in that short timespan he became one of the finest writers in modern history. Most who keep flyrods in the trunks of their cars have read *A River Runs Through It* at least twice. I have no idea how many times I've read it but it is as close to a Maclean autobiography as we'll ever get and it has become a reference book in the still unfolding story of my own life.

Though lesser known, *Young Men and Fire* is maybe even better than *A River Runs Through It.* Not just because it teaches a story about a big wildfire – there are lots of those – but because Maclean's second book holds a gripping description of what it must be like to die in a firestorm.

The young men in Maclean's story were smokejumpers stationed at the county airport in Missoula, Montana. They were overrun by searing heat and flames on a grassy slope in Mann Gulch, a rocky canyon that rises above the Missouri River, not far from Helena, Montana, August 5, 1949.

The two jumpers who survived – Bob Sallee and Walter Rumsey – outran a wall of flames. When he was still a teenager, Maclean outran a terrifying inferno on Fish Creek, west of Missoula. He wrote about it in "Black Ghost," a sad remembrance about a fire he fought on Fish Creek, southwest of Missoula, Montana. I have fished there and know it to be very rugged country.

"I kept looking for escape openings marked by holes in smoke that at times burned upside down," Maclean wrote. "Behind, where I did not dare to look, the main fire was sound and heat, a ground noise like a freight train. Where there were weak spots in the grass, it sounded as if the freight train had slowed down to cross a bridge or perhaps enter a tunnel. It could have been doing either, but in a moment it roared again and started to catch up. It came so close it sounded as if it were cracking bones, and mine were the only bones around. Then it would enter a tunnel and I would have hope again. Whether it rumbled or crackled I was always terrified. Always thirsty. Always exhausted."

Maclean was summering in his cabin on Seeley Lake, north of Missoula, when news of the Mann Gulch tragedy reached him. Unable to put it out of his mind, he headed for Willow Creek, not far from Mann Gulch, picked up his brother-in-law and headed for the scene of the still smoldering fire. There, crossing a small creek, they met their black ghost, a still living deer that had been horribly burned because it, too, had been unable to outrun the flames.

"The deer was hairless and purple," Maclean wrote. "Where the skin had broken, the flesh was in patches. For a time, the deer did not look up. It must have been especially like Joe Sylvia, who was burned so deeply that he was euphoric. But when a tree exploded and was thrown as a victim to the foot of a nearby cliff, the deer finally raised its head and slowly saw us. Its eyes were red bulbs that illuminated long hairs around its eyelids."

The deer was able to steady itself, bounded a few feet, stumbled and fell headfirst into a fallen log. Maclean's brother-in-law had left his rifle in their borrowed pickup so there was nothing they could do but watch tragedy unfold.

"The deer lay there and looked back looking for us, but, shocked by its collision with the log, it probably did not see us," he wrote. "It probably did not see anything – it moved its head back and forth, as if trying to remember at what angle it had last seen us. Suddenly, its eyes were like electric light bulbs burning out – with a flash, too much light burned out the filaments in the blubs, and then the red faded slowly to black. In the fading, there came a point where the long hairs on the eyelids were no longer illuminated. Then the deer put its head down on the log it had not seen and could not jump."

I saw those same "electric light bulbs burning out" in the eyes of my best fishing buddy the moment he drew his last breath in 2002. I thus know the emptiness that enters our still living souls when the life of your best fishing pal fades to black and you are left alone with nothing more than the waters of memory.

Maclean's son, John, finished *Young Men* after his father died in 1990. "Black Ghost," a short story the elder Maclean wrote several years earlier, is the book's forward – and it the perfect lead-in to a heart-breaking tragedy memorialized in song by James Keelaghan. "Cold Missouri Waters" will put a lump in your throat.

There are no pictures of the Mann Gulch Fire consuming its young men, only photos of the Forest Service stretcher bearers carrying canvass-wrapped bodies across barren slopes. But you can go on the world wide web and find thousands of photographs of the West's wildfire pandemic, none more haunting than John McColgan's August 6, 2000 digital image of elk standing in the East Fork of the Bitterroot River near Sula, south of Missoula. The Sula Complex Fire burned 365,000 acres.

I have often wondered if they survived. Or did they become black ghosts.

Our friend Peter Kolb thinks the Sula Complex is one of his best outdoor classrooms. When NBC interviewed him following the fire, he went to great lengths to explain how rolling "fireballs" had incinerated the trees for as far as you could see, plus the organic and mineral soil in which they flourished. He also showed the camera crew a neighboring forest that its owner had thinned. When the fireballs reached the boundary line they crashed back to earth and crawled through trees no crown fire could touch.

Another friend, Pat Connell, a University of Montana forestry school graduate who served in the state legislature for several years, sent me a picture he took of elk killed in a wildfire near his Bitterroot Valley home. Skulls and skeletons were all that remained, but one skull facing the direction of the oncoming fire wore the horns of an old warrior who had challenged the flames to protect his herd.

I wonder if his bellowing sounded like horses screaming in a burning barn. My grandfather and I tried to rescue them but the searing heat kept us from getting close enough to the barn doors to open them. Sixty-six years later, I can still hear them screaming and kicking at burning walls.

The West's wildfire pandemic has belately attracted the attention of science reporters at *Knowable* Magazine, an electronic publication of non-profit Annual Reviews, a Palo Alto, California organization supported by the Gordon and Betty Moore and Alfred P. Sloan Foundations. What all the black ghosts saw is explained by Alexandra Witze in a March 19, 2019 post titled "Untangling the Physics Behind Drifting Embers, 'Firenadoes' and other Wildfire Phenomena." If the title sounds tedious, the essay is not. It reminded me that Harry Gisborne fathered wildfire behavior research from

Earth's Climate Kids need to visit with woodworkers who get their hands dirty every day supplying them with the comforts of daily life. Danny Schwartz, a self-employed log truck driver from Grangeville, Idaho starts his day at one a.m. His wife, Dixie Ray, handles the office duties from home. Although big machines do most of the logging today, many loggers still pack chainsaws.

a platform he built in the treetops overlooking the Forest Service's Priest River Experimental Forest Station in northern Idaho in 1922. Four years later, he was transferred to the agency's Rocky Mountain Research Station in Missoula.

What neither Norman Maclean nor Harry Gisborne were ever able to explain about wildfire behavior is explained in this fine essay which begins by noting that acres burned in the Pacific Northwest have increased 5,000 percent since 2003.

Of California's deadly 2018 wildfire season, Janice Coen, an atmospheric scientist in Boulder, Colorado told Witze, "Nature has given an astonishing sequence of events, each one outdoing the one before. Is this different from the past? What's going on here?"

To answer the "what's going on" question Coen and a small cadre of fire behavior analysts have turned to physics, lasers, radar and computer models to peer inside small fires in hopes of identifying the forces that transform them into megafires or, worse, firenadoes, a self-explanatory word that describes the convergence of high winds and wildfire.

Neil Lareau, a meteorologist at the University of Nevada notes that research has often been based on "what people have seen fires do in the past." "That deep personal experience is really valuable," he told Witze. "But it breaks down when the atmosphere goes into what I would call outlier mode – when you are going to be witnessing something you've never seen before."

Until I read Witze's story, I did not know there are certified fire chasers who stalk big fires in the same way midwestern storm chasers track tornadoes from vehicles loaded with monitoring equipment. Fire chasers carry laser-scanning equipment capable of penetrating ash and smoke plumes. The birth of a firenado goes something like this:

- The fire creates a plume of hot, turbulent air and smoke.
- Cooler air mixes with the plume as it rises.
- Somewhere around 15,000 feet altitude, the plume cools enough for water vapor to form. More heat is released into the rising plume, turning it bright white at around 40,000 feet.
- Instability in the atmosphere transforms the cloud into a thunderstorm, forming a pyrocumulonimbus cloud. Beneath the cloud, air rushes upward at speeds in the 130-mile-an-hour range.

Picture a figure skater pulling her arms over her head during a spin. As her spin accelerates, a coherent or orderly vortex is formed. That's a firenado. They are very different from your garden variety fire whirl.

From the comfort of his office, Lareau watched a firenado form in real time during the Carr Fire at Redding, California in July 2018. Some 1,000 homes were lost and eight were killed. Among them, a firefighter whose pickup was sucked into a 143 mile-an-hour firenado and tossed 100 yards into a grove of burning trees. More than 230,000 acres of forest and rangeland were blackened.

Coen observed the same phenomenon as the deadly Camp Fire approached Paradise, California, not from the comfort of her office but from a conference room at Stanford University where she was about to deliver a presentation titled "Understanding and Predicting Wildfires."

"I could tell by the winds and by how badly the evacuation was going that it was going to be a terrible event," she told Witze. "But at that point we didn't know it would be the deadliest fire in California history."

The Forest Service has been studying wildfire behavior at its lab in Missoula for decades. Satellite imagery and Light Detection and Ranging equipment [LIDAR], which uses pulsed laser light to create three-dimensional images of its target, are now the tools of trade. There are also wind tunnels and burn chambers that replicate the thresholds and limitations of fire spread.

Harry Gisborne would have loved this stuff, but he did not live to see it. He collapsed and died on the torturous trail leading to Mann Gulch in November 1949. Against the advice of his doctors, he had gone there to see what he could learn about how a forest fire became a grass fire and then a killer of young men. To my knowledge, he is the only fire scientist to die chasing a wildfire.

Every scientist who studies wildfire behavior goes on high alert as our godawful wildfire seasons unfold. Forest Service Chief, Vicki Christiansen, who has scads of wildfire experience, described it in her own way in a June 5, 2019 National Public

Radio interview. One billion acres of land across these United States were "at risk of wildfires like last fall's deadly Camp Fire in northern California."

Robbo Holleran, a Vermont forester

"We really don't have fire seasons anymore," she said of her estimate covering risks on multiple federal, state and private forest ownerships. "Wildfires are now a year-round phenomenon."

Asked to explain why this is happening Christiansen pointed to our nation's long history of fire suppression, rampant home development in high fire risk areas and changing climate. While these factors have certainly made matters worse, the main reasons are lousy forest policy, regulatory gridlock, and a Forest Service failure to use congressionally approved management tools to best advantage.

Ms. Christiansen can't say these things without bringing down the wrath of environmental groups that enjoy characterizing most forest restoration projects as "logging without laws." It's not true but it makes good press. How else to explain the June 12, 2019 *Los Angeles Times* headline: "Forest Service seeks to exempt some logging and mining from environmental review laws." More propaganda. Yet another unfounded attempt to scare the public silly.

What the Forest Service is attempting to do – with congressional blessing – is speed the pace and scale of project reviews mandated by the 1970 National Environmental Policy Act by consolidating and streamlining numerous approval processes. Currently, NEPA analysis can take two to four years – an unacceptable time frame in an era of megafires and firenadoes.

Remember, we're talking here about one *billion* acres. Frankly, I think she's high on her estimate given the fact that the greatest risks involve *80-90 million acres* of neglected and mismanaged national forestland. But let's give her points for trying to make a valid point. Her estimate reminded me of an observation attributed to the late Everett McKinley Dirksen, a reliably quotable U.S. Senator from Illinois. "A billion here, a billion there, pretty soon you're talking about real money," Dirksen once said of a budget debate that wasn't going well for Senate Republicans. He later denied the quote but said he liked it so much he never disputed it.

I also want to give Ms. Christiansen points for having the media savvy to participate in June 6, 2019 groundbreaking ceremonies for a first-of-its-kind engineered wood basketball arena at the University of Idaho. The 62,000 square foot arena will be constructed entirely from mass timber – pre-fabricated beams, columns, walls, floors and roofs assembled from wood components milled from small-diameter trees – the very trees the Forest Service wants to remove from overcrowded forests *before* they burn.

"This ground breaking comes at an exciting moment for the mass timber market in the United States," Christiansen said. "A thriving mass timber market can help reduce excess vegetation in our overstocked forests, leading to safer and more resilient communities. It can also support rural economic development, providing an opportunity for the Forest Service to contribute to a more sustainable building sector."

So far as I know, Ms. Christiansen is the first Forest Service Chief to connect these disparate dots in one easily understood sentence. She said the Forest Service is open for business. That's leadership. Here's hoping.

Ms. Christiansen isn't the first Forest Service Chief to try to break free of the political confines of the hall monitors in her Washington office, some of them holdovers from the Clinton years. We had to deal with their nonsense during a Q&A interview we did with her while she was still Interim Chief.

Nor is Ms. Christiansen the first Chief to be blindsided by a bonehead decision made by

Photo courtesy of Jim Petersen

PhD forest scientist, Bob Zybach, then a student at Oregon State University, successfully challenged government assertions that the Pacific Northwest had once been "a vast sea of old growth timber."

bureaucrats who didn't even bother to consult her on a matter that surely embarrassed the daylights out of her. Such was the Trump Administration's earlier explained decision to jettison the Forest Service's decades-old Job Corp Conservation Center program.

The Evergreen Foundation is a non-profit 501(c)3 corporation. It's illegal for us to lobby or litigate and we have a long history of not picking fights with presidential administrations, but the decision seemed so unwarranted that I wrote an opinion piece for our website in which I rhetorically asked why we didn't simply ship Job Corps kids to some far off gulag.

"Maybe they should shoot Smokey, too," I wrote. "Hell, he's 75 years old, more than twice the lifespan of your ordinary, garden variety black bear. Never mind the fact that his image is the most recognizable advertising image on earth or that he's helped reduce wildfire damage from 22 million acres in 1944 to an average 6.7 million acres today."

The decision made no more sense to me than the Administration's earlier announced plan to sever all federal financial ties to Special Olympics, an ill-advised verdict from which the President himself quickly retreated.

The Job Corps decision was roundly criticized by many including my colleague, Michael Rains, the National Association of Forest Service Retirees and god only knows how many parents who had crossed their fingers and enrolled a troubled child in the Job Corps program in hopes that working and learning in the great outdoors would help them find their way forward in life.

I don't know how much taxpayers have invested in the Job Corps, but I guarantee you the annual cost of housing, feeding and training some 3,000 struggling kids is chump change compared to the cost of housing them in prison cells or treating their drug addictions.

Reading between the lines of a press release quoting Ag Secretary, Sonny Perdue, left me wondering if the administration thought its decision would miraculously refocus the Forest Service's attention on its core mission: *Caring for the land and serving the people*. We're all for that. Not much caring or serving has gone on over the last 30 years, though the reasons why go well beyond anything the Forest Service could have done on its own steam.

The Job Corps program is the only Forest Service program that even remotely resembles the celebrated Civilian Conservation Corps. I'd think that the Trump Administration – or any administration for that matter – would be much better served by doubling down on the CCC's.

Here's my main point. Most youngsters long to do their part to "save the planet," whatever that means in their vernacular. These kids cling to social media on their cell phones. They prowl the world wide web constantly. They are relentless and very intelligent. Why aren't we harnessing their passion?

This sad story has an instructive sidebar. A smiling Sonny Perdue appears in several recent full-page advertisements in the Wall Street Journal. "Do right and feed everyone," he declares in bold type above a headline declaring that, "FOOD MANUFACTURING IS BOOMING!" The $280,000 ad is sponsored by the Pratt Foundation and Pratt Industries. The ad bears the signature of by Pratt's Executive Chairman, Anthony Pratt.

And who is Anthony Pratt? He's an Australian billionaire whose company is the largest privately owned paper and packaging company in the world. In 2016, he launched a new paper mill near Chicago. Vice President, Mike Pence, who was then Indiana Governor did the honors.

The following spring Pratt opened his sixty-eighth box manufacturing plant in Beloit, Wisconsin. Two months later – in the presence of President Trump – he pledged $2 billion to create 5,000 new manufacturing jobs in the Midwest. Good for him. You can bet Sonny Perdue has him on speed dial. And why not? He's the Agriculture Secretary and ag is all about farming and Pratt packages food. But you have to ask yourself: Where are the full-page *Wall Street Journal* advertisements featuring a smiling Perdue with a grinning western lumberman who is trying to help the Forest Service develop sustainable markets for small-diameter trees?

Part of the problem here is that the Forest Service is barely a blip on the Department of Agriculture's radar screen. I'd guess the West's wildfire crisis is mainly an aggravation for Secretary Perdue. He's from Georgia. Most forestland there is privately owned and well managed. Wildfires are rare. Good Fire is used to tamp down wildfire risk. I can imagine Perdue wondering what's wrong with the Forest Service. Why can't they act more like Georgia timberland owners?

What a powerful signal Secretary Perdue could send to the country if he appeared in a few full-page Wall Street Journal ads thanking lumbermen like Duane Vaagen, Roger Johnson and Chuck Roady for investing millions of their own dollars in better national forest conservation and management.

Duane has been one of the guiding lights behind forest collaboration and restoration in the West for many years. His father and uncle started Vaagen Lumber Company near Colville, Washington when Duane was still a boy. His Colville sawmill is a technological marvel. He has risked millions of dollars of his own money to help the Forest Service do more with less. He personally paid more than one million dollars for environmental impact studies on a thinning project the Forest Service had proposed. A gutsy move considering the fact that he had no say in the outcome of the study.

Roger Johnson has doubled down on his family's Pyramid Lumber Company at Seeley Lake, Montana so many times I've lost count. He was the first lumberman to buy into the Forest Service's stewardship contracting vision. Trading trees for which the government had no market for infrastructure work it could not afford was controversial. But the Clearwater Stewardship Contract stands as a shining example of what is doable when big ideas are set in motion. Pyramid got timber it needed and the Forest Service got new toilets in campgrounds and new culverts in aging road systems. Rumor has it Roger lost $600,000 on the deal, but he later told me he thought the project had been a great learning experience. Pyramid is still leading the way in forest restoration work in western Montana.

Chuck Roady is vice president and general manager of the F.H. Stoltze Land and Lumber Company at Columbia Falls, Montana. Stoltze is the oldest continuously operating sawmill in Montana. It has been a fixture in northwest Montana since 1912. The company is owned by the fifth-generation heirs of F.H. Stoltze, who first came west with the Great Northern Railway in the 1890s.

Chuck is the fourth Stoltze general manager I have known since the early 1970s. Though no two have been the same, they've all had a practical streak in them. It's the hutzpah that keeps the company going despite periodic economic downturns that are especially challenging for small family-owned businesses.

The first mill manager I knew was a lovely guy named Royce Satterlee. Ours was an unusual connection. He grew up dirt poor on a small farm just up the hill from my grandfather's sprawling cattle ranch on Gold Creek, northeast of Sandpoint, Idaho. The old Satterlee place was abandoned by the time my memories begin, but I heard stories about how my grandfather kept the Satterlee family fed during the Great Depression. Royce confirmed the story for me decades later. He was so thrilled to learn that my grandmother was still living that he jumped in his airplane and flew to Sandpoint to take her to lunch. Royce was the real deal.

Royce was the real deal and so is the Wisconsin-based Stoltze family. I find it remarkable that they continue to invest their capital in a far-off business they rarely visit. There have surely been years when the mill lost money. But there is a sense of duty in family-owned lumber companies that you won't find in the big publicly traded outfits. The DNA is different. Employees, families and communities are more than decimal points on balance sheets.

If I were Sonny Perdue, I'd be damned proud to stand beside Chuck Roady or Duane Vaagen or Roger Johnson. The future of our diseased and dying national forests rests on their willingness to continue investing their hard-earned capital in technologically advanced wood processing equipment and markets that don't require taxpayer subsidy. I've said it before and I'll say it again: No mill, no market, no forest.

We can't fix what ails our national forests by leaving them to nature. We can't fix them by building a bigger and better fire department. And we can't fix them with managed fire. The National Park Service has allowed most of its wildfires to run their course since the 1970s. The plainly visible results aren't pretty.

Around Lake McDonald in Glacier National Park, 30 miles east of Stoltze Lumber. It isn't pretty. Last summer, the historic Lake McDonald Lodge was nearly lost in the Howe Ridge Fire, just as the 104-year-old Sperry Chalet in Glacier's backcountry was lost in 2017. But it's natural.

There is only *one* fix for the wildfire pandemic that is reducing the West's great national forests to ash and ruin: thinning and prescribed fire. A one-two punch with a long history of success. Thinning as a tool for reducing forest density before wildfire strikes. Intentionally set Good Fire as a tool for cleaning up woody debris after the thinning work is done. And when and where wildfires occur, the first goal ought to be to put the damned thing out as quickly as possible!

Why don't the climate kids know about this stuff? Do they know anything about what insects, disease and wildfire are doing to their national forest heritage? Has anyone shown them the growth and mortality data for western national forests? Do they even know what growth and mortality mean?

I fear the answers to all three questions is "No." And to the extent that the climate kids think loggers and lumbermen are "killing the planet," what's left of the West's timber industry has only itself to blame. I get the part about lobbying Congress for regulatory relief, but these kids are going to vote for the first time when they are 18. Who and what do we think they'll vote for?

Why aren't we engaging these youngsters? Do they know that our wildfire pandemic is anything but natural? Do they know why their grandparents and great grandparents worked so damned hard to stuff the Wildfire Genie back in her bottle? Do they know that putting out forest fires was the cornerstone of our country's conservation ethic for more than a century?

Was it wrong? No, it wasn't wrong – and it still isn't wrong. The public no longer favors timber harvesting in our national forests. Does this mean the public thinks we should "let nature take its course" just because the luddites among us think nature knows best? I hope not.

Remember, nature doesn't give a damn what we want or need. Whatever we want and need from our national forests we have to get on our own – and the process begins with crafting federal forest policies that allow the Forest Service to do its job to the best of our ability using the tools and technologies that science and technology provide.

I'd like to introduce these kids to Duane Vaagen, Roger Johnson and Chuck Roady. I want them to tour their sawmills. Then I want to take them to the woods with my friend, Dave Ehrmantrout. This gentle man and his sons have turned logging into an art form.

There are other loggers as good as Dave, but I know Dave and I know he'd invest the time in showing them what thinning and forest restoration looks like where the rubber meets the road. It isn't about "chopping down all the trees" or "logging without laws." It's about saving forests from wildfire.

I also want these kids to walk in the utter devastation that wildfires leave in their wake. I want them to understand that there is no ecological precedent for these wildfires in modern ecological history.

Yes, our climate is changing and, yes, climate change is adding to our wildfire crisis, but we can't fix this mess by demanding that coal trains not transfer their cargo to ships in Seattle or insisting that liquified natural gas not be off-loaded at coastal sea ports. And more wind and solar power aren't going to do a damned thing to save our national forests from fiery death.

Rob Davis, Show Low, Arizona, is an exceptionally inventive consumer of small diameter trees. His Forest Energy Corporation manufactures everything from kitty litter to animal bedding to EPA approved wood stove pellets – enough to heat 25,000 homes in the Southwest.

These kids also need to spend a day in the woods with our friend Peter Kolb, not because he's a PhD eco-physiologist but because he's very good at explaining how forests grow and the natural forces that shape them through time. Peter is a quiet and purpose-filled man who cares deeply about his work as a college professor and Montana State extension service forester. Even his kids like him!

I'd like to think that some of Peter's devotion will rub off on our climate kids. We will soon need many more young scientists who care as much as Peter cares – foresters, biologists, botanists, biometricians, ecologists, dendrologists, statisticians, forest biometricians and eco-physiologists – than we have now. And we need them to know how we got ourselves into this wildfire mess and how to get us out of it.

There are other fine forest scientists in the woods today, but there are also imposters with PhD's and dubious motives whoring for federal grants in hopes of sabotaging the whole idea of human-led forest restoration work. In their conceit, they have put science on the path to irrelevance in the public arena.

I recently read a speech by Robert Lackey, a PhD fisheries biologist at Oregon State University. For 27 years, he led the EPA's national research laboratory at Corvallis. He is best known for his work involving the interplay between science and policy, which no doubt explains why the Society of American Foresters invited him to be a plenary lecturer at their 2018 annual convention in Portland. We've never met but I'd like the climate kids to meet him.

"Using science to push personal or employer policy preferences is now widespread," Lackey said. "And such now common behavior has consequences for everyone: scientists, natural resource managers, appointed bureaucrats, elected officials and the public."

One result, Lackey continued, is "the all-too-common view that anyone, no matter how poorly informed, no matter how dubious the source of quoted information, anyone has the right to his or her own facts."

Worse, Lackey asserted, many scientists are contributing to the erosion of public trust. Having spent years investigating the scientific basis for listing the northern spotted owl as a threatened species, I know Lackey is correct. How else to explain the fact that notes made daily by so-called "owl scientists" assembled in Portland were shredded and bagged every night, ultimately trucked to a powerplant at Boardman, Oregon.

I think their notes should have been Scotch-taped to the front door every morning. But it was locked so the unwashed could not enter.

"When I travel outside the confines of my cloistered professional world, I run into many people who are highly skeptical of what scientists say and write," Lackey said. "And skepticism comes from both the political right and left. Oh, they still value scientific information, but increasingly they have simply lost faith in the policy neutrality of scientists themselves."

Lackey's assessment is harsh – maybe a little too harsh – because the political left and right have both become very adept at cherry-picking the science that best fits their agendas. We end up with conflicting environmental policies and regulations that make it impossible for federal natural resource management agencies to do their jobs the way the public expects the job to be done.

"Call it advocacy science, fall it junk science, call it policy-biased science or stick with normative science, regardless of what you call it, it is deceitful and it has no legitimate place in policy deliberations," Lackey declared. "Its rampant prevalence threatens to marginalize the legitimate and essential role that science ought to play in natural resource policy and management."

Science, Lackey declared, should be policy neutral and based on "information gathered in a rational, systematic, testable and reproducible manner."

Lackey understood that all scientists have their personal biases, but he warned that the policy preferences of scientists have no more value than those offered by anyone else and he reminded his audience of something Nobel Laureate and theoretical physicist, Richard Feynman has once said: "I believe that a scientist looking at non-scientific problems is just as dumb as the next guy."

Phil Aune's knowledge of the forces that have shaped and reshaped western national forests is encyclopedic. He worked for the U.S. Forest Service in planning and research in California for 40-some years. Now retired, he is a leader in the widely respected National Association of Forest Service Retirees.

We need to equip the climate kids with good bullshit meters. How else to insulate them from the barrage of advocacy that is swamping rational thought?

"In science," Lackey concluded, "when you see the words 'natural,' 'healthy,' 'degraded' or 'biological integrity,' these terms, and many others have embedded assumptions about what someone or some organization regards as a desirable value choice, a preferred policy choice. These and similar words have no place in science. They are classic examples of normative science. Their use in scientific publications is simply policy advocacy disguised as science."

A great deal of normative science has been invested in proving that salvage logging following a wildfire is "like mugging a burn victim." I want to tour our climate kids through a salvage logging job. No, they need to see two salvage logging jobs – one in process and one completed a few years ago. The visual transformation, which takes about two years, is astonishing.

I'll bet none of these kids know that salvage logging is common in all but federal forests. States and tribes salvage log and replant promptly. Private landowners salvage log and replant quickly. The Forest Service salvage logged and replanted quickly for decades. The visible results refute normative science.

But our federal government has ditched salvage logging in favor of natural recovery. We allow fire-killed trees to rot where they stand. Quite usable trees become magnets for insect infestations. Reburns are common because no effort has been made to clean up the mess. Often there isn't sufficient organic soil left to support much more than brush. It will be two or three hundred years before the half-million acres burned in the 2002 Biscuit Fire is again a forest. Some of the area has already reburned twice. In whose warped mind is this a good idea?

If our climate kids could see what the Siskiyou National Forest looks like today compared to what it looked like when I first saw it in 1971 they'd understand why this book is titled *First, put out the Fire!* and why their forebearers – the men and women who built this country – worked so hard to put out forest fires as quickly as possible, and why it is still important that we put these damned fires out as quickly as possible.

I want these kids sitting in on conference calls when the Forest Service attempts to explain why it is slow to jump on wildfires when they are small. Julia and I sat in on such a call last year following the 2017 Milli Fire near Sisters, Oregon. We still can't figure out what possible motivation the Forest Service had for watching the fire for several days before realizing that it might overrun Sisters. The Forest Service insists this isn't "policy." Okay, then what is it?

These kids are mostly computer whizzes. So let's introduce them to the Forest Service's Forest Inventory and Analysis Program. FIA's colorful interactive story maps will keep our climate kids busy for years especially after they discover FIA's Space Shuttle partnership with NASA. Good bullshit metering tools, too.

Layer upon layer of data gathered from some 125,000 forest inventory plots located on private and publicly-owned forestlands scattered across our nation's 3.53 million square mile landscape, some dating from the 1930s. Close to 200 forest characteristics measured at each plot and more than 1.5 million trees are measured to evaluate their volume, condition and vigor. Less known are FIA's 4.5 million remote sensing plots and its 9.43 million aerial photographic points. 3.1 million covering forestland and another 6.3 million covering non-forest.

Kids can click on the story map of their choice and be guided to county-level data sets for every county, parish and borough in the United States. Pick a forest value and "click" and there it is – displayed in color on digitized maps representing dozens of values: green trees, dying trees, dead trees, insects, diseases, wildfire, carbon in the air we breathe, carbon in the soil, land use changes, urban sprawl, water quality, fish and wildlife habitat – all of the measurables that act as proxies for the big five: clean air, clean water, abundant fish and wildlife, a wealth of year-round recreation opportunity and immeasurable forest beauty.

I want these kids to have an opportunity to join a stakeholder forest collaborative near them. They want them to witness *and learn to respect* the give and take that goes on between the citizen members of these all volunteer groups that are trying to help the Forest Service solve some of its most vexing management problems. I want them to wrap their minds around the amazing cultural diversity that sits at collaborative tables across the West.

By all means, kids, take your laptop computers with you so you can dial up all those FIA story maps for your neighborhood. You'll quickly earn the mutual respect of other forest stakeholders.

Our climate kids are very concerned about Carbon in our atmosphere. That's great, but has anyone bothered to tell them that without Carbon – Symbol C and Atomic Number 6 on the Periodic Table – there would be no life on earth? Have they ever seen a Periodic Table? Do they know that the 118 elements displayed by their atomic numbers are the building blocks of life on earth? Do they know that their bodies are 18 percent carbon atoms? Or that those atoms were once in the food we eat and before that the air, oceans, rocks and other life forms? Do they know carbon is an element born of exploding stars or that 90 percent of the earth's carbon resides beneath us, deep in the Earth?

What do our kids know about the connection between the element Carbon and carbon sequestration? What do they know about photosynthesis – the completely natural process by which plants use the free, non-polluting energy of the sun to convert water, complex carbohydrates and carbon dioxide – the chief culprit in global warming – into cellulous.

Do they know that cellulose is what gives plant walls – and thus wood – its structural integrity. And do they know that the byproduct of this completely natural process is labeled Atomic Number 8, Symbol O on the Periodic Table. It's called Oxygen. We breathe it. Now we're talking miracles!

Do our climate kids know we can measure the amount of carbon stored in a tree? We can. One process is called "sonic tomography." It relies on a device that sends sound waves through tree trunks to gauge their density. The denser the tree, the more carbon stored inside. Think of it as a CAT scan for trees.

The Forest Service's Forest Inventory and Analysis Program does this work on a grand scale using more sophisticated technologies – satellites, drones and laser scanning – to compute forest carbon loads for entire states. These reports tell us a great deal about how much carbon dioxide trees are sequestering and how much oxygen they are releasing for us to breathe. Do our kids know this?

Speaking of the air we breathe, I want our climate kids to have the unfortunate opportunity to breathe the same damned lousy air we breathe for months on end every summer. I want them to know that inhaling wildfire smoke is as dangerous as smoking cigarettes. Then I want our kids to reconsider the idea that these big wildfires are just "the new normal." This is nonsense. There is nothing normal or natural about this disgusting mess. Our problem is fixable. We just haven't had the courage to tell the luddites who live among us to go to hell.

Do our kids know that wood is the only structural building material on earth that is renewable, recyclable and biodegradable? Do they know it takes less energy to manufacture things from wood than from steel, aluminum or concrete? Do they know that less water is needed or that there is far less air pollution? Trust me. They don't know. We aren't teaching this stuff in schools.

I wish our climate kids could meet my friend Wink Sutton, who has PhDs in chemistry, botany and biometrics. Wink believes scientists will someday break through the molecular barrier that holds wood's deepest secrets.

When that glorious moment comes, cellulose from trees and plants can replace fossil fuels, including the fuel we burn in our cars. What youngster interested in the environment or climate change or air quality wouldn't want to be part of such a marvelous discovery?

Someday, someone is going to unlock the genetic codes that enable some trees to grow faster, straighter and taller while producing better quality wood than trees of the same species standing right next to them.

Someday, someone is going to figure out how to saw logs without saws, eliminating wood waste altogether. Lasers or high-frequency sound?

Someday, someone is going to build a mechanical harvester that operates off solar panels and leaves no visible footprint in its path. You can bet that Dave Ehrmantrout and his sons will be very interested.

Why can't that someone be one of your kids or grandkids, maybe a niece or nephew, or that nice girl that lives across the street or the high-energy kid down the street who's always trying to sell you a big bag of popcorn?

Our climate kids are never going to understand any of this if we continue to allow bullshit artists to fill their heads with goofy ideas about the environment and the planet and how people are bad and, if we just left everything to nature everything would be fine.

We need to teach our kids how to recognize the difference between superficial, feel good crap and a more meaningful and certainly more measurable approach to living green than simply eschewing paper bags and plastic straws.

Do our kids know that most shopping bags are made from recycled paper? Do they know that it takes 1,000 times as much energy to deliver the bottled water they insist on storing in their designer metal and plastic Starbucks bottles?

What on earth is wrong with tap water? Most of it comes from the same forested watersheds where the bottled water con artists get their water – publicly-owned water for which outfits like Nestle pay pittance. What's up with that?

Even New York City's millions get their drinking water from well managed forests in the Adirondack's but take a stroll down any of the city's busiest streets and all you'll see are people sucking on water bottles. I don't get it. Do you?

Do our climate kids know that the much ballyhooed Green New Deal doesn't speak to our wildfire pandemic. Its main goal is to rid us of our dependence on fossil fuels by 2050 – less time if possible. That's fine. Go back a few paragraphs and you'll see that Wink Sutton believes that cellulose molecules hold the key. I hope he's right. But it takes energy to make energy.

Wind and solar power are great, but if the wind isn't blowing and the sun isn't shining what do we do? We still need power – and lots of it – to heat, light and cool our homes, offices and factories.

Our best known sources of clean power are hydroelectric dams and carbonless nuclear power but most greens don't like these. Natural gas might work but the greens don't like it because it's a fossil fuel.

The late T. Boone Pickens, who made billions investing in oil and gas exploration, advocated for natural gas-powered vehicles and wind turbine power for our homes and industries but environmentalists hated the idea of all the new transmission lines leading from wind farms to customers. What to do?

Our climate kids need to know that transitioning from centuries of fossil fuel use to clean energy sources isn't simply a matter of passing new environmental laws that favor one energy source over another. Politicians will promise anything to get elected but people tend to vote their pocketbooks and I don't see anyone volunteering to give up their job in a factory powered by coal or natural gas.

Meantime, we have a lot of carbon that needs to be stored. Estimates vary, but over the last 25 years our forests have stored the equivalent of 11 percent of our country's carbon dioxide emissions – more when we count the carbon stored in wood products.

This looks like part of a hopeful solution to me when we consider that trees are powered by the free, non-polluting energy of the sun. We need to be planting and growing more trees. It's the part of this that has me wanting our climate kids visit with some Forest Service retirees.

Maybe 15 years ago my late friend, John Marker, whom I mentioned earlier, helped organize the National Association of Forest Service Retirees. John was a class act, a real gentleman and a big, big thinker who devoted his entire professional life to the Forest Service. Some 700 Forest Service retirees are members of NAFSR. By my back of the envelope estimate their combined careers represent some 21,000 years of experience managing our national forests.

What insights might these dedicated men and women offer our climate kids? What might they say about their boots-on-the-ground years? What might they suggest concerning career opportunities? What sciences? What needs doing?

Here I think of three retirees I know well: Michael Rains, Phil Aune and Rich Stem.

Michael is one of the smartest guys I've ever met. He holds five college degrees from five different universities. His was a 48-year career. He lives in Pennsylvania now and he tutors kids with limited physical and emotional strengths. Read his speech[70] he delivered when he was still Director of the Northern Research Station and Forest Products Laboratory. Read it here to understand this gentle man's depth of experience.

Before he retired from the Forest Service, Phil Aune was Research Program Manager for the Redding, California Silviculture Laboratory. He is a walking encyclopedia where managing wildfire risk is concerned. I was fortunate to be invited to join a wildfire tour of the Lake Tahoe Basin that he hosted. One of the properties we visited is a small forest that belongs to Mike Love of Beachboys fame. A logger had done some thinning work to protect his home. It looks west over Lake Tahoe from high atop the crest that separates California from Nevada. To say the least, the view is breathtaking.

Many Lake Tahoe homeowners – all of them wealthy – have hired loggers to thin the forests that surround their hideaways. Others, less fortunate, lost their homes in the 2007 Angora Fire. Although Angora was small by wildfire standards – 3,100 acres – 242 homes at the south end of the lake were lost.

Phil is devoted to helping forestry students learn all they can about the practical aspects of managing land. I've seen him in action at many conferences and he's amazing to watch. His suggestions for tackling the regulatory mess that impedes Forest Service restoration work are spot on. Here you can see one of his many PowerPoint presentations. And here you can study – and I do mean study – a presentation he made before the Senate Energy and Natural Resources Subcommittee on Public Lands and Forests in 2007.

Rich Stem is his own tour de force and a good friend of many years. We met in the late 1980s, not long after I started *Evergreen* Magazine. We were drawn together by the 1987 Silver Fire, the first of three big burns on southern Oregon's Siskiyou National Forest. Rich and his skilled multi-disciplinary team had been tasked with preparing an Environmental Impact Statement justifying the merits of salvage logging on part of the burn. Their report was completed and implemented in record time. I was amazed by their expert professionalism.

Now retired, Rich and his wife own a beautiful home overlooking the Ruby Reservoir near Virginia City, Montana. My mother's first teaching job was in the historic town's one-room schoolhouse. When I was a boy, I fished the Ruby River often, despite its

70

The depth and breadth of technology found in forestry, logging and wood products manufacturing today is astonishing. Do our Climate Kids know that it's all precisely controlled and monitored computers much like their own – many of them linked to satellites orbiting the earth?

rattlesnakes. If Julia and I could steal Rich and Karen's home we would, but we think they'd notice.

Rich is a NAFSR board member – as are the six living Forest Service Chiefs: Max Peterson, Dale Robertson, Michael Dombeck, Dale Bosworth, Abigail Kimbell and Tom Tidwell. He likes to keep his head down now, but Rich and several NAFSR board members collaborated on several letters to Agriculture Secretary, Sonny Perdue, outlining strategies for increasing the pace and scale of forest restoration work in our national forests.

Our climate kids need to spend a day in the woods with Rich. They can also catch him playing with a country western band at the Bale of Hay Saloon in Virginia City. My mother played the piano there on weekends in the late 1930s. Yes, kids are welcome as long as they're with their parents.

I also want these kids to know that we all owe our national forests a great debt for saving our butts during World War II. Few today know that a 36-foot plywood boat built by a brash Louisiana lumberman named Andrew Jackson Higgins changed the face of World War II.

Supreme Allied Commander, Dwight D. Eisenhower – a man not given to rash statements – called Higgins "the man won the war for us." I cannot watch film of young men going ashore at Omaha Beach on June 6, 1944 without being moved to tears. Higgins would tell you that it was they who won the war.

Shallow-draft Higgins boats, with their unique drop-down bow, participated in every major amphibious landing in World War: Normandy on D-Day, Sicily, Italy, Guadalcanal, Tarawa, Saipan, Tinian, Okinawa and Iwo Jima. Ike said open beach landings would have been impossible without Higgins boats. Hitler called Higgins "the new Noah." They were both right.

I'd like to know what our climate kids know about the American Tree Farm System – if anything. God only knows how many trees have been planted in our nation's forests since it was created in October 1941. It had been Bill Greeley's vision for years. When he gave up his Forest Service Chief's job in 1928, it was to pursue his reforestation vision as chief executive of the West Coast Lumberman's Association. The association's members included some of the largest timberland owners in the Douglas-fir region.

Despite the fact that West Coast lumbermen had their backs to the Pacific Ocean, they initially scoffed at Greeley's replanting dreams. Timber was cheap and plentiful. Best get it before it burns in a wildfire.

To their credit, they had formed their own wildfire cooperatives following the 1902 Yacolt Burn – the goal being to join forces with other private timberland owners. But it would be another 22 years before Congress reluctantly funded similar efforts by the Forest Service – and then only because Greeley, who was then Forest Service Chief, had greased the skids with U.S. Senate members who favored his ideas about protecting national forests from wildfire.

But now here was Greeley telling members of the West Coast Lumberman's Association that they needed to create a nationwide network of certified Tree Farms. What sense did that make?

It made a great deal of sense to Greeley because his entire forestry career had been shaped by wildfire. He had assumed command of the Forest Service's newly formed District 1 on September 1, 1908 – 41 million acres spanning 22 national forests: all of Montana, Idaho north of the Clearwater River, the northeast corner of eastern Washington and South Dakota's Black Hills National Forest.

When the disastrous 1910 fire swept over three million acres of virgin timber in northern Idaho and western Montana, it fell to Greeley to organize the near futile effort to battle the conflagration and to supervise the burial of 78 firefighters, most of them burned beyond recognition. Small wonder that he continued to press his case for replanting cutover timberland after the West Coast Lumberman's Association hired him in 1928.

In January 1942, with America at war on two continents, WCLA's members certified the nation's first Tree Farms – 16 in all – and all of them in western Oregon and Washington. Weyerhaeuser's 130,000-acre Clemons Tree Farm near Montesano, Washington holds Tree Farm Certificate No. 1.

Bill Hagenstein, my mentor for nearly 40 years, kept the minutes at the October 1941 meeting. He was 26 years old and would soon depart for the South Pacific where he built and ran sawmills for island-hopping Marines. God only knows how many trees have been planted in public and privately owned forests since then.

Do our climate kids know any of this history? Have any of them read Greeley's autobiography? *Forests and Men* is packed with information and perspective they need to consider. So is *Breaking New Ground*, Gifford Pinchot's autobiography. Likewise, *Fernow* by Andrew Denny Rogers III.

I want to ask our climate kids if they think its "okay" to allow our nation's forest heritage to burn to the ground because some screwball thinks it's more "natural" than removing dead and dying trees before they burn. How do we square this nuttiness with the tens of millions of tons of carcinogenic carbon our wildfire seasons are belching into the air we breathe.

I want our climate kids to have the opportunity to visit with some of the gifted men and women I've interviewed over the last 34 years. Professional foresters like Phil Aune and Rich Stem. Between them, their Forest Service careers span more than 80 years.

Or Robbo Holleran, a Vermont forester who is one of the keenest observers of nature I've ever met. Or my friend, Bob Zybach, a PhD environmental scientist in Oregon, who was a reforestation contractor for many years before he decided to go back to school. Bob is a student's dream come true.

How about my thoughtful friend, Mike Petersen, a first-rate conservationist and respected leader in the West's forest collaboration and restoration movement. Mike is quiet, polite and exceptionally skilled at bringing people together.

Or Rob Davis, an entrepreneurial genius from Show Low, Arizona, who is transforming small trees and woody biomass into an array of consumer products so commonplace we don't think much about them. Or Gordon West, a methodical craftsman who makes beautiful furniture from ponderosa pine logs and limbs that would otherwise be burned.

Or the men and women of the National Association of Forest Service Retirees. Their careers represent more than 28,000 years of accumulated knowledge and experience. Talk about a resource! These are the professionals our climate kids should be questioning.

Then there are the hundreds of men and women who get their hands dirty every day in sawmills and on logging jobs. I've interviewed dozens of them and I have yet to have one of them say, "Oh, I just want to chop down all the trees." Yet that's the story told by the bullshit artists who live among us. It isn't true.

I also want to offer our climate kids my apology for the horrible way that we adults are caring for their forest heritage. In our selfishness and stupidity, we are destroying what they will inherit from us. What we are doing to these youngsters is ethically and morally repugnant. We should be ashamed of ourselves. Many of us are but some of us are so twisted we see nothing wrong with our utterly inexcusable behavior.

I'd like to think that our climate kids will develop what my late friend, Jack Ward Thomas, often called "some by-God humility" about what they think they know. Start by remembering what Nineteenth Century humorist, Josh Billings, had to say about all of our by-God certainties: "It ain't what you don't know that gets you in trouble. It's what you know for sure that just ain't so."

Many of us aren't very humble about what we insist we know for sure. We are disrespectful know-it-alls with no regard for the beliefs and opinions of others. Some of us haven't even learned to say "please" and "thank you," simple courtesies many of us learned when we were kids.

Lightning strikes, errant campfires and mismanagement aren't the root causes of our nation's dreadful wildfire pandemic. The root cause is the raging political fire that is searing our soul in Washington, D.C. Until we get this fire under control, we have no hope for saving our cherished national forests from fiery death.

Know that this isn't a game. Remember that hope is not a strategy and science is a process, not a religion. Forests are dying. People are dying. Animals are dying. We are surrounded by black ghosts.

If you are contemplating college, get a good education in one of the forest sciences, roll up your sleeves and get to work. We need your passion and your dedication. If college isn't in your future, there are still plenty of good jobs in forests and in forest products manufacturing. We need you, too.